GLORIOUS GARDENS

GLORIOUS

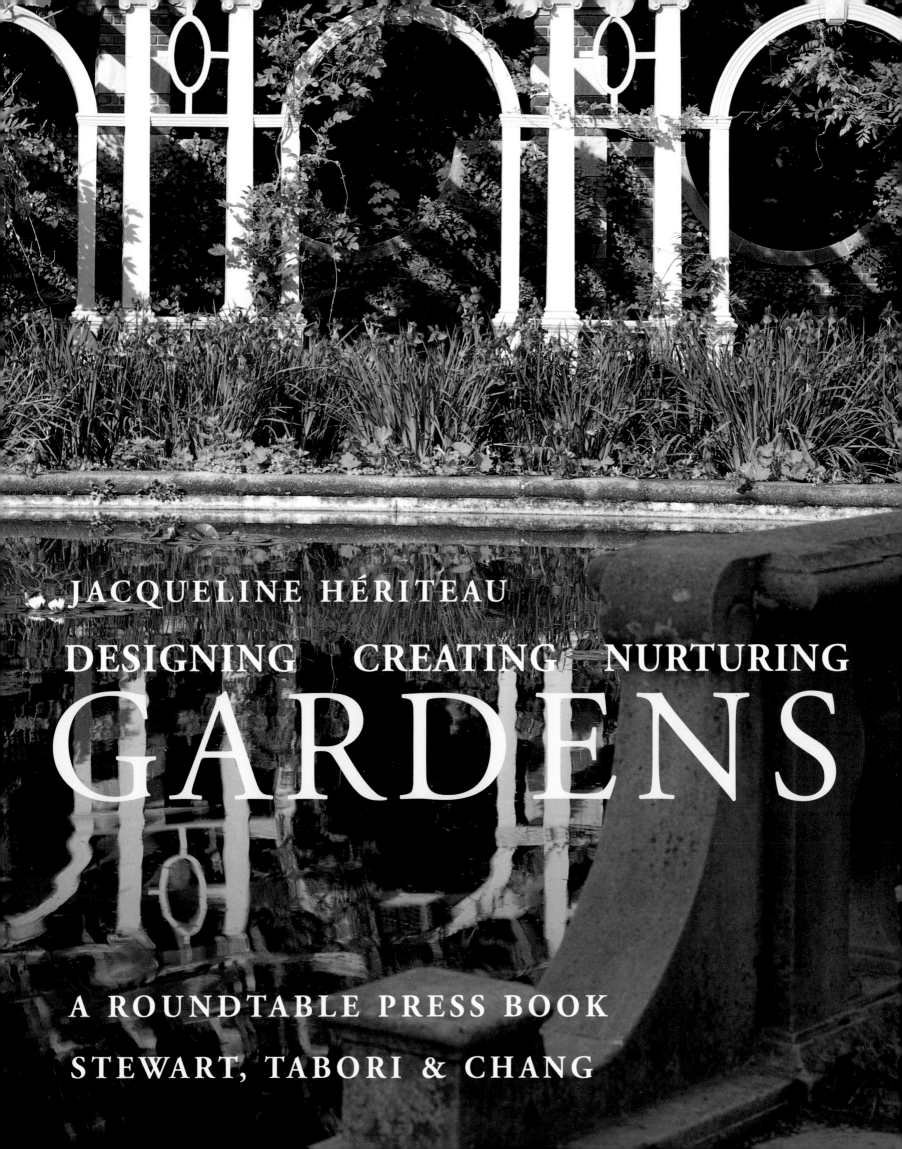

JACQUELINE HÉRITEAU

DESIGNING   CREATING   NURTURING

GARDENS

A ROUNDTABLE PRESS BOOK

STEWART, TABORI & CHANG

To Earl Hubbard, the artist whose love guides my life.

For Roundtable Press, Inc.
Directors: Susan E. Meyer, Marsha Melnick
Executive Editor: Amy T. Jonak
Project Editor: Jennie McGregor Bernard
Designer: Nai Y. Chang
Photo Editor: Sarah Longacre
Horticultural Consultant: Mary Mantuani
Assistant Editor: Abigail A. Anderson
Production: Steven Rosen
With thanks to Holly Shimizu and Paul Lindell

Published in 1966 by
Stewart, Tabori & Chang
a division of U.S. Media Holdings, Inc.
575 Broadway
New York, New York 10012

Distributed in Canada
by General Publishing Co. Ltd.
30 Lesmill Road, Don Mills
Onterio, Canada, M3B 2T6
Distributed in Australia and New Zealand by
Peribo Pty Ltd.
58 Beaumont Road
Mount Kuring-gai
NSW 2080, Australia
Distributed in all other territories by
Grantham Book Services Ltd.
Isaac Newton Way
Alma Park Industrial Estate
Grantham, Linconshire
NG31 9SD, England

Library of Congress Cataloging-in-Publication Data

Hériteau, Jacqueline.
    Glorious gardens : designing, creating, nurturing / Jacqueline
Hériteau.
        p.   cm.
    "A Roundtable Press book."
    Includes index.
    ISBN 1-55670-485-2
    1. Landscape gardening. 2. Gardens—Design. 3. Gardens.
4. Landscape gardening—Pictorial works. 5. Gardens—Pictorial
works. I. Title.
SB473.H437   1996
635—dc20   96-22295
                              CIP

Printed in JAPAN

PHOTO CREDITS

Rosalind Creasy: pages 6, top right;58;61; and 62.

Derek Fell: cover and pages 48, left;51, top;54, bottom;81;103;141;166;172-173;198;204;205;and 224-225.

Tria Giovan: page 44.

Mick Hales: pages 2-3;30, bottom right;69, right;108-109;116-117;169; and 219.

Jerry Harpur: backcover and pages 6, bottom right and top;7, bottom left, bottom right and top right;8(Great Dixter);18-19(Great Cornard Country Park);23(Designer: Mrs. Annie Fisher);26, bottom and top(Rodmarton Manor);30, top(Bennington Lordship);36(Designer: George Cooper);42(Designer: Peter Place);43, bottom and top left(The Dingle, Welshpool, Wales);45, bottom right;51, bottom left(The Dingle, Welshpool, Wales);56, right(The Dingle, Welshpool, Wales);60, bottom left;74(Designer: Daniel Pearson);80(Designer: Christopher Masson);82(Wave Hill);83(Designer: Penny Crawshaw);84, bottom left(Bourton House Garden, Gloucestershire);86-87(Designer: Penny Crawshaw);92(Designer: Lisette Pleasance);120(The Beth Chatto Gardens, Essex);124;126(The Beth Chatto Gardens, Essex);148-149(Designer: Isobelle Greene);160, bottom(The Beth Chatto Gardens, Essex);160, top(The Beth Chatto Gardens, Essex);161(The Beth Chatto Gardens, Essex); 164;165; 175(Designer: Isobelle Greene);183, left;188;193;210;213; and 230.

Andrew Lawson: pages 7, top left;11;12, bottom and center;31, right;38;40, bottom right;41, bottom;48, right;60, bottom right;63, left;68, left and right;88, left;90, left;93;94-95; 96;106, top;130-131 (all);132, center and right;133;134;139;140;142;146, left;153, bottom right;154, left;158;162, bottom and top;168;174;178, bottom right;179;180;182, bottom and top;183, right;196;203;207, right;209;211; and 228.

Clay Myers/The Wildlife Collection: pages 33, right and 99.

Clive Nichols: pages 6, bottom center, bottom left, center, and top left;14;15;16(Duckyls, Sussex);25;27(The Beth Chatto Gardens, Essex);34;35;37(The Beth Chatto Gardens, Essex);41, top(Ramster, Surrey);45, top left and top right(Designer: Jane Fearnley-Whittingstall);48, center(Keukenhoff, Holland);52-53(Coates Manor, Sussex);66-67(Cecily Hill House, Gloucestershire);69, left;72-73(Designer: Nigel Colborn);76(The Country Living Garden, Chelsea, '95: Designer: Rupert Golby);78(Designer: Daniel Pearson);84, bottom right(Vale End, Surrey);84, top left and top right(Bourton House Garden, Gloucestershire);88, right(The National Asthma Campaign Garden, Chelsea, '93, Designer: Lucy Huntington);89, left(The Anchorage, Kent);98(Designer: Douglas Knight);104-105(Little Coopers, Hampshire);111(Bennington Lordship, Hertfordshire);118(Designer: Richard Coward);119;121(Brook Cottage, Oxfordshire);129(Designer: Anne Waring);136-137(The Woodland at Great Thurlow Hall, Suffolk);138(The Dower House, Barnsley, Gloucestershire);143(Villa Hanbury, Italy);144;145(Mottisfont Abbey Gardens, Hampshire);146, top(Designer: Jo Passmore);147(Glazeley Old Rectory, Shropshire);150(Turn End Garden, Buckinghamshire: Designer: Peter Aldington);156, top(The Beth Chatto Gardens, Essex);157(The Beth Chatto Gardens. Essex);176-177(The Dingle, Welshpool, Wales);181(Abbottswood Garden, Gloucestershire);184(Designer: Vic Shanley); and 214-215(Babbacombe, Devon).

Carole Ottesen: pages 12, top;30, left;55;170-171;and 200-201.

Hugh Palmer: pages 1;13;40, top right;51, bottom right;54, top;77;79;90, right;135;223; and 226.

Jerry Pavia: pages 20;22;28;32;40, top left;45, bottom left;46-47;56, bottom and top left;63, right;65;68, center;70;89, right;106, bottom;115;122;125;132, left;152;153, bottom and top left;154, center and right;155, left and right;156, bottom;163;172, left;178, bottom left and top ;194, top;195;197, bottom;206;218; and 222.

Curtice Taylor: pages 10;59;97;100;112-113;159;184-185;190;194, bottom;199, left;202(Designer: Virginia Purviance, Middletown, RI); and 208, right(Designer: Carol Mercer, East Hampton, NY).

Michael S. Thompson: pages 9;29;31, left;33, left;40, bottom left;43, right;60, top left and right;69, center;71;101;105, right;151;155, center;189;197, top;199, right;207, left;208, left;212;216;217;220-221 (all); and 228.

FOREWORD

We were finishing our first garden together. My granddaughter Emily, who is known as Miss Pink, had selected pink tulips, yellow daffodils, and white crocus. She named the flower colors for her crayons and she wasn't interested in conventional flower border design. She wanted the flowers planted in wavy lines, just like the wind was blowing. Each year Emily and I have added to her garden other types of plants, and flowers for other seasons of bloom, but her idea of the design has never wavered. She still loves flowing lines and living colors. Anyone who gardens should feel just as free to express ideas as does our Miss Pink.

Gardening is one of the most satisfying of all vehicles for expressing individual creativity. It has become our number one hobby because it rewards freedom of expression with profound pleasure. There's no right and no wrong way to landscape, as the photographs of the beautiful gardens in this volume make abundantly clear. The rules of landscape design have been relaxed. We see the opportunities offered by the site, and we delight in creative ideas that meet the challenges present. Turn the pages and you will realize that in every type of setting the contemporary and the traditional now live side by side. Indeed, in some of the most exciting gardens I have visited recently they cohabit. Flowering meadows and flowering allées are no longer strangers, and a natural garden can encompass a tree rose along with ornamental grasses and groves of native trees and shrubs. Avant-garde homes have kitchen gardens, some planted right by the front entrance. Walks, fountains, lawns, screens, beds, water gardens, and play areas are planned not for their effect on the guests, but as a personal environment and the space from which you view the world. Any plant is appropriate providing only that it is environmentally suited to the site, and that the climate, the light, and the soil you bring it to enable it to be the most it can be.

Jacqueline Hériteau is the consummate garden writer, and her passion for beauty and her knowledge of gardening reality have been brought to fruition in this volume. She is one of very few contemporary authors whose prose has the ability to communicate both the soaring vision and the earthy guidance you need in planning a garden. You will find here understanding of the many variables you have to play with, and you will discover environmentally sound solutions on which to base gardens whose beauty can be sustained for years to come. Following Jacqui's "green thoughts" and losing yourself in contemplation of the glorious gardens portrayed will help you to explore the many unique opportunities afforded by your own property. Jacqui's discerning eye, wisdom, and down-to-earth knowledge of what makes these gardens beautiful will free the artist in you, and open your thought to ideas leading to the creation of a dream garden that is truly your own.

Rejoice with us in the liberated creativity and natural beauty that are the principles driving landscape design today, and join Miss Pink in creating gardens that flow with the wind and that are as joyful as a child's crayon colors.

Dr. H. Marc Cathey, President
American Horticultural Society
Alexandria, Virginia

CONTENTS

INTRODUCTION

By viewing Nature, Nature's handmaid Art,
Makes mighty things from small beginnings grow.

JOHN DRYDEN

A garden is many things to many people. For some, it is a communion, a connection with the earth and its beauty. For some it is a source of serenity, a means of imposing order on the untamed forces of nature. And for some, a garden is a wellspring of joy and inspiration, an ever-changing display of color and form just outside the door. To me, a garden is all of this and more. Large or small, formal or wild, a garden is the embodiment of a creative vision. At its foundation, a garden is a work of art.

Like all artists, we gardeners engage in the hopeful work of turning a dream into a reality. The fine artist uses paints and canvas, wood and clay and stone to shape a work of art; the garden artist uses head and heart and hands, light, water, earth, the nature of the plants, the contours of the land itself. Planning a garden is a painterly project. It is a bringing to life of the gardener's vision, an act of faith awesome in its ability to transform. Truly glorious gardens are created by men and women who have a love of nature's limitless beauty and who trust their own creativity, taste, and intuition. Beauty is born of a liberated imagination.

THE EYE OF THE ARTIST

When we set out to create our works of art, gardeners look at the environment creatively: What can I make of this? Where does this garden (or portion of the garden) fit? And then we use knowledge and commitment and imagination to turn those questions into living, flourishing answers.

Almost any site—city or country, hilly or flat, wet, arid, rocky, sandy, windy—can be home to a beautiful garden. What will define the success or failure of your creation is your ability to really *see* the site, the space, and the light, and to filter that vision through your love of nature and your own appetite for beauty. The exquisite Shade Gardens in this book weren't created simply to solve the *problem* of too little sunlight. They grew out of an appreciation of the shade as a place of cool respite from the world outside, a secret room filled with the soft whisper of leaves and the sweet fragrance of nicotiana and four o'clocks.

The gorgeous Hillside Gardens we've pictured are *not* just hard-to-plant slopes that present problems of runoff and erosion. Rather, the garden artists who landscaped those slopes saw in them dramatic waves of earth and stone frozen in motion, exciting natural settings for plunging waterfalls, flowering meadows, and terraced gardens evocative of the romantic old hilltop towns in Provence and Italy. In Rock Gardens, the dreamer with an eye for rugged beauty envisions a stone-strewn barren slope as an ideal site to create a miniature of a high mountain meadow. These aren't spaces where roots can't take hold, they're vistas where glaciers melt, great winds dwarf the trees and shrubs, and drifts of blue-green rock cress, silvery lady's mantle, purple blue anemones, buttercup-yellow hypericum, and other lovely little alpine plants can flourish.

A windy seashore property can be challenging, but it also can be home to a bold romantic garden where cool humid nights heighten the color of the cottage pinks and the fragrance of the roses. In Seashore Gardens, wetlands and salt marshes

OPPOSITE:
Scarlet poppies, yellow threadleaf coreopsis (*Coreopsis verticillata*), and lavender blue sea holly (*Eryngium*), with scarlet *Crocosmia*, at Great Dixter, in Sussex, a 15th century property restored by architect Sir Edwin Lutyens, a close associate of Gertrude Jekyll. Jekyll created exquisite cottage gardens using plant colors, forms, and textures. In formulating the trend away from the stiffly patterned beds of European chateaux and Victorian manor houses, Jekyll's gardens inspired the natural plantings admired today.

ABOVE:
Golden feverfew (*Tanacetum parthenium* 'Aureum') blooms with blue love-in-a-mist (*Nigella damascena*), a Jekyll favorite.

Narcissi and grape hyacinths (*Muscari*) bloom together in a carefully chosen and bloom-timed color module typical of the Jekyll legacy that combines cottagey mixtures of bulbs, perennials, and annuals in orchestrated harmonies. To acquire the knowledge that made this photograph possible, and that produced the exquisite flower combinations on the following pages, takes a lifetime of seeking, experimenting, and learning, as Gertrude Jekyll's writings make abundantly clear.

are exactly the backdrops needed to wed the ornamental grasses of the garden to the beach and to the water beyond. In Small Gardens, a small space doesn't demand a small dream. A minute courtyard can house tubs of exotic lotus and elephant's-ear, even a fountain. A sunny city balcony decked out with an espaliered pear, a chaise longue, and tubs filled with perfumed heliotrope evokes Colette's earthly paradise, and might on a luminous summer evening be visited by the spirit of the great poet herself.

Every home, every space, offers a myriad of opportunities to combine the elements of site, light, climate, and personality, into glorious gardens of any scale.

THE ARTIST'S TOOLS

For most artists, the creative process provides as much satisfaction as the finished work. For gardeners, this is a universal truth: The reward isn't so much the product as the process. Earth and plants, light and water are the tools of the gardener's art. And, like a sculptor molding clay or shaping wood, the gardener must understand the nature and properties of these materials in order to make the most of them.

Become intimate with your garden. The first soft day of early spring, go bare-foot along a sun-warmed path. Close your eyes and step from the hard-packed dirt to the spongy loam in the flower bed. Forever after, that feeling will prevent your heavy booted feet from compacting soil which must remain air-filled to sustain the delicate roots stretching out below, growing cell by cell. Use naked hands to work spring's loose, cool earth. Bare fingers are the finest tools. They spare small treasures that garden gloves are blind to: emerging buds, baby worms, seedlings volunteered by last summer's snapdragons. On your hands and knees, invest an enchanted hour following strands of myrtle and small-leafed ivy in their wanderings.

Rub good garden dirt between your palms. Become very still, and slowly and easily breathe in the rich, musky earth smell. It is deeply satisfying after a winter away from the yard. Rejoice in the silky texture of soil that has digested the chopped leaves you fed to it last fall; it will remind you that now is the time to fertilize the trees and shrubs that provided those leaves. Inhale the aroma of crushed mint and lemon balm. Tuck parsley seeds in around the parsley plants, and use fingers, not a rake, to comb away old parsley stems and winter-killed branches of thyme and oregano. The clean, pungent smells will awaken your appetite for lavender and roses—and in the presence of the dream, you'll find enlarging the herb garden is no trouble at all.

Watch the flowering plums and cherries for planting cues. Traced against blue sky, bare branches with just one or two fat buds open have a beauty that is breathtaking. This precious time of birth is ideal for setting out finicky plants. Too soon the trees will flower over and leaf out, the petals will fall in blizzards of pink and white—and the very best days for early spring planting will have gone by.

The dominant sounds in the spring garden are the busy-ness of baby squirrels and the flutter of wings. But the rhythm of the rain is the sound the garden loves best. To feel the rain the way the garden does, plant in the midst of a gentle shower. As the first drops fall, open a big umbrella at the edge of the flower bed and tuck in under it. Propped between your knees, the umbrella handle holds the canopy at just the right angle to shelter you, the seedlings, and the soil. Your hands are free to work. The rain patters and drums overhead, close and intimate as you firm seedlings into their soil pockets. When the plants are all in, sit under the umbrella sipping tea and see them washed and watered by the sky. Dream.

THE HEART OF THE ARTIST

Creating a garden is an act of faith: faith that your own knowledge, instincts, and vision can produce a thing of beauty. Approach the planting of your garden with an unintimidated reverence, and expect to delight in its magic. Welcome mysteries. Try doubtful experiments. Failures, like unexpected successes, are just information—not the final judgment. Don't worry a lot about your plants. Life on earth—blossoms, you, me, birds, bees, trees—rests in the care of vast forces determined to succeed. Open up! Invite them in! Submit to them, and your garden will flourish.

To carry out a great new plan for the porch garden, I made fall cuttings of some spectacular hot pink geraniums and a frost-tender pink florist's hydrangea. The cuttings spent the winter in a corner of the yard, deep inside a big garbage pail filled with damp peat moss. It was a mild winter and four of the geraniums came through and bloomed all summer in the porch baskets. When I uncovered the hydrangea cuttings, I was thrilled to see fat green buds paired all the way up the stems, ready to unfold. Cleaned and set in water, all four cuttings began to root. Then three died, and with them my plan for the porch garden. The big terra cotta planter for which they were destined got a hot pink geranium tree instead—not my kind of plant, it was a gift—and at its feet I planted Persian violets, puffy blue ageratum, and cascades of variegated vinca and crisp pink and white petunias. The planter turned out to be the summer's pride and joy. The surviving hydrangea cutting I stuck directly into the soil in a

Evergreens and flowering shrubs, bold-leaved hostas, and soaring astilbes and kniphofias provide the structure that orders the natural arrangement of perennials mirrored like an exquisite impressionist painting in the still waters of a millstream pond. A beautiful garden can be installed almost anywhere if you'll allow your creativity to have its way. This beautiful garden wasn't seen by its designer as a ruin of outmoded technologies that needed to be cleared away. Rather, the garden artist saw an opportunity to surround a living mirror with the soaring spires and colorful spheres of a flowering border and other elements to create a living work of art.

Marigolds and Caladiums (Ollesen)

Pansies and 'Bismarck' Hyacinths (Lawson)

'Windsong' Iceland Poppies (Lawson)

12

Early frost bejewels a spider's web and outlines the creamy white variegations of *Hedera helix* with the precision nature applies to all its works. Finding space on your property for flowering meadows and woodlands, however small, invites wildlife by providing sources of food and shelter, secure areas for courting, and places where young animals can safely learn and grow. You will assure the health of the natural system if you replenish the earth by restoring to it some of the foliage it produces annually in the form of compost and mulch. A garden is a whole, to some extent self-perpetuating, and most successful when the elements that were a part of the original habitat are retained and kept in balance.

The most beautiful gardens are those that are most loved. Become intimate with your garden. Approach the planting of your garden with a reverence that can't be intimidated by site or inhibited by other landscapes, however glorious, and expect to delight in the magic of your own creativity.

The ultimate glory will never quite be achieved in the garden at hand: We always have a yearning for more, and that is the planet's song, luring us on.

rose bed where it grew lustily. So I thought I knew everything I needed to know, and forgot about it. With summer, it lost its sunlight, its water, and its life to the roses. And so I learned once more that precious cuttings had best grow up in pots of their own.

ABOUT THIS BOOK

Gardening, like all art, evolves. Every new creation is the product of wisdom and inspiration gained through experience and exposure. The ten chapters in this book are filled with breathtaking garden portraits, whose primary purpose is to release your own creativity. Beautiful, natural, interesting, and original, they can inform your vision, heighten your intuition, and inspire your dream. The text is also filled with ideas and recommendations—from my own experience and the wisdom of other gardeners whose work I know and admire. I think you'll find yourself instinctively matching our gardens to the opportunities that your own property offers.

Creativity is strengthened by knowledge, so I have included a section called Gardening Basics, a compilation of reassuringly simple how-to information. To help you make the right choices for your garden, I have listed outstanding species for all of the different gardens, plant type by plant type, and I have included some sources for these plants. *Glorious Gardens* is designed and written to provide the inspiration *and* the knowledge you need to let yourself create freely. Enjoy! Let the artist in you turn your every garden dream into a glorious, beautiful reality.

NATURAL
GARDENS

I believe a leaf of grass is no less than the journey-work
    of the stars,
And the pismire is equally perfect, and a grain of sand,
    and the egg of the wren,
And the tree toad is a chef d'oeuvre for the highest,
And the running blackberry would adorn the parlors of
    heaven.

WALT WHITMAN

A natural garden is loose and flowing. The plants grow in undulating drifts, poised to unfold beyond the immediate horizon, to follow the birds that inhabit, it to infinity. It is forever becoming—there are chores, of course, but the garden never *looks* as though weeding, pruning, cutting, cleaning up, grinding, composting are needed to make it complete. A natural garden is never messy, never off balance because it is never on balance. It dissipates tension and puts its guests at ease.

Within a natural garden there's a comfortable place, however small, for every aspect of the planet's life systems. There's a sunlit meadow. Bright with buttercups and daisies, milkweed and clover, it will attract butterflies, feed the bees, and fill the air with the sweet scent of meadow grasses. There's a shaded woodland. The trees and shrubs shelter nests and provide gentle shade for the lovely wild things that grow in dappled light—beautiful pink bleeding heart and snowy white trilliums, the green, green ferns and velvet mosses. And there's a place off in a lost corner where everything grows up and goes wild, where thick brambles hide nests and burrows and there's water in a tiny pond for the little animals—the birds, the chipmunks, the frogs, and the darting dragonflies.

Look for traces of the wild gardens that were on your land before your home was built. Early morning is my favorite time to probe the garden's history. Go out before dawn and settle down in the most welcoming spot on the property, and as the day brightens let the land speak to you. You will see what is there in a new light. Sunny slopes and the tops of trees and tall shrubs catch the sunrise first and tell you where meadow flowers and miniature woodlands can flourish. Even if it's a very small yard locked into a very big city, traces of its original affinities are present where the thieving squirrels settle, where the moisture-loving mosses stubbornly soften and green the earth.

Trust the land to reveal what to plant where, and your own receptivity will acknowledge it. This may seem mystical, but it is very practical advice. A natural garden thrives when it imitates the landscape that originally was there. Plants flourish, flowers reseed themselves year after year, and wildlife comes to places that resemble their native habitats.

MEADOW GARDENS

An open space, flat or slightly sloping, filled with sunshine, is an invitation to create a meadow garden, where colorful flowers will bloom in the midst of tall grasses. The flowers need six hours of full sun daily, and a well-dug, well-drained soil. A good soaking rain, or watering, two or three times a month will keep the flowers flourishing all season long.

The showiest flowers you can plant in a meadow garden are garden ornamentals that go wild. Some examples are the many small-flowered sunflowers and daisies, the daylilies, especially the spotted wild tiger lily, a variety of poppies, and if there's a wet patch, blue flag (*Iris versicolor*) and sweet flag (*Acorus calamus*). They require a little more effort to establish than wild meadow flowers, but the large colorful blossoms are very effective, and with any luck at all the plants will multiply. The many regional beauties that won't go wild in my area fill me with envy—perhaps they will grow in

PRECEDING SPREAD:
Left: Rich, dense, textured, naturalized azaleas and yellow species rhododendrons follow a crystalline waterfall downhill at Leonardslee Gardens in Sussex, England. When ornamentals are planted with compatible natives, a fluid design emerges and the environment does much of the plant maintenance. Leaf fall here provides mulch and helps maintain the acid soils in which azaleas thrive.

Right: A river of naturalized daffodils flows through open woodlands at Great Thurlow Hall, in Suffolk, England. I have found daffodils invulnerable, even to squirrels, and able to bloom, multiply, and spread into open land as long as the foliage is allowed to yellow before the plants are cut back.

OPPOSITE:
English bluebells (*Hyacinthoides non-scripta*) carpet a natural garden of copper beech and Ghent azaleas that attracts birds, our most effective insect control. Here the architecture of trees and tall shrubs replaces the man-made structures of formal gardens: Plants seem to follow the prevailing winds and creep along paths created by light, moisture, and wildlife.

OVERLEAF:
Brilliant in crimson satin and black velvet, corn poppies blanket a ploughed field. One of the showiest garden species included in wildflower mixes, under good conditions *Papaver rhoeas* will reseed itself and spread.

your meadow. I especially love the tall pink plumes of Wisconsin's queen-of-the-prairie (*Filipendula rubra*), and I am wild about California's confetti-colored wild poppies, the evening primroses, *Geum triflorum*, and starry, blue-eyed *Sisyrinchium bellum*.

A handful of naturalized garden flowers makes an outstanding contribution to the meadow garden, but the bulk of the flowers comes from mixtures of wildflower seeds suited to various regions. Many of the garden catalogs offer seed mixtures that are better suited for different regions of the country. Yarrow, bachelor's buttons, coreopsis, sweet William, baby's breath, assorted coneflowers, lupines, and daisies turn up in most of the mixtures, but beware—some wildflower mixtures contain a lot of weed seeds. The wildflower mixtures I've found in the gift shops of local botanic gardens and arboreta seem to have more that are special to the area. Consider planting sturdy perennial plants throughout your seeded meadow, to give them a head start on the annuals and weeds that will grow vigorously the first year. If your space for a meadow garden is small, consider installing wildflower turf. It is distributed by sod growers to nurseries and garden centers. It will bloom the first year and last, as perennials do, four to six years before it needs dividing or renewing.

White evening primrose (*Oenothera speciosa*) romps through a garden landscaped with plants that thrive in, blend with, and enhance the existing terrain. Large numbers of trees aren't necessary to create the impression of a woodland. A small grove, even a single tree, can achieve the visual effect and provide many of the growing conditions woodland plants require.

Ornamental grasses also are an integral and beautiful part of the meadow garden. They are the background against which the flowers thread their colors, and they give the meadow the softness and movement of a wild garden. In early spring before seeding the meadow with flowers, weave seedlings of ornamental grasses through the meadow—tufts of wiry fescue, fountain grass, *stipa*, and *calamagrostis.*

Some of the meadow flowers included in regional seed mixtures will come back to grace your garden every year. Some will need to be renewed. Even if those planted in your meadow fail after a year or two, new seeds will fly in on the wind or be sown by birds. Flowers that grow wild along the sides of the roads and in empty fields in your region are the surest bets. Graceful Queen Anne's lace will decorate your summer meadow and, as summer draws to a close, the ubiquitous goldenrod will brighten your meadow with a sea of golden yellow plumes. (Goldenrod does not, by the way, cause hay fever.) The goldenrods likely to establish residence are the *Solidago canadensis* and *S. virgaurea*, and I recommend them highly for their color. But also look for seeds of *Solidago odora*, which, while not as colorful, makes sweetly scented bouquets.

The daisies in the wildflower mixes tend to stay, but they make a better showing when new seed is sown every spring. The white oxeye daisy (*Leucanthemum vulgare*) brightens fields all over the United States and Canada in early summer. Enduring, hardy perennials with golden central discs, they often flower from seed the first year. The daisylike black-eyed Susan (*Rudbeckia hirta*) blooms reliably from midsummer to fall, even in the hot south. After its petals fall, the sooty black cones remain, ripening seed that feeds the birds and replants the meadow. While they are biennials that flower the second year after seeding, these coneflowers will also need occasional reseeding by you, as will two other worthwhile meadow flowers, the lovely blue chicory (cornflower to Canadians) and purple joe-pye weed (*Eupatorium purpureum*).

The meadow's colors also can be maintained by planting chosen spots not just with your own favorite meadow flowers, but with some of the showy cultivars, native flowers recast as garden flowers. One such flower is the tall, stately, vivid purple coneflower (*Echinacea purpurea*). It's not my favorite in a cultivated garden, but in the sea of green and pastels that is a meadow garden it stands out. Huge, daisylike, deep orange-bronze cones are surrounded by rich, dusky rose-purple petals that angle backwards a little and are set off and beautifully balanced by dark green foliage. A tough, long-lived native, it is dear to butterflies, and finches relish the seeds. Extremely long-flowering, it comes into bloom in late spring, May or June in the South, or in early summer and continues to bloom intermittently into fall, especially if it is deadheaded.

Nor can I imagine a meadow garden without the milkweeds! Common milkweed (*Asclepias syriaca*) produces only a modest floral display in a faded shade of old rose, but in the fall its handsome seedpods split and spill silky white threads to the winds. The sculptural castings left behind are so striking you will want to gather and dry them for winter arrangements. Common milkweed tends to appear in the meadow garden whether you plant it or not, but you my have to plant its very desirable cousin, butterfly weed (*Asclepias tuberosa*) unless it already grows in your area. A striking perennial, it is native to meadows and prairies and competes well with grasses. Like its relatives, it is a major source of food for the exquisite orange and black monarch butterfly; its flowers are a clear orange that is just beautiful against the meadow's golds and greens. The flowers are long-lasting and sweetly fragrant, and the seed-

Coarse dark green foliage sets off the rich, dusky rose petals that make the purple coneflower (*Echinacea purpurea*) a superb choice for meadow gardens. Dear to butterflies and finches, the purple coneflower is one of many outstanding native plants that have been recast as cultivated ornamentals.

OPPOSITE:
The bright, long-season flowers of our native Indian blanket (*Gaillardia pulchella*) color a flowering meadow that has been overwhelmed by grasses. Though changing combinations of plants are welcomed, a meadow garden needs help to maintain a show of colorful flowers. To serve the wildlife so essential to the health and beauty of the garden, cut back the plants after they have ripened their fall gifts: seedheads and silky tassels for lining nests and decomposing vegetation for feeding earthworms and nourishing beneficial insects.

pods are attractive in the fall. Butterfly weed is slow to start from seed and slow to emerge in spring, but it is easy to grow and well worth the wait!

At least one species of wild aster blooms almost everywhere in North America. Asters grow so vigorously—I've seen clumps 6 feet tall in the hills around Chautauqua, New York—they could be expected to crowd out other meadow flowers, but they, too, may need periodic reseeding. The exuberant plants top themselves with masses of tiny, long-lasting, fluffy pink, purple-pink, blue, or white blooms. Sow lots of seed for the pale pink asters—with goldenrod, they make gorgeous fillers for late summer bouquets.

Many of the meadow flowers are biennials and perennials that bloom only the second year from seed. Even though it is included in many of the regional wildflower mixtures, every spring sow seeds of the brilliant little annual, *Gaillardia pulchella* (Indian blanket) to bridge color gaps. It has the longest bloom period of any summer flower. The bright, daisy-faced blooms, a showy, yellow-tipped red, are a real asset—butterflies love them and, like many other wildflowers, they develop interesting seedheads.

PREPARING AND PLANTING THE MEADOW

Fall is the best time of the year to prepare the soil for these plants. One of the best ways to avoid growing lots of unwanted native plants (weeds) is to strip away the sod to a depth of about 2 inches. Or burn out the potentially troublesome seeds by baking the area under heavy black plastic for eight weeks during the hottest weeks of late summer. Then remove the plastic and cover the area with 4 inches of organic mulch; the dead sod below will decompose to some extent during the winter.

In early spring, as soon as the ground is dry enough to be worked on, rototill what remains of the mulch and the turf into the soil; rake the area smooth and discard clumps of turf, woody roots, and rocks. Better still, don't rototill at all, and you'll avoid bringing to the surface weed seeds buried deep in the soil, just lying in wait. Instead, just loosen the surface of your mulch with a rake and seed on top of it. Don't be tempted to fertilize. Fertilizers encourage the wild grasses that crowd out wildflowers.

Before planting meadow flower seeds, mix them with slightly damp sand. Following the instructions given on the seed containers, broadcast the seeds evenly over the meadow area. Tamp them with your feet to firm them onto the soil. Right after sowing, water by hand with a fine spray. Keep the soil moist for the next several days until the seedlings are showing green against the earth. Sharp little tufts of crabgrass and quickgrass will come up with the flower seeds; root out as many of these as you have patience for the first year, and again early each spring. Without some control, grasses and weeds tend to take over, obscure, and eventually engulf the flowers.

Give the meadow garden a haircut every autumn when the flowers have gone by and before winter storms flatten the stalks. Don't cut until the meadow has prepared its many gifts for wildlife—birdseed ripened in the stiff, dry seedheads, feathery tufts that float on the air, silky tassels for lining nests, decomposing organic materials that eventually will feed the earthworms and the beneficial insects.

Scythe the meadow, or cut it with the blade of your lawn mower set as high as possible. Leave the brush to dry where it falls. When it has completely dried, if you gather it and shake it to free and to scatter the remaining dried seeds, you will be helping the plants to reseed the meadow and providing a winter banquet for birds. An annual cutting opens up the area to more health-giving light and air and readies it for next year's displays. You can also leave the attractive, graceful grasses and flowers standing all winter, and mow early in the spring instead.

OPPOSITE:
In spring the lake at Leonardslee Gardens mirrors the azaleas. Home to an immense variety of creatures, the trees and shrubs shelter nests and burrows and provide shade for the lovely wild plants that thrive in their dappled light—pink bleeding heart and snowy white trilliums, lacy ferns and velvet mosses. A natural garden can provide water for the wildlife.

---

* Z refers to hardiness zone numbers.
See Zone map on page 233.

WOODLAND GARDENS

A lightly wooded site or a yard where a few trees cast dappled light invites a woodland garden. The grade can be flat, sloping, even steeply sloping. The light filtered by trees allows you to grow a wonderful variety of woodland plants that would not survive in a bright, sunny meadow garden; woodland plants thrive in shade.

I love to see a path cut through a woodland, a path that flows through the dappled light and disappears off somewhere. The path can wander through free-form drifts of flowers and ferns, drifts that are repeated, and repeated yet again in the distance. The glades of dappled light that occur here and there in the woods can be carpeted with pretty ground covers like heart-shaped wild ginger (*Asarum europaeum*) and silvery Japanese painted fern (*Athyrium nipponicum* 'Pictum'). Other ground covers that should do well in a sunny glade include *Chrysogonum virginianum*, *Cornus canadensis*, *Lamium maculatum*, *Polygonum bistorta*. Local varieties of ferns purchased from nurseries, of course, should adapt well to your woodland. If nature hasn't put them there already, they're gorgeous placed in front of rocks and by old tree stumps. Make it a point to provide an old tree stump and a fallen log or two that time will color with golden lichens and green moss.

I like to give the garden the appearance of greater depth and to add a touch of mystery by partially screening some areas. Try planting flowering evergreen shrubs at intervals near the path and set the larger shrubs up front with the smaller shrubs farther back. Azaleas, rhododendrons, and elegant mountain laurel will fill the woodland in spring with gorgeous flowers in a wild array of colors—pinks, purple, red, rose, orange, mauve, lavender, white. Where winters are mild, plant camellias, *Skimmia*, whose evergreen leaves are aromatic when crushed, and the cherry laurel (*Prunus laurocerasus*) for its graceful, cascading form.

To furnish the woodland with song—and to keep the insects under control—plant a few trees specially for birds. They like to nest in the branches of evergreens, such as Canada hemlock (*Tsuga canadensis*), and white pine (*Pinus strobus*), and they eat the fruit of American holly (*Ilex opaca*) and red cedar (*Juniperus virginiana*). Flowering fruit trees are veritable larders for birds, especially the beautiful new cultivars whose fruit hang on for months, such as the crab apple *Malus* 'Narragansett'. Where I live in Washington, D.C., a pair of cardinals dines on our Chinese dogwood and weeping cherry all winter. Many native trees bear fruits attractive to the birds. The American hornbeam (*Carpinus caroliniana*) is a lovely shade tree, bears fruit, as does the wild red cherry (*Prunus pensylvanica*) and the chokecherry (*P. virginiana*). The flowers and fruits of the native species are smaller, but birds love them, and the leaves color nicely in fall.

The way I guarantee spring color in my little woodland is to plant shade-loving garden flowers. They are, after all, just the woodland flowers we chose to tame because, even in their wild state, they were the showiest and the most beautiful. In mild winters, narcissus bloom under the fringe tree as early as November. They are followed in late winter and early spring by drifts of miniature daffodils and splashes of vibrant color from small species tulips. Then the wood hyacinths (*Hyacinthoides hispanica*) display their pastel bells under the Kousa dogwood, and soon the quilled columbines are nodding in pristine white and rich purple above foliage as dainty as maidenhair fern. If cut back when it begins to fade, columbine foliage returns to carpet the forest floor for the rest of the season. In May, drifts of lily-of-the-valley unfurl their broad green leaves, and dozens of slender stems rise through them bearing up to

twenty tiny, pure white bells. For the next few weeks, that patch of woodland is graced by one of the world's greatest floral perfumes, the essence of the perfume Joy. But for me, the high point of spring isn't when the first daffodil glows yellow, nor even when the first violet lifts its incandescent purple head—it's when I come upon a tuft of pastel primroses in bloom.

Summer is the most difficult time to provide a sure show of color in a woodland garden. The candy pink and white heart-shaped blossoms of bleeding heart (*Dicentra spectabilis*) appear in late spring and early summer. When the flowers fade, the beautiful, lacy foliage remains. In the hottest months I rely on the annuals, such as the little wax begonias and brilliant impatiens, spectacular planted with matching caladiums, and a few shade-loving perennials, such as the indestructible spiderworts (*Tradescantia* × *virginiana* hybrids), a few hardy cyclamens, and summer-flowering, lemon-yellow straw foxglove (*Digitalis lutea*). The last flower to bloom in the wood-

A rustic bridge and an open gate mark the transition between two areas of the garden and offer access to paradise—a host of golden daffodils. Many spring-flowering bulbs are used to provide early spring color for flowering meadows and gardens of ornamental grasses. Narcissus thrive in full sun as well as in light shade, and when set out in drifts of at least twelve, they spread rapidly.

Stately plants 3 to 4 feet tall, Russell lupines are often included with other cultivated flowers in regional wildflower seed mixes. Others you can plant to brighten the soft green, gold, and russet of wildflower meadows are golden yarrow and coreopsis; blue bachelor's buttons; purple and red sweet William, coneflowers, and poppies; and white baby's breath and oxeye daisies. Most of the seeds used in regional mixes are those of modest natives that have had millennia to adapt to the variables of their habitat.

land garden is the Japanese toad lily (*Tricyrtis hirta*), which bears modest, but quite lovely, orchidlike flowers on gracefully arching stems.

The purist plants a woodland garden only with authentic, native woodland wildflowers. Although many are easy to grow, some are fussy, with narrow, sometimes unusual, soil, water, and light requirements. To succeed with the most particular species is a labor of love that requires patience and perhaps years of trial and error. The difficult ones that finally become established are the treasures of the woodland garden. The woodland wildflower I love best isn't easy to find either in the woods or in established gardens. In fact, I've only come across it once in the wild years ago in midspring on Cape Cod. Perhaps the most fragrant of all wildflowers, trailing arbutus, or mayflower (*Epigaea repens*), is a slow-spreading, 6-inch-high evergreen creeper with bright green leaves. In spring it bears, almost hidden by the leaves, clusters of pink-tinged flowers rather like tiny, incredibly scented apple blossoms. It is Massachusetts' state flower.

The easiest woodland wildflowers to grow are the ones native to the woods in your area. In eastern United States, where soils tend to be acid, woodland plants, except those native to limestone outcrops, are likely to do best in acid, humus-rich soils, the same soils in which the rhododendrons and azaleas thrive. If your soil isn't acid enough (pH 4.5 to 6.0, a little lower for the fussy species), you can amend the soil with chemicals (see page 234) or, even better, with peat or acid compost.

Many easy-to-grow, perennial woodland flowers are sold at local nurseries and through mail order catalogs, among them the exquisite native bleeding hearts and Solomon's seal. Both the fringed bleeding heart (*Dicentra eximia*) and the Pacific bleeding heart (*D. formosa*) are small, delicate-looking plants with blue-green, fern-like foliage, and rose-purple, pink, or white flowers. They are surprisingly hardy and bloom all summer. Solomon's seal (*Polygonatum biflorum*) hangs pairs of bell-shaped, greenish white or pale yellow flowers below its leaves on long, arching stems and follows these with blue-black berries. Plant bleeding hearts and Solomon's seal with ferns and hostas in drifts, and repeat them along the woodland path. Solomon's seal planted in a carpet of wild ginger (*Asarum caudatum*) is beautiful splashed through the woods. The clumps increase slowly over time, making a distinctive ground cover, and the golden leaves of the Solomon's seal contrast beautifully with the dark green leaves of the wild ginger in the fall.

Two of the most beautiful wild woodland flowers that grow successfully in cultivation are the trillium and the lady's-slipper. With the first real flush of warmth, immaculate, almost orchidlike, the great white trillium (*Trillium grandiflorum*) unfolds its three ascending petals. Each rhizome sends up one stem with three leaves and a three-petaled blossom, which may be pure, glowing white or pink. Other trilliums have deep maroon-red or purple-brown flowers. With luck and care, trilliums will form colonies and spread, forming a fine, tall ground cover. The beautiful lady's-slippers are real orchids. The most successful of this challenging genus that I've seen grown in cultivation is the large yellow lady's-slipper (*Cypripedium calceolus* var. *pubescens*). It has large, strongly ribbed leaves and in spring sends up 12-inch stems tipped with one or two very fragrant, pouchlike, large yellow flowers streaked with brown. The delicate pink lady's slipper (*C. acaule*) is almost impossible to grow except where it occurs in nature.

Another wilding worth trying, perky Jack-in-the-pulpit (*Arisaema triphyllum*) is loved by children. It's one of the first wildflowers of the year. Children love to be

WOODLAND FLOWERS

Black cohosh, bugbane
Cimicifuga racemosa Z3-8

Bloodroot
Sanguinaria canadensis Z3-9

Bunchberry
Cornus canadensis Z2-7

False Solomon's seal
Smilicina racemosa Z3-7

Fringed bleeding heart
Dicentra eximia Z4-8

Golden Star, Green-and-Gold
Chrysogonum virginianum Z5-9

Jack-in-the-pulpit
Arisaema triphyllum Z4-9

Japanese toad lily
Tricyrtis hirta Z4-9

Mayflower, trailing arbutus
Epigaea repens Z4-8

Oconee bells
Shortia galacifolia Z5-8

Solomon's seal
Polygonatum biflorum Z3-9

Speckled wood lily
Clintonia umbellulata Z4-8

White baneberry, white cohosh
Actaea alba Z4-9

White giant trillium
Trillium chloropetalum 'Album'
Z4-9

White wood aster
Aster divaricatus Z4-8

Wild Ginger
Asarum caudatum Z6-8

Rue-anemone
Anemonella thalictroides Z4-9

Yellow lady's slipper
Cypripedium calceolus Z5-8

27

the first to discover it, and sometimes they taste the plant to test adult warnings that to put any of it in the mouth causes a long-lasting, painful pins-and-needles feeling. Which it certainly does. Jack can be established in moist, acid, humus-rich soil and will develop small colonies. Jack-in-the-pulpit are followed in the fall by a cluster of bright red berries.

One way to add new wildflowers to your woodland garden is to to gather seed in the wild. Sow fresh seed as soon as you collect it, in late summer or early fall. *Never* dig wildflowers in the wild—many are protected by conservation laws. Always buy from reputable nurseries; many wildflowers are now available as container plants. You will find more exotic woodland species in the catalogs of specialists. Botanic gardens and arboretums in your area will be able to suggest other sources.

Spring is the best time for transplanting most woodland plants in most regions. To prepare the soil, in fall mulch the areas to be planted 6 inches deep with chopped or ground dried leaves, and add a light application of an acid fertilizer. Since the ideal soil for most woodland plants is acid, use acidic mulches, such as leaf mold (half-composted leaves or composted pine needles), lime-free compost, and peat moss. In early spring top the mulched area with 3 inches of sharp sand, add another application of fertilizer, and dig everything into the soil.

A woodland garden benefits from a yearly half-strength application of a slow-release acid-type fertilizer in November and again in early spring before growth begins. Fertilizers and soil amenders identified as acid, lime-free, or suitable for azaleas, rhododendrons, and evergreens are right for woodland plants.

FERNS AND MOSSES

A shaded, damp site where mosses grow naturally is an invitation to plant ferns and mosses. These are plants whose ancestors greened the planet before coniferous and flowering plants evolved. They often flourish where other plants fail, in the deep shade of a wooded north slope, for example, on dry, rocky soil, or where drainage is poor. And, because they're shallow-rooted, they avoid competition with tree roots for moisture and space.

With the first real warmth of spring the ferns raise their fiddleheads, a soft, cool presence unlike any other in the woods. Local garden centers and farmers' markets sell container-grown ferns native to the area. (Make sure they are nursery-propagated, not collected in the wild.) They will do better than those offered in catalogs. They spread more rapidly and adapt more easily to their new situation. Planting beds ideally should have forest soil that is 50 to 75 percent humus or decayed, shredded leaves fertilized with composted cow manure.

Plant a fern with its crown just below the soil surface. Mulch all around with shredded leaves, leaf compost, or peat moss. Avoid deep cultivating; weeds should be pulled by hand, gently. Fern rhizomes must be free to creep over or just under the surface soil and colonize their territory. A little overhead watering in hot weather is helpful. In late winter scatter a light application of acid fertilizer under the foliage. Allow the duff (layer of decaying vegetation that covers the soil) to remain undisturbed.

Many mosses will volunteer and thrive in a woodland environment in which azaleas, rhododendrons, shortias, and ferns grow well. They are extremely hardy and need no supplementary water or fertilizer. Mosses grow in a wide variety of habitats, even in the dense shade under a canopy of beech and in highly acid soil (pH 5.5 or lower). If your soil isn't acid enough for the variety of moss you plan to grow, prepare the soil in early spring by spreading aluminum sulfate or ferrous sulfate on the moist

Ornamental grasses give a naturalized garden the softness and movement of a wild prairie. This collection at Longwood Gardens in Pennsylvania includes: in the foreground, *Leymus secalinus*; behind it, to the left, *Miscanthus sinensis* 'Gracillimus', and on the right, Japanese blood grass (*Imperata* 'Red Baron'); the stand of orange-gold grass is *Calamagrostis*, and the yellow-banded grass on its left is *Miscanthus sinensis* 'Zebrinus'; the tall bold green grass in the background is the giant reed called *Arundo donax*.

OVERLEAF:
Top left: A sunny meadow bright with daisies and scented by rosy sweet clover attracts bees and butterflies that, along with the wind, pollinate flowering plants. Enduring and hardy, the oxeye daisy (*Leucanthemum vulgare*) has naturalized in fields and by the roadsides of North America, but its homelands are Europe and Asia. Many species of garden plants have escaped to join our native wildflowers and color the natural landscape.

Bottom left: Siberian iris foliage turns rich orange-gold-brown in fall, and the viburnums color their berries lipstick red; their maroon foliage matches the maroon of the dogwoods. Shrubs whose flowers are followed by colorful berries and autumn foliage give life and beauty to the garden in the cold seasons.

Right: A sophisticated collection of shrubs and trees borders a narrow path brightened in spring by masses of dainty pink *Primula polyneura*. On the right are a low-growing weeping hemlock and a tall, slim weeping blue Atlas cedar (*Cedrus atlantica* 'Glauca Pendula'). Among the background plants are rhododendron 'Bowbells' and behind it a beautiful little red Japanese maple (*Acer palmatum*).

ground. In about two weeks the pH of the soil should be at or below pH 5.5. You can buy moss spores from a garden catalog or wait for the mosses to appear on their own. You may be able to salvage unwanted mosses from a building site or from your neighbors; press them down onto the prepared soil and keep them moist until they are established. Do not collect large quantities of naturally growing mosses. An unusual method I've tried is to process a quarter cup of moss and a cup of yogurt in a blender and to spread the blend over acidified soil. The yogurt provides the nourishment needed to get the mosses off to a quick start.

Keep a new bed of moss free of leaves during the winter. Gently sweep the leaves away, or spread netting over the moss before the leaves start to fall. When all the leaves are down, roll up the netting and recycle the leaves for compost.

GARDENS FOR WILDLIFE
Flowering meadows and woodlands invite wildlife by providing sources of food, water, shelter, and places where young animals can safely learn and grow. All these

FERNS FOR WOODLANDS

American maidenhair fern
Adiantum pedatum Z3-8

Beech fern
Phegopteris hexagonoptera Z3-8

Christmas fern
Polystichum acrostichoides Z3-8

Cinnamon Fern
Osmunda cinnamomea Z3-8

Hay-scented fern
Dennstaedtia punctilobula Z2-8

Interrupted fern
Osmunda claytonia Z3-8

Japanese holly fern
Cyrtomium falcatum Z9-10

Japanese silver painted fern
Athyrium nipponicum 'Pictum'
Z3-8

Lady fern
Athyrium felix-femina Z3-8

Leather fern
Rumohra adiantiformis Z9-10

Marginal wood fern
Dryopteris marginalis Z4-8

New York fern
Parathelypteris novaeboracensis
Z2-8

Ostrich fern
Matteuccia struthopteris Z2-8

Royal fern
Osmunda regalis Z3-9

Spinulose wood fern
Dryopteris carthusiana Z3-8

Western sword fern
Polystichum munitum Z5-8

Paper birch with woodland ferns
Betula papyrifera

TREES THAT ATTRACT BIRDS

American holly
Ilex opaca Z5-9

American hornbeam
Carpinus caroliniana Z3-9

Chinaberry
Melia azederach Z7-10

Chinese dogwood
Cornus kousa var. *chinensis* Z5-8

Crab apples
Malus cultivars Z5-8

Choke cherry
Prunus virginiana Z2-8

Cornelian cherry
Cornus mas Z5-8

Eastern hemlock
Tsuga canadensis Z4-8

Eastern Red cedar
Juniperus virginiana Z3-9

Eastern white pine
Pinus strobus Z3-9

Hackberry
Celtis occidentalis Z2-9

Pin cherry
Prunus pensylvanica Z3-8

Pitch pine
Pinus rigida Z4-7

Red mulberry
Morus rubra Z5-9

Shadblow, serviceberry
Amelanchier spp. Z3-8

Washington hawthorn
Crataegus phaenopyrum Z4-8

31

Winterberry
Ilex verticillata Z3-9

elements can be fitted into a surprisingly small space. The wildlife habitat maintained by The American Horticultural Society in Alexandria, Virginia, includes a couple of trees, brambles, wildflowers, rocks piled to make little caves, and water. The habitat occupies a mere 20 by 40 feet. Leave a dead tree standing and an astonishing collection of creatures will make their homes in and around it. The insects digesting the wood provide food for woodpeckers and other creatures, and holes in the tree are occupied by bats, owls, squirrels, and song birds. Raccoons like to perch high up, curled and snoozing safely in the fork of a branch. Hollow out a fallen tree at either end, and it will soon shelter a variety of animals.

To invite wildlife into the yard, the first step is to provide water. Locate it where you can watch the animals without disturbing them. What kinds of animals will come depends on the size of the body of water and its location. Equip a condo balcony with a container of water 2 feet in diameter, or even less, and there will be dragonflies, butterflies, and birds. To attract frogs and other small creatures, create a small marshland by installing a pond with a muddy shelf that leads naturally into the deeper water. Build hollow rock piles at the edge to provide cover, and sink short lengths of plastic pipe for crayfish. Install a 10-square-foot pond in an isolated corner of a yard in the suburbs, and it will attract birds, local small animals, raccoons, opossums, and even deer.

To protect your garden from chipmunks, rabbits, and woodchucks, install their water supply a long distance away, and provide a master burrow near the water. A burrow can be made of short pieces of plastic tubing—1 1/2 to 3 inches in diameter—positioned to act as entrances to the interior of a hollow rock pile, a slat house set over the pipe, or a hole in a stone wall. The size of the pipe governs the size of the occupant and protects it from larger predators. For chipmunks, which need a grass-lined nesting chamber, create a weep hole in a brick or a stone wall, or in a pile of rocks. Make the only access to the hole a short piece of 1 1/2-inch plastic tubing buried under soft soil.

Rabbits, in particular baby rabbits of which there is a never-ending supply, are sweet little thieves that can be kept out of the kitchen garden only by chicken wire fencing that rests on top of folded hardware cloth sunk deep into the soil all around. They may be less destructive if water, an inviting habitat, and good pickings are provided well away from your own garden. Allow a tangle of wild roses, raspberries, or forsythia to grow up and they will make their home there. Or build a brush pile: Arrange logs, stones, cinder blocks, or bricks around a 6-inch sloping depression, top this with two or three 4-inch logs set parallel, and cross with logs facing the opposite direction. Cover it with a criss-cross of stalks of underbrush about an inch in diameter. The rabbits will burrow under the pile and up into the hidden chamber. Plant a generous supply of natural forage plants near their domain, and wildlife may be more likely to stay out of your garden.

To attract butterflies and hummingbirds, plant splashes of brightly colored flowers that remain all season. Both of these flighty little creatures haunt tubular single blossoms rich in nectar. Their favorite colors are intense shades of purple, yellow, orange, and red. Single blossoms are preferred over double because the nectar is easier to get at. Both are irresistibly drawn to the butterfly bush (*Buddleja davidii*) whose beautiful lavender flowers are fragrant and will bloom all summer and fall if deadheaded. There are other colors—deep purples, pinks, reds, and white—but the species, which is lavender, is the most fragrant and has the greatest appeal to wildlife.

A brilliant cultivar of bee balm (*Monarda didyma*).

The flowers are borne on new wood, so where it doesn't die to the ground, cut it back in late winter before growth begins to stimulate the strong new growth that produces the best flowering. Lantana is another favorite. Hummingbirds are partial to red and regularly visit the trumpet vine (*Campsis radicans*), red bee balm, coral bells, scarlet runner beans, honeysuckles, fuchsias and hibiscus, and firebush (*Hamelia patens*).

Once you have succeeded in attracting adult butterflies to your garden, you may decide to plant the species that support their larvae. Butterflies need different host plants for their larval and adult stages. Each species needs a particular host on which to lay its eggs and to feed its larvae. Monarchs lay eggs on milkweeds; black swallowtails, on parsley; and tiger swallowtails, on tulip trees and wild cherry. *Passiflora* × *alato-caerula* and *P. caerula*, vigorous tropical vines that bear fragrant flowers, are the host plants for gulf fritillary, zebra, and Julia butterflies. In cool regions the tropical passion flowers can be grown as annuals.

Birds need a high observation post from which to study a water supply before they come down to it and a safe place to retreat to a short distance away. They usually fly first to a distant branch, then come in closer to check out the territory, and finally fly on in. They also need a clear flight path and tend to follow the same approach pattern. An ideal landing site is a broad stone that slopes gently up from the edge of the water, making a platform for drinking and bathing.

In summer birds can find plenty of insects, seeds, and berries to eat. In winter they are easily drawn to a bird feeder station. They are relatively selective about the grains they eat. While extensive lists of preferred foods are available from the Audubon Society, I've enjoyed experimenting on my own by placing a variety of seeds in lots of two teaspoonfuls along a wall, or some other safe place. The seeds that vanish in less than two hours suggest which birds you can easily attract. Then set out plants that produce the seeds for your favorite group. Goldfinches, for example, love thistles. Not too near the house, plant a stand of Scotch thistle, *Onopordum acanthium*. It's a much-branched, silver-blue, ornamental biennial 9 feet tall with sharply toothed, hairy leaves and fuzzy white or purple thistle flowers. Dig a garden bed around it and fill the bed with regional wildflowers. It will make a pretty flowering border that will become a feeding station for goldfinches.

PLANTS THAT ATTRACT BUTTERFLIES

Bee balm, Oswego tea
Monarda didyma Z4-9

Butterfly bush, summer lilac
Buddleja davidii Z5-9

Butterfly weed, pleurisy root
Asclepias tuberosa Z3-9

Cosmos cultivars
Cosmos bipinnatus Annual

Daylily species and hybrids
Hemerocallis spp. Z3-9

Flowering tobacco
Nicotiana alata Annual

Jupiter's beard, red valerian
Centranthus ruber Z5-9

Lantana, yellow sage
Lantana camara Z9-10

Lavender
Lavandula angustifolia Z 6-9

New England aster
Aster novae-angliae Z3-9

Petunia
Petunia hybrida Annual

Pineapple sage
Salvia elegans Z8

Pitcher sage
Salvia azurea Z5-10

Purple coneflower
Echinacea purpurea Z4-8

Swamp milkweed, red milkweed
Asclepias incarnata Z3-8

Monarch butterfly
Danaus Plexippus

WEEKEND
GARDENS

I built my soul a lordly pleasure-house
Wherein at ease for aye to dwell

ALFRED, LORD TENNYSON

The New American Garden style is ideal for the weekend gardener. Its beauty derives from groups of plants that are carefree once they are established, such as trees and shrubs, flowering bulbs, indestructible perennials, and, above all, the beautiful ornamental grasses. These willowy, whispering, wind-tossed plants, the grasses, are the trademark of a prairielike landscape where simple plantings become increasingly artless as they move away from the dwelling, until they merge seamlessly with the countryside. Seasonal changes and nature's own vibrant sound-and-light shows are the main events. The garden in snow is as exciting as the garden in bud or bloom. Often it features broad, rustic walks and comfortable stopping places that invite contemplation. The design is essentially low-maintenance and it works as well in a city yard as it does on a country estate. The difference is one of scale. A weekend garden allows you to play at gardening in a space that invites recreation, meditation, and escape from everyday mindsets.

There are no grand beds of labor-intensive perennials here, but I find that simple plantings provide a completely satisfying, ever-changing, year-round kaleidoscope of color, texture, sound, and movement. In early spring, sweeps of naturalized bulbs push up between the cut-back ornamental grasses. There are daffodils and narcissus, crocus and hyacinths, and varieties of tulips that open throughout spring: perky species tulips, little Greigiis, and water lily, lily-flowered, bouquet-flowering,

fringed, and parrot tulips. On the first warm days of February groves of witch hazel come into bloom, followed by shadblow (which you may know as serviceberry) and flowering plums. Crows and swallows skylark with the wind. In June bees drone over lavender in the field that has replaced the intensive-care lawn, then tall sedums and black-eyed Susans bloom amid the rising grasses. With the coming of fall rains, the flowers of jade-green sedums turn russet-pink-coral, then rust-brown. The leaves of the sweet gums and sourwoods, azaleas and winged euonymus flame into red, coral, yellow, maroon, and the grasses bleach to gold and disperse their seeds. In October the greens remaining in the garden become so intense that at dusk they are almost black. Birds fly in for feasts of bright berries and stay to chatter in the treetops. In winter, birds scour the blackened coneflowers for the last few seeds, and snowdrifts build at the feet of tall golden grasses.

In this very comfortable garden you can allow the plants to develop throughout the year without pruning, staking, spraying, or deadheading. The seedheads of the grasses and the flowers can be left to ripen and stand through fall and winter before you cut them back in early spring. By maintaining a 3-inch layer of mulch, you can avoid having to deal with weeds. The watering system is a system of leaky hoses, or it is installed underground and is automated. The design and the maintenance plan promote a healthy ecological balance that encourages birds and does not exclude insects. I find that there is a healthy balance between harmful and beneficial insects when the garden is composed of a variety of plants and resembles a naturally evolved ecosystem.

DESIGNING THE WEEKEND GARDEN

In planning your weekend garden, I recommend that you make the first element of the design a large, comfortable terrace or deck for dining and lazing about. Because your garden will require minimal maintenance, you'll be spending a lot of time there enjoying the scent of rain on the wind and watching the clouds go by. Surround the terrace with a prairielike, grassy field that fans out towards thickets of flowering and fruiting shrubs and small groves of evergreens and flowering native trees. These vertical landmarks, along with stands of tall upright grasses, will define the boundaries of the property and edit views that lie beyond. If you want to follow the New American Garden style, you should plant the field with masses of medium-height ornamental grasses and spring-flowering bulbs, and with irises, stately giant onion, Indian and foxtail lilies, and some of the enduring summer-blooming perennials suggested below. Or, if you wish to use the space for flying kites and catching butterflies, you'll want to plant a casual lawn. A casual lawn is one that is friendly to weeds, supported by an automatic watering system run by a timer or allowed to go dormant during drought, and mowed only when you feel like mowing. With either approach you can design a rustic path ambling off through the grasses toward wild thickets of berry-laden shrubs and roses, and leading on to groves carpeted with perfumed pine needles and furnished with benches, where you can contemplate the views, and meditate, and sing off key, and walk alone. You can use these design elements to landscape the small backyard of a suburban lot or even a tiny town house garden. As in a bonsai, everything is reduced in scale. The grassy meadow would cover just a few square yards; the path could be a few yards long, or it could cut horizontally through a long, narrow space; and the grove and the view could be symbolized by a stand of tall ornamental grasses backed by evergreen azalea and forsythia and a small tree with spreading branches, perhaps a flowering crabapple.

OPPOSITE:
Cultivars of *Erica* × *darleyensis*, a hybrid of winter heath *(Erica carnea)* and Irish heath *(E. erigena)* are covered with tiny nodding flowers in late winter and early spring. The twiggy heathers are drought-resistant, carefree, evergreen shrubs. They are excellent choices for the easy-care landscape.

MAINTAINING A NEW AMERICAN GARDEN

LATE WINTER
Cut the meadow back to the ground and mulch.

EARLY SPRING
As new foliage begins to emerge, fertilize with a slow-release fertilizer (10-6-4, at 5 pounds per 100 square feet).

SPRING/SUMMER/FALL
Allow the plants to develop throughout the season without pruning, staking, spraying, or deadheading. Water the garden only during an extended drought.

OPPOSITE:
Rustling, swaying grasses are the trademark of the New American Garden style, a prairielike landscape designed to merge seamlessly with the countryside. Reading clockwise: seedheads of *Miscanthus sinensis* 'Silberfeder' golden yarrow, striped eulalia grass (*Miscanthus sinensis* 'Variegatus'), yellow-banded *Miscanthus sinensis* 'Zebrinus', and plumes of pampas grass (*Cortaderia selloana*).

LEFT:
Rhododendrons and golden species azaleas bloom in a spring garden. I love a path that moves through dappled light past colorful clumps of shrubs and flowers that are repeated farther along.

BELOW:
A cultivar of *Astilbe* × *arendsii*, a species often used with the New American Garden style.

Create no straight lines, no clear-cut borders. Let the planted spaces flow one into the next, punctuated by the trees and shrubs and by stands of tall upright ornamental grasses. Small casual plantings of sprawling, naturalized flowers, such as coreopsis, are delightful lapping at the feet of the trees and shrubs or softening the angles of masonry steps and stone walls. Try to bring together flower species that contrast in texture as well as in color, and choose plants that will be appealing from shoots to fruits. Include perennials like rudbeckia and the long-lasting astilbes, whose dried seedheads will counterpoint the grasses in autumn. The ornamental grasses used in a prairielike field should be medium-tall varieties, planted in clumps in long curving island beds, and interplanted with masses of several varieties of flowering bulbs and

TYPICAL BLOOM SEQUENCE FOR SPRING BULBS

1. Winter aconite
2. Snowdrops
3. Crocus
4. *Iris reticulata*
5. Squill (*Pushkinia*)
6. Miniature daffodils
7. Narcissus
8. Siberian squill (*Scilla siberica*)
9. Glory-of-the-snow
10. Hyacinth
11. Species tulips
12. Grape hyacinth
13. Tulip
14. Wood hyacinth
15. Giant snowflake
16. Ornithogalum
17. Fritillaria
18. Spring starflower (*Ipheion uniflorum*)
19. English bluebell (*Hyacinthoides nonscripta*)
20. Alliums
21. Foxtail lilies
22. Fall crocus

RIGHT:
Rambling roses allowed to go a little mad and a few tall, magnificent perennials give this city garden lavish color without intense labor. The very fullness of the plantings inhibits any inclination to tidy up. The scarlet oriental poppies and purple Giant Pacific delphiniums thrive in their comfortable green jungle, yarrow multiplies at will, and the plants develop throughout the season without pruning, spraying, or deadheading.

OPPOSITE TOP:
Luminous pampas grass (*Cortaderia selloana*) and a scarlet Japanese maple are framed by the orange-red foliage of staghorn sumac (*Rhus typhina*). With the cold of early autumn, gold invades the ornamental grasses, and trees and shrubs chosen for their fall colors easily outshine summer's most brilliant flowers.

OPPOSITE BOTTOM:
Higher up along the path the valley view opens out. The orange below is repeated here by a different plant, white enkianthus (*Enkianthus perulatus*), and the scarlet by another Japanese maple. A variegated holly separates the two groups of bright color. A secluded place in nature where you can contemplate the changing of the seasons, meditate, and sing off key is a great joy.

perennials. Vary the widths of the planting beds to avoid any formality. Combine upright grasses, fountain grasses, and grasses of different hues and textures. You will quickly learn to love, as I have, the grasses' freedom from restraint and speed with which they grow from their cut-back, until their shining, airy inflorescences are bending and swaying with the slightest breeze.

As you lay out the design of the field and choose positions for specimen trees, thickets, groves, and rocks, try to imitate the patterns you see in the countryside and plan for a year-round show. Include native rocks here and there on the property where they will be half hidden by plants during the growing season, but bare to the sky in winter. Close to the dwelling and the terrace plant trees and shrubs that are especially interesting in early spring, fall, and winter, and attractive enough to stand alone. Let a tree shelter a big rock, a stand of golden grasses, ferns, patches of evergreen ivy, and

RIGHT:
Nurturing divinely beautiful, fragrant, and usually vulnerable roses is one of many garden fantasies you can indulge when the landscape has been planned to provide maximum enjoyment with minimum labor.

OPPOSITE:
Top left: A contemporary entrance garden intersperses geometric planting beds with brick-edged paving stones and gravel. Among easy-care ground covers growing here are vinca and masterwort (*Astrantia major*), which bears purple floral bracts and pinkish flowers in early summer.

Top right: A Japanese-style entrance garden combines familiar plants with symbolic elements used in Oriental dry landscape designs. In a bed of blue-gray gravel, carefully chosen stones are planted with tiny greens, a representation of water and cliffs. Among the plantings are hostas, *Ajuga reptans*, maroon heuchera 'Palace Purple', gold *Lysimachia nummularia* 'Aurea', and exotic, grassy, purple-black *Ophiopogon planiscapus* 'Arabicus'.

Bottom right: Tokyo's Ryoan-ji Temple garden, the most famous "dry garden" today, is a study in tension and balance whose subtleties the viewer is invited to fathom. The composition is exquisite during a rainfall when the rocks glisten with moisture. Dry landscaping was developed by Zen Buddhists as a focus for contemplation and for spiritual exercise.

Bottom left: Fall in the Japanese Garden, in Portland, Oregon. Bamboo fencing and cherry trees are other elements that are used in dry landscaping. Here the rocks represent islands.

a few brilliant early tulips and narcissus. You'll enjoy seeing from the house the first velvety red buds in early spring, new pale green leaves opening, the first streaks of fall color. A small, graceful evergreen tree, such as Japanese cedar (*Cryptomeria japonica* 'Elegans', for example) is memorable the morning after a snowstorm.

If at all possible, arrange to install a water feature somewhere within hearing distance of your terrace or deck—a little waterfall, a gurgling stream, a gently dripping fountain, or a reflective pool whose light shimmers on a nearby wall.

INDULGING IN A GARDEN FANTASY

With a little of the time freed for recreation by your low-maintenance landscape, indulge in one demanding, fabulously delightful garden fantasy. It can be labor-intensive or difficult—a kitchen garden for example, or a collection of brilliant poppies—as long as it is small, a joy but not a chore, an extra bubble in the champagne. One of my favorite tear-my-hair-out projects is growing any rose, a tea rose, for example, that may be vulnerable to pests and diseases, but whose perfume makes you eager to get out of bed in the morning. Coral red 'Fragrant Cloud' and the soft lavender 'Lagerfeld' are among my favorites. You may prefer to try a pair of perfumed bicolors, such as the cream and crimson 'French Perfume' and 'Double Delight', or an antique rose, such as the exquisite 'Souvenir de la Malmaison', with pale pink, almost white blossoms and an exquisite scent. This rose grows rampant in a sunny place by our kitchen steps and displays a generous dose of black spot every summer; I like to imagine that the Empress Josephine grew it at Malmaison, *sans* black spot. I've always wanted to try a literary English rose. 'Jane Austin', described as an exquisite noisette with pale yellow petals that flush to deeper apricot, and 'Brother Cadfael', a pink Victorian rose round and plump as a peony, would make a handsome couple. Or you could devote your garden play time to building an arched trellis and training the luscious scarlet 'Blaze' to climb it. A less demanding rose project is keeping in bounds an enthusiastic, scrambling, rambling polyantha climber, such as the luscious, lovely, clear pink 'Cécile Brunner'.

A garden project with a much larger dimension than the growing of a rose is the creation of a small garden for meditation, a garden that embodies the spiritual concepts East Asian plantings intend to express. Zen Buddhism influenced the development of kare-sansui, or dry landscaping. The ultimate Japanese garden in this style is the famous Ryoan-ji garden near Tokyo where fifteen rocks are arranged in a bed of

small stones. The garden symbolizes a study in tension and balance whose subtleties are yours to fathom, and it is described as exquisite during a rainfall, or immediately after, when the rocks glisten with moisture. You might enjoy thinking through a Westernized interpretation. Or, you might select a grove to be your Japanese tea house and develop the elements of a Japanese tea garden within it—a path of stepping stones directing your footsteps past places to stop and reflect, perhaps a bonsai mounted as a statue, a fabulous weeping cherry tree, a pink azalea, or a bamboo cane dripping water into a small bowl.

CHOOSING THE PLANTS

In the New American Garden, the whispering field grasses are the chorus and the trees and the shrubs are featured players. Close to the house I like to see trees that have interesting bark. Beautiful bark comes into its own in the winter, a revelation of texture and color obscured during the leafy months. The chalky white bark of the paper birch standing against evergreens and stormy winter skies is a familiar treasure. There are other lovely barks, including some that peel away periodically exposing new bark with contrasting color. If you are inclined towards a birch, choose the Japanese white birch (*Betula platyphylla* var. *japonica* 'Whitespire') which is pest- and disease-resistant. It has distinctive white bark with contrasting black triangles at the bases of the lateral branches. Variegated foliage is another good choice for a close-in

OVERLEAF:
Spring in the Japanese Garden, in Portland, Oregon. One extraordinary tree can satisfy the hunger for beauty.

45

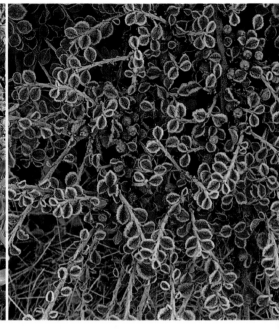

ABOVE:
Summer color for this opulent little garden is provided by durable perennials, such as phlox, and self-sowing annuals, such as gaillardia, that take care of themselves. Morning glory volunteers are allowed to grow up and clothe the rustic gate in green and old rose.

ABOVE, CENTER:
Spring in a sheltered corner comes with grape hyacinths, raspberry rhododendrons, and *Tulipa greigii* 'Toronto'. Greigiis are among the few tulips that naturalize, but you can coax many of the tall varieties to return year after year by planting them 10 to 12 inches deep.

ABOVE, RIGHT:
Early winter frost jewels the dainty white-edged leaves and bright red berries of rockspray, cotoneaster (C. *horizontalis*) 'Variegatus'. A slow-growing shrub that needs little attention, this outstanding cultivar has flat, layered branches 2 to 3 feet high and a spread of 5 to 8 feet.

position. Far off, even the brilliant variegated hollies fade to soft, and not-always-interesting lime green, but up close, they are striking. In a west coast garden you could use a young Pacific madrone (*Arbutus menziesii*), a beautiful tree with lustrous dark green leaves, whitish underneath, and warm brown bark that sheds somewhat untidily every year. In spring it bears lovely, bell-shaped flowers followed by clusters of orange or orange-red berries.

A grove, large or small, is a major feature in this type of landscape, one you will enjoy either augmenting if the basic elements are present or creating from scratch. In addition to marking the boundaries and providing a comforting sense of intimacy—where the swing is, where you picnic, where you shelter from rain—it should include a variety of trees and shrubs that present fascinating colors and changes in every season. Be sure to retain and encourage native trees and shrubs already growing on the property. Semi-mature evergreens, such as hemlocks, cypress, junipers, and pines, and broad-leaved hollies, laurels, rhododendrons, and azaleas are especially valuable. When fertilized, even skinny wildings will soon fill out and knit your garden into the surrounding countryside.

I use evergreens primarily as anchor, counterpoint, and foil to the deciduous trees and shrubs, the plants you will look to primarily for colorful flowers and foliage. Evergreens capture the drama of the fourth season, the months of rain, ice, and snow that darken and lighten bark and bare branches and embellish them with changing textures. Position a tall pyramidal or columnar evergreen towards the center of the grove and place in front of it little flowering trees with spreading branches. I find such airy, horizontal branching outlined against the dark upright evergreens very beautiful. If native evergreens aren't available, use garden plants such as arborvitae and easy-going topal holly (*Ilex* × *attenuata* cultivars) or 'Blue Maid' holly (*Ilex* × *meserveae*), a deep green cultivar that withstands more cold and heat than most. To knit the groves of trees together visually, use both evergreen and deciduous shrubs, along with groups of low-growing perennial plants that have bold contrasting foliage. The big-leaved hostas and *Bergenia cordifolia* make a striking backdrop for ferns and other dainty woodland plants. Another magnificent bold-leaved plant is American spikenard (*Aralia racemosa*); its foliage is dramatic, and birds love the berries. The deeply cut, gray-green foliage and stately streaming plumes of the plume poppy (*Macleaya cordata* syn. *Bocconia cordata*) are magnificent in a grove. These plants can be set against big rocks and planted with a rich variety of naturalized ground covers such as European wild ginger (*Asarum europaeum*), the Japanese silver painted fern (*Athyrium nipponicum* 'Pictum'), blue plumbago (*Ceratostigma plumbaginoides*), silvery lamb's-ears (*Stachys byzantina*), and creeping thyme (*Thymus praecox* ssp. *arcticus*). The grove can be enhanced by one or two large clumps of upright grasses.

Don't bother to plant vines. They tend to go rampant, and chances are good that in time nature will be more than generous with volunteers of bindweed, woodbine, and honeysuckle. The goal is to create groupings that in two or three years will look as though they have always been there but that don't need a lot of pruning to stay in balance. A grove that *looks* a little overgrown is appealing; a grove that actually *is* overgrown, like Jack's beanstalk, promises a monster pruning job ahead.

FLOWERING TREES

The flowering trees with the showiest blooms include ornamental varieties of plum, cherry, peach, and pear. But in a grassy New American landscape I find the more modest native flowering trees, or their cultivated varieties, quite as attractive and more interesting. The first to bloom is the slightly crooked, slow-growing witch hazel (*Hamamelis vernalis*). It's particularly lovely planted with a few little yellow and white crocus at its feet. The fascinating witchhazel flowers consist of four yellow ribbon-like petals tipping gray-barked branches. They roll up on very cold days to avoid frost damage. Some varieties are fragrant, just a gentle sweetness on the cold air of early spring. Yellow witchhazels are showier than the reds, but the devotion this plant inspires in those who know it has more to do with courage than with color. Watching as the fragile petals of a young, shrub-size witchhazel face a late burst of Arctic wind and snow is awe-inspiring. They do endure! The next tree to flower is the graceful shadblow, or serviceberry (*Amelanchier laevis*), a small tree that grows wild in open woodlands. In early spring it bears clusters of delicate white flowers followed by rather sweet, berrylike fruits attractive to birds. In fall the foliage turns yellow to orange and dark red. *Chionanthus retusus*, the graceful, airy little fringe tree, blooms next in our garden, with a mist of fragrant, fringelike white flowers. It is stunning combined with two or three dwarf white azaleas. In fall the fringet ree is the last of our trees to turn color. Overnight every leaf turns from green to solid gold, and, just as suddenly, they all fall to the ground. The dainty little redbud (*Cercis canadensis*), which is perfect for the front of the grove, blooms at about the same time as the dogwoods, each slim branch covered with showy, red-purple buds that appear before or with the foliage. *Cornus florida*, the dogwood that grows wild in woodlands and in many eastern gardens, now is available in disease-resistant Rutgers hybrids (Stellar Hybrids, C. × *rutgersensis*) that are a cross with the disease-resistant Chinese dogwood (*C. kousa* var. *chinensis*). Like the Chinese dogwoods, they bloom late and perch their flowers like great creamy white butterflies above their dark green leaves. In fall there are bright red fruits for the birds, and the leaves turn maroon-red. The bark of the Chinese dogwood mottles as the plant matures.

Of the natives that bloom in late spring and early summer I find the sweet bay (*Magnolia virginiana*) the most beautiful. The flowers are big and creamy white and the leaves, which have beautiful silvery undersides, and the conelike fruits are fascinating in flower arrangements. The Franklin tree (*Franklinia alatamaha*) bears

VARIEGATED TREES AND SHRUBS

Bigleaf hydrangea
Hydrangea macrophylla 'Variegata' Z6-9

Chinese holly, horned holly
Ilex cornuta 'O'Spring' Z7-9

Five-leaved aralia
Eleutherococcus sieboldianus 'Variegatus' Z4-8

Gold dust tree
Aucuba japonica 'Variegata' Z6-8

Hiba arborvitae
Thujopsis dolobrata 'Variegata' Z6-9

Holly olive
Osmanthus heterophyllus 'Aureo-marginatus' Z7-9

Japanese rose
Kerria japonica 'Picta' Z5-9

Lily-of-the-valley bush
Pieris japonica 'Variegata' Z5-8

Rockspray or rock cotoneaster
Cotoneaster horizontalis 'Variegata' Z5-9

Siberian dogwood
Cornus alba 'Elegantissima' Z2-8

Thorny eleagnus
Eleagnus pungens 'Maculata' Z7-9

Threadleaf Japanese maple
Acer palmatum 'Dissectum Variegatum' Z5-8

Variegated Privet
Ligustrum japonicum 'Silver Star' Z7-9

Variegated weigela
Weigela praecox 'Variegata' Z4-6

Variegated wintercreeper
Euonymus fortunei 'Gracilis', *E. f.* 'Emerald 'n' Gold' Z5-8

fragrant white camellialike flowers from August to mid-fall; it is a southern native with beautiful, bright green foliage that turns orange-red with the onset of cold.

Azaleas, rhododendrons, forsythia, and a few other showy garden shrubs look very much at home in a grassy landscape, and they add welcome touches of color at various seasons. I also like *Cotoneaster multiflorus* and *C. bullatus* var. *floribundus*. Siebold viburnum (*Viburnum sieboldii*) offers outstanding displays of white flowers and generous crops of crimson fruits. At the edge of a grove the fountain butterfly bush (*Buddleja alternifolia*) is a beautiful filler covered with lilac-purple flowers in mid May. The lilac I prefer in this setting is the Japanese tree lilac 'Ivory Silk' (*Syringa reticulata*, syn. *S. amurensis* var. *japonica*). The beautiful dark green leaves set off huge trusses of creamy white flowers that appear shortly after the Chinese dogwoods bloom. It will grow in acid soil where most lilacs languish.

If you would like some brighter colors in your weekend garden, look to the rugosa roses. These big, stiff-caned plants really do take care of themselves. They open their sweet-scented, single or double flowers in spring and summer and follow with gorgeous orange-red rose hips. There are pink- and red-flowered varieties, as well as beautiful whites, such as 'Sir Thomas Lipton'. The winter color of the Siberian, or red-barked dogwood (*Cornus alba* 'Sibirica') has made it a favorite of mine. It's a multistemmed shrub of medium height whose bark is a spectacular coral red in winter, brilliant in a snowy field. The color is most vivid when the shrub is cut back in late winter to encourage the production of young shoots.

CHOOSING FOLIAGE AND BARK FOR COLOR

When you choose trees for both specimen trees and groves, look variety in shape and color in fall and winter as well as in other seasons. Etched against the horizon, the leafless limbs and glossy red-brown bark of the pretty little amur cherry (*Prunus maackii*) appears very different from the limbs of the magnificent lacebark pine (*Pinus bungeana*), an evergreen whose young stems are green with white and brown. Red maples become enveloped in a red haze as their buds swell and bloom in late winter, while the catkins and young leaves of the golden weeping willow (*Salix* × *sepucralis* var. *chrysocoma*) inscribe the beautiful tree in gold. Summer leaves are not all shamrock green, and evergreens can display a range of color from green-blue to green-silver and even to a vivid yellow. Varieties of the deodar cedar (*Cedrus deodora*) may be light to grayish green, blue-green, silver, or yellow and they are very pretty in a grove. The narrow and dramatic Italian cypress (*Cupressus sempervirens*), which gives so much style to any planting, comes in blue and golden forms, and there's also a golden Hinoki cypress (*Chamaecyparis obtusa* 'Tetragona Aurea').

From a few yards away, yellow foliage will look like yellow flowers and used with discretion, can be very effective. *Spiraea* 'Mellow Yellow', a big arching shrub, contributes bright yellow foliage to the landscape after its showers of white flowers go by. There's a yellow Boston ivy (*Parthenocissus tricuspidata* 'Fenway Park'), in addition to the more common red species, that glows orange when the weather cools; the new leaves of 'Ginza Lights' are bright pink and white against the green of the mature foliage. The foliage of the elegant threadleaf Japanese maple (*Acer palmatum* 'Dissectum Atropurpureum') is a good solid red and so deeply cut that the leaves look almost like lace. 'Osakazuki', a yellow cultivar, turns blood red in autumn. Stand these elegant plants out in the open where they can be seen from many perspectives. I find that the foliage of red and yellow variegated plants needs full sun to

Redbud (*Cercis canadensis*) and pink azaleas bloom against a background of golden forsythia. Redbud is a dainty little native tree that grows in open woodlands and blooms in spring at the same time as the dogwoods.

The chalky white bark of the paper birch standing against dark evergreens is a delight in fall and winter. The crimson shrub is *Disanthus cercidifolius*, a native to the mountains of Japan, in its breathtaking fall color.

Boston ivy (*Parthenocissus tricuspidata*) in dynamic autumn red. Its close relative, the Virginia creeper, or woodbine, is a beautiful but not-always-welcome volunteer.

51

From a distance the rich yellow leaves of fast-growing *Catalpa bignoides* 'Aurea' look like flowers. The tall evergreen to the left is Chinese juniper (*Juniperus chinensis* 'Stricta').

SHRUBS WITH BRIGHT BERRIES

American bittersweet
Celastrus scandens Z4-8

Cranberry cotoneaster
Cotoneaster apiculatus Z5-8

Japanese barberry
Berberis thunbergii 'Vermillion'
& *B. t.* 'Atropurpurea' Z4-8

Red chokeberry
Aronia arbutifolia Z4-8

Rugosa rose
Rosa rugosa Z4-9

Scarlet firethorn
Pyracantha coccinea Z6-9

Viburnum species and cultivars
V. betulifolium Z5-9
V. × *burkwoodii* 'Mohawk' Z5-9

Winterberry
Ilex verticillata Z3-9

SHRUBS WITH COLORFUL FALL FOLIAGE

American smoke tree
Cotinus obovatus Z4-8

Coral bark maple
Acer palmatum 'Sangokaku'

Dwarf winged spindle tree
Euonymus alatus 'Compacta' Z3-8

Japanese maple
Acer palmatum 'Osakazuki' Z4-8

Korean barberry
Berberis koreana Z5-9

Large fothergilla
Fothergilla major Z4-8

Siberian dogwood
Cornus alba 'Sibirica' Z2-8

Staghorn sumac
Rhus typhina Z3-8

Swamp azalea
Rhododendron viscosum Z3-9

Swamp haw
Viburnum nudum Z6-9

Sweetspire
Itea virginica Z5-9

Willowleaf cotoneaster
Cotoneaster salicifolius 'Autumn Fire' Z6-8

color well. It seems to be most effective left untrimmed, and that's ideal for the weekend gardener.

If you choose your plants well, the fall and winter show will be even more interesting than the spring and summer displays. The maples, sweet gums, and sourwoods are brilliant cold-weather performers, but even the evergreens color up. Many junipers and mahonias turn to plum, and the Sawara cypress, silvery green in summer, is grayish blue in winter. From Minnesota to the Florida Keys, the red or swamp maple (*Acer rubrum*) cultivars 'October Glory' and 'Red Sunset' can be counted on for a glorious mix of red and orange leaves. In colder regions plant instead the extra-hardy 'Autumn Flame' and 'Northwood'. On the West Coast from British Columbia through Northern California, the little vine maple, *A. circinatum*, gives the best fall color. I have heard arborists describe the display of the big American sweet gum (*Liquidambar styraciflua*) as the most spectacular of all. It ranges from true red to dark crimson and yellow. The lovely native sourwood (*Oxydendrum arboreum*) has gorgeous crimson color in fall, and the showy, drooping racemes of fragrant white flowers it bears in summer leave behind attractive, lacy fruits. It also has round, deeply grooved bark, which makes it a good choice as a featured specimen.

Many of our flowering garden shrubs color in fall and winter, the evergreen azaleas and viburnums, for example, and a few are spectacular. The one I find most beautiful is *Euonymus alatus* 'Compacta', the shrub-sized dwarf winged spindle tree; in the fall, it stands out like a flame in pink-crimson-coral. Chittamwood, the little American smokewood (*Cotinus obovatus*), is enveloped in fluffy, pink-gray fruiting panicles in June and its leaves turn brilliant orange-red in the fall. Both these shrubs have interesting corky bark. Chokeberry (*Aronia arbutifolia* 'Brilliantissima') is another splendid compact shrub that turns red in autumn and has long-lasting, glossy red berries. It bears white flowers in spring.

Add to the fall show and welcome birds by planting shrubs that produce showy berries. *Ilex* 'Sparkleberry' and other winterberries are deciduous hollies that remain covered with shiny red berries after the leaves fall. In snow they are stunning. 'Sparkleberry' will give its very best show it if is pollinated by 'Apollo'. Firethorn (*Pyracantha coccinea*) is a handsome, thorny evergreen shrub valued for its fine foliage and attractive mid spring flowers followed by clusters of brilliant scarlet fruit in fall. Plant cultivars that are pest- and-disease-resistant: 'Mohave', which has masses of orange-red berries, 'Shawnee', if you prefer yellow fruits. American bittersweet (*Celastrus scandens*) is a climber that produces thick clusters of showy yellow-orange fruits with crimson berries. It looks wonderful tumbling over rocks or covering a stump, but you mustn't plant it where it can smother a live tree. The barberries, slow-growing, thorny deciduous or evergreen shrubs, grow into impenetrable thickets and hedges; in fall the foliage glows crimson and orange, and bright red berries ripen for the birds. *Berberis thunbergii* 'Crimson Pygmy' is a spectacularly colorful dwarf.

GRASSES AND FLOWERS

Movement, not color, is the gift of the grasses. Movement and sound. They whisper in the wind. Their colors are gentle—buff and tan, sea green and green, gold and pale gold—dominating the bright spires, rounds, and clumps of flowers planted with them. Late in the growing season, as the flowers begin to fade, the grasses raise fascinating, straw-encased seedheads, feathery inflorescences that remain until the plants are cut to the ground in late winter. The inflorescences are silvery, bronze, beige-gold,

BULBS FOR COLOR

Bear grass, Indian lily
Camassia quamash Z4-10

Giant onion
Allium giganteum Z5-10

Grape hyacinth
Muscari armeniacum Z3-9

Narcissus species and cultivars
Z3-9

Siberian squill
Scilla sibirica Z1-8

Snowdrops
Galanthus nivalis Z3-9

Spanish bluebell, wood hyacinth
Hyacinthoides hispanica Z4-9

Star-of-Bethlehem
Ornithogalum umbellatum Z5-10

Single early tulips and yellow pansies
Tulip cultivars
(lily flowered, emperor) *Tulipa* spp. Z3-8

OPPOSITE, TOP:
Frost outlines the white-edged foliage of *Hedera helix* 'Argenteo-variegata', one of the indestructible ivies. The variegated form is delightful carpeting the ground under tall trees.

OPPOSITE, BOTTOM:
Ilex verticillata 'Sparkleberry' is spectacular with evergreens behind and snow all around. One of the winterberries, 'Sparkleberry' is a deciduous holly that remains encrusted with shiny red berries after the leaves fall. For a generous crop of berries, plant 'Apollo' nearby.

55

ORNAMENTAL GRASSES

Australian fountain grass
Pennisetum alopecuroides Z5-9

Autumn moor grass
Sesleria autumnalis Z5-9

Big bluestem
Andropogon gerardii Z3-9

Blue grama grass
Bouteloua gracilis 3-10

Feather reed grass
Calamagrostis × *acutiflora*
'Stricta' Z5-9

Fountain grass
Pennisetum setaceum Z7-10

Japanese blood grass
Imperata cylindrica 'Red Baron'

Large blue fescue
Festuca amethystina Z4-9

Little bluestem
Schizachyrium scoparium Z4-9

Maiden grass
Miscanthus sinensis 'Gracillimus'
Z5-9

Pampas grass
Cortaderia selloana Z6-10

Prairie cord grass
Spartina pectinata Z5-9

Sedge 'Bowles Golden'
Carex 'Bowles Golden' Z5-9

Silver spike grass
Spodiopogon sibiricus Z5

Variegated Japanese sedge
Carex morrowii 'Aureo-marginata'
Z5-9

dun. I find the full, luminous, creamy white seed plumes of pampas grass (*Cortaderia selloana*) the most beautiful of all.

The grass-to-perennial flower ratio suggested by Wolfgang Oehme and James van Sweden, the landscape architects most often identified with prairielike gardens and the new direction in landscaping, is one-third flowers to two-thirds grasses in sunny places, and one-third grasses to two-thirds flowers in light shade. In their larger designs, Oehme and van Sweden mass perennials in minimums of fifty and routinely set out 120,000 grass and perennial plants and bulbs. Every inch of the soil is covered. Oehme believes that mass plantings make a small space look larger; even for a smaller garden, he recommends planting perennials in clumps or clusters of no fewer than six.

What makes a mass planting of grasses exciting is a mix of plants chosen for contrast and texture, form, and colors. The plantings are most successful when you use fewer varieties and more of each, rather than lots of varieties and few of each. Once you begin to work with grasses, you will realize how different they are, one from another. Some grow upright, stiff as reeds, others imitate fountains, still others droop gracefully, for example, prairie cord grass (*Spartina pectinata*). Some are very fine textured and some coarse textured. Some are small enough to edge a low flowering border, while others are tall enough to use against a wall in place of a high-maintenance espaliered plant. The quintessential fine grass is the little mosquito grass, or blue grama (*Bouteloua gracilis*): open, upright clumps of nodding foliage that in summer raise reddish purple inflorescences as ephemeral as the flitting of mosquitos. In second place are the fine-leaved fescues (*Festuca*), a genus that includes familiar lawn grasses as well as big, handsome ornamentals. They form tufts of fine, wiry leaves, rolled in some species, and their inflorescences are elegant, narrow, green-white or purplish panicles familiar to anyone whose lawn has gone to seed. One of the coarsest grasses is the low-growing Japanese blood grass (*Imperata cylindrica* 'Red Baron'). It is used in nearly all the grass gardens, placed where the maroon red foliage will catch the sun and justify its name.

The upright grasses that invariably cause me to stop and stare are the silver grasses (*Miscanthus*). The most graceful is *M. sinensis* 'Gracillimus'. In late summer and fall, tall, silky, silvery-tan plumes stand above the foliage. *M.s.* 'Zebrinus' is a striking species 6- to 8-feet tall with leaves banded horizontally with yellow. *M. sinensis* 'Variegatus', the striped eulalia grass, is another beauty, robust, upright, 4 to 6 feet tall, with foot-long inflorescences that start pale pink or reddish and open silvery white. The inflorescences of the variety 'Silberfeder' have very beautiful silvery accents. *Miscanthus floridulus* is the giant silver grass, 10 to 12 feet tall, a huge, upright, clump-forming grass that stands in winter until the wind blows away the leaves leaving only the stalks of the flowers behind.

The flowers that stand out planted with ornamental grasses are the same species that dominate a meadow garden, but in the weekend garden the grasses decidedly dominate. In addition to masses of spring-flowering bulbs and brilliant and unusual tulips, Oehme and van Sweden usually include in their designs the bright color palette presented by rudbeckia 'Goldsturm', sedum 'Autumn Joy', fernleaf yarrow 'Coronation Gold', purple coneflower, foxgloves, yellow and purple loosestrife, astilbe 'Fanal', species daylilies, and the spider flower (*Cleome spinosa* 'Pink Queen'). For lavenders and blues they often use wild asters, English lavender 'Hidcote', blue salvia, and huge stands of tall, smoky, romantic Russian sage.

ALTERNATIVES TO LAWNS

Bergenia hybrids and cultivars
B. 'Ballawley', *B.* 'Morgenrote'
Z3-8

Blue plumbago
Ceratostigma plumbaginoides Z5-8

Bugleweed cultivars
Ajuga reptans 'Alba'
A. r. 'Bronze Beauty' Z3-8

Creeping juniper cultivars
Juniperus horizontalis Z3-9

Creeping thyme
Thymus praecox ssp. *arcticus* Z5-7

English ivy
Hedera helix Z5-9

European wild ginger
Asarum europeum Z4-8

Japanese spurge
Pachysandra terminalis Z5-8

Lamb's-ears
Stachys byzantina Z4-9

Lilyturf
Liriope muscari Z6-10

Moneywort
Lysimachia nummularia Z4-8

Periwinkle, creeping myrtle
Vinca minor Z4-8

Pussytoes
Antennaria dioica Z4-7

Red epimedium
Epimedium rubrum Z5-9

Rose daphne
Daphne cneorum 'Ruby
Glow' Z5-8

Rose verbena
Verbena canadensis Z6-10

Siberian tea
Bergenia crassifolia Z3-8

Spring heath
Erica carnea Z5-8

OPPOSITE:
The red, white, and green of the winter holiday season are represented by the silvery plumes of pampas grass, the scarlet bark of Siberian dogwood (*Cornus alba* 'Sibirica'), and the rich green foliage of spruce.

KITCHEN
GARDENS

There's rosemary, that's for remembrance; pray, love remember.
And there is pansies, that's for thoughts.
There's fennel for you, and columbines; there's rue
For you, and here's some for me; we may call it herb of grace
*   o' Sundays.*

WILLIAM SHAKESPEARE

Imagine near the kitchen entrance a small garden overflowing with lush salad plants and treasured vegetables, aromatic herbs and sunny flowers. I can think of no more profound pleasure than being able to run down the kitchen steps just before serving a meal to gather mesclun and arugula, sweet ripe muskmelons and tomatoes still warm from the sun, a few fresh flowers for the table. Even looking at the garden through the kitchen window fills me with deep satisfaction.

As you plan your own beautiful kitchen garden, choose vegetables for color as well as for flavor. A wonderful array of food plants in sparkling colors is available to the garden artist—ruby-stemmed chard, red-flowered bush beans and red oakleaf lettuce, peppers in every shade of the rainbow, lavender eggplants, purple basils. Grouped in the garden with flowers in complementary shades, these vegetables fairly glow. Most vegetables, as well as some of the best herbs for cooking, are annuals, and annual flowers grow well right along with them. Vivid zinnias and snapdragons tall and small, perky nasturtiums and calendulas bright as orange juice, golden marigolds and blue sage are among the many cut-and-come-again flowers that thrive with vegetables. Colorful climbing vines make heavenly backdrops to a kitchen garden. Morning glories are gorgeous intertwined with the great white bugles of the moonflower, whose beauty and fragrance enchant the dusk. The brilliant blossoms of the scarlet runner bean, a vibrant climbing beauty, and sweet-scented white and purple blossoms of the hyacinth bean (*Lablab purpurea*) are followed by succulent edible pods. (As they ripen, lablab's pods turn a striking shiny dark purple; the mature seeds contain toxins and are edible only after they have been well cooked in several changes of water.)

I like to use the herbs as fillers and edgers for my kitchen garden. They're almost all foliage plants; their differences in leaf texture and plant structure help to create the dynamic tension that makes a planting interesting. Some herbs are tall and shrubby, like needle-leaved rosemary and tarragon. Some are low-growing, richly colored greens like curly parsley and mâche (corn salad). Others have amazing variations

PREVIOUS SPREAD:
Left: Harvest time in Roz Creasy's sumptuous kitchen garden whets the appetite with varieties the best food shops don't carry. The picturesque mound includes purple violas, fragrant sweet alyssums (*Lobularia maritima*), hybrid nasturtiums (*Tropeolum*), and marguerite daisies (*Argyranthemum frutescens),* with leaf lettuces, bok choi, carrots, parsley, broccoli, and other vegetables and herbs.

Right: Sunny *Helianthus annuus* is the symbol of the family kitchen garden, a visual treat, and a feast for birds, squirrels, and humans.

OPPOSITE:
As you plan your own kitchen garden, choose vegetables for color as well as for flavor. Reading clockwise, colorful companions are: leaf lettuce 'Red Sails' and 'Royal Oak'; Boston-type butterhead lettuce 'Jericho' and African marigolds; red cabbage and the greenish white flowerheads of parsley; Brussels sprouts and jewel-bright strawflowers (*Helichrysum bracteatum*).

LEFT:
Roz Creasy's playful variation on a traditional herb garden is a wheel centered on a birdbath and surrounded by geraniums, roses, cerise celosia, pink cosmos, daisies, and Peruvian lilies (*Alstroemeria*), which are lasting cutting flowers. Thyme, sage, rosemary, and other kitchen herbs share the center of the wheel with fragrant sweet alyssum. The spokes are planted in blue star creeper (*Laurentia longiflora*).

and variegations: tricolor sages, white-splashed mints, purple basils. Be sure to plant perennial herbs like thyme and rosemary where they won't be uprooted when you cultivate the kitchen garden in spring. Or you can fudge a little, as I have done, by growing them as annuals, replanting seedlings every year.

I encourage you to make the kitchen garden fun, too. This is a garden where you can play! Dare a little, be whimsical. Let your scarlet runner beans grow all the way up a penthouse drain pipe. Attract smiles with miniature pumpkins ripening on a rose arbor. If you have a lot of space, plant seeds for giants and dream of an 800-pound pumpkin and a 300-pound watermelon. If your garden is very small, think and grow small: 'Tom Thumb' tomatoes, miniature eggplant, tiny-but-fiery Thai peppers. Plant squash that will look like geese, mile-long cucumbers, and zinnias shaggy as a cactus and bright as a paint box.

Choosing plants that afford true pleasure is a key to success in any garden; a well-loved garden is well tended. There are many varieties to choose from, and much to learn, but the learning and the doing are fascinating and fun. The weather varies from year to year, and no plant performs the same way two years in a row. There will always be surprises, and occasionally, a small disaster, but one of the great things about annuals is that there aren't any serious mistakes to make. What goes in comes out within weeks or months, and you have time to try again. Vegetables that mature quickly are usually sown as seed; they can be sown again if seeds or seedlings fail. Vegetables that are slow to mature and that must be planted in warm weather, like eggplant, cucumbers, tomatoes, and sweet peppers, I set out as lusty seedlings to hurry them along. I start them early in cold frames or hotbeds, or indoors under grow lights. You can also get the jump on spring by setting out seedlings of cool-weather leaf crops like lettuce and Chinese greens, as well as cold-tolerant broccoli and Brussels sprouts. If seedlings fail, replacements are available at garden centers.

Perennial vegetables don't belong in the kitchen garden beds that are deeply cultivated every year. I grow asparagus and a few strawberries in beds of their own, as well as artichokes and rhubarb plants. They are all quite beautiful—and delicious!

CHOOSING THE RIGHT SITE AND SIZE

The kitchen garden can be any shape that enhances the garden, and almost any size, but it must have well-drained soil and receive full sun. To be as productive as they can be, the plants that grow in the kitchen garden need six to eight hours of direct sun. There are exceptions, of course. Some lettuces, spinach, broccoli, and squash tolerate some shade, as do some herbs, including basil and borage, chervil, lavender,

SALAD BAR

Arugula, cress, and watercress

Carrots and cucumbers

Chicory, endive, escarole, and radicchio

Florence Fennel

Lettuce: Buttercrunch, Red Sails, Salad Bowl

Mâche/corn salad

Peppers: green, purple, red, and yellow

Radishes, daikon

Scallions

Sorrel and spinach

Tomatoes: Sweet Million, Yellow Pear, and 'Subarctic'

OPPOSITE:
In Rosalind Creasy's marvelous edible garden, the outer perimeter of her herb wheel, California poppies (*Eschscholzia californica*), sweet alyssum, and lady bells (*Adenophora confusa*), thrive with lettuce and ruby chard, rosemary (*Rosmarinus officinalis*), onions, parsley, and nasturtiums.

LEFT:
The airy marrow arch in Rosemary Verey's potager at Barnsley House, in Gloucestershire, England, lets through enough light to bring into bloom sunny rudbeckia, nasturtiums, and sunflowers. *Potager,* French for "kitchen garden," is derived from the word *potage,* "soup." Grape, other food-bearing vines, and fruit trees may also be trained to grow upward.

63

OPPOSITE:
The pretty apple-bearing tree called 'Winter Banana' hosts an early spring crop of maroon red ruby chard and clear orange pot marigolds. The pot marigold is the edible "marigold" of Shakespearian plays and ancient herbals, and the petals still are used today to add color and flavor to salads, cream-cheese dips, and desserts. The monastery gardens of the Middle Ages included nasturtiums in the herb garden, along with sweet violets, spicy pinks, and perfumed roses, all of which were used to flavor food and medicinals. Whenever the botanic name of a species is *officinalis* you can be sure that it was originally one of the herbs grown in the pharmacopeia.

mint, and chives. In fact, most leafy plants can handle light shade in summer and may benefit from it where summers are very hot, but tomatoes, cucumbers, melons, beans, root crops, and many annual flowers need at least six full hours of direct sun, more in the far north.

The frequent sowing and harvesting typical of a high-yield garden is much easier if the site is fairly level. A gentle rise is a fine site as long as the planting rows run across the slope to minimize runoff. The soil on a sloping site needs to be well mulched. Mulch to help minimize runoff and soil erosion; it may be applied before or after planting, depending on what you plant and what you use for mulch. If a steep slope is your only site, then terrace it and it will be beautiful and easy to work. If you have a choice, select a south-facing slope over a north-facing slope. It will warm more quickly in spring and the hill will protect early and late plantings from icy north winds, which can damage early-start seedlings.

Ideally, the site will be airy as well. The dense foliage typical of intensive cropping benefits from a bit of a breeze. Air movement helps with pollination, keeps insects from lingering, and discourages diseases. On the other hand, a sheltered site will allow you to plant earlier and harvest later. If you can, avoid siting the garden near big shrubs or trees whose roots will rush in to take up the fertilizer and moisture provided for the plants.

The size of your kitchen garden is important. I've learned the hard way to avoid creating a garden that will demand more time than my hands, head, and heart are willing to give it. A comfortable size for your first kitchen garden is about 12 feet long by 10 feet wide, the size of a small room. This is just enough space for six rows 2 feet wide. Think of it as 60 feet of 2-foot-wide planting rows. Once it is established you will find it very easy to manage.

By using highly productive techniques such as intercropping and succession planting, those six rows easily can fill your salad bowl from mid-spring to late fall. There's also room for two zucchini plants, tomatoes, green beans, cucumbers, chard or other greens, and herbs. Cut-and-come-again zinnias, snapdragons, and other annual flowers at the row ends are charming additions. Pick flowers and branches of mint and purple basil to make fragrant kitchen bouquets, and the plants will continue to branch and produce until frost.

For every additional 2 feet of width available, the garden can accommodate one long-season vegetable, like melons, or two in-and-out vegetables, such as early spring peas followed by zucchini, or mid-season lettuce followed by tomatoes. You may be able to harvest a third crop of cool-weather vegetables such as Oriental greens, mesclun, kale, and radishes, if your winters are mild or if you use covers and other season-extending techniques.

A smaller kitchen garden, say 8 feet by 6 feet, has space for spring and fall lettuces; for tomatoes, peppers, cucumbers, dill, parsley, basil; radishes in early spring and fall; and a few midsize marigolds. If you grow the tomatoes and cucumbers on trellises at the north end of your garden, you'll even have room for a row of beans and a couple of eggplants. You can further increase your harvests without committing yourself to a larger garden by growing some things in containers, as described below.

DESIGNING FOR BEAUTY AND RESULTS

Traditionally the kitchen garden is laid out as one or more rectangular beds surrounded by grassy or pebbled paths. Wide paths provide easy access to the plants that grow

in regimented rows. Herbs are planted in a bed of their own, and flowers at the front or the back of the garden. The outer boundaries may be defined by fruit trees—typically, apples and pears in the North, citrus fruits in the South.

I love the order and the harmony of the traditional kitchen garden layout, but you may prefer a modern version. One design that is attractive and very practical is a series of narrow rectangles intersected by broad grass or mulched paths that keep all sides of the beds within your reach so they can easily be worked. Another version raises the rectangles knee-high and provides them with retaining walls with wide cap stones. I like the walls because they offer a place to sit as I work in the garden. These are spacious, gracious, orderly designs.

For a more contemporary garden, emphasize abundance, color, and diversity. A broad path that curves sinuously between colorful borders of closely planted vegetables, herbs, and flowers is delightfully inviting. If you want to sow the path in grass, make it the width of your lawn mower. Or you can pave it with bricks, loose flagstones, or wooden pavers, or just top it with shredded redwood bark. The rows can be designed as swirls, drills, or clumps emanating from the path, with the borders edged with parsley, thyme, and low-growing red zinnias, or small, frilly, green lettuces and orange nasturtiums.

Consider including some of the accessories of a flower border. Have the path between the beds wind towards a trellised arch supporting a wild array of red and white climbing roses, or climbing nasturtiums and white miniature pattypan squash. A bird bath, a small fountain that cools and humidifies the air, and a garden seat are simple additions that emphasize that this garden is savored and enjoyed.

CONTAINER KITCHEN GARDENS

The kitchen garden can also be a movable feast. Vegetables succeed in tubs, planters, hanging baskets, plastic flower pouches, even big pots. There are tomato varieties developed just for hanging baskets—Burpee's 'Tumbler Hybrid', for example. The smallest window box can accommodate small herbs, including parsley, bush basil, thyme, oregano, arugula, mâche, and several of the little French marigolds. A single clay pot 14 to 16 inches in diameter can host a thriving mini-kitchen garden of a staked small tomato variety, parsley, thyme, basil, Madagascar periwinkle, and a pair of the little French marigolds. Larger tomato plants do better in tubs 18 inches deep.

An entire kitchen garden can be fitted into two or three planters 30 to 36 inches long, 19 inches wide, and 18 inches deep. A planter 3 feet long, 8 inches wide, and 12 inches deep will accommodate smaller plants and herbs, but on a balcony in midsummer it will need watering at least once a day. The same plants growing in a tub 16 inches square by 18 inches deep can make do with watering every three or four days. Self-watering planters are expensive but worth investigating, because they encourage unchecked growth. Food growing in containers becomes a focus of attention, so choose the most beautiful varieties of vegetables and herbs. Select plants that are naturally smaller, and compact varieties of the larger vegetables. Red radicchio,

Decorative as well as delicious, red and green oakleaf lettuces planted in a colorful pattern brighten a corner of the potager at Cecily Hill House. One of the great virtues of leaf lettuce, which graced the royal gardens of Persian kings more than 2,500 years ago, is that it germinates quickly in spring and is ready for harvest in a matter of weeks.

ANNUAL HERBS

Anise (biennial)

Borage

Caraway

Chervil

Chili peppers: Jalapeno, Ole!, Serrano, Super Cayenne, Thai, Yatsufusa

Cilantro/Coriander/Chinese parsley

Dill: Fernleaf, Tetra

Fenugreek

Holy basil

Lemon mint (biennial)

Marjoram (tender perennial)

Nasturtium and pot marigold

Parsley: curly or flat-leaved (biennial)

Perilla

Summer savory

Sweet basil: Anise, Fino Verde, Genovese, Lemon, Lettuce Leaf, Opal, Thai

---

deep green arugula, and mâche are lovely, naturally small vegetables. Larger ruby chard is a colorful, bold-leaved plant that can be used for background in a container garden. Interesting dwarf and miniatures varieties are offered by the catalogs. 'Tom Thumb', a tiny 4- to 6-inch heading lettuce, makes an elegant salad for one person. Baby cantaloupes and watermelons are well worth trying, as is 'Dwarf Bees', a miniature red-flowered bean plant 20 to 24 inches high. It flowers all summer long and produces long, flat snap beans: harvested young they can be cooked as green beans; allowed to mature they become shelling beans.

PLANNING A HIGH-YIELD GARDEN

To keep the kitchen garden growing exuberantly all season, provide fertile, well-drained soil in a raised bed and follow an intensive cropping plan. Intensive cropping is an approach to vegetable gardening that has every foot of the soil producing from early spring until the end of the growing season. Succession cropping, intercropping, and close-spaced planting are the simple, common sense techniques that produce great results. In a traditional vegetable garden about 30 percent of the surface soil is planted; intensive cropping uses 70 to 80 percent.

Succession cropping keeps every garden row occupied with crops all season long. You can begin the yearly round by sowing seeds for frost-tolerant peas and the quick-sprouting radishes, early spring's first harvest. Radishes, by the way, are great row markers for more slow-to-germinate vegetables, such as carrots. These can be followed with seeds or seedlings of the hardy leaf lettuces, spring crops that fade in summer heat. When the weather warms, you can set out seedlings of tomatoes and peppers, eggplants, and other warmth-loving plants that will go on producing until real cold comes. As space becomes available, make successive sowings of beans, carrots, and other vegetables tolerant of summer heat. Once the weather begins to cool

MARIGOLD 'RED SEVEN STARS'

FLORENCE FENNEL, ANISE

COSMOS SENSATION STRAIN 'PINKIE'

a little, sow seeds for another set of the cold-hardy salad plants such as arugula and corn salad. If enough growing weather remains, try for crops of broccoli, kale, winter carrots, parsnips, and other cold-tolerant vegetables. Carrots can be harvested until the ground freezes, and parsnips can stay there all winter.

Intercropping has companion crops growing in the same space at the same time. Seeds for fast-growing plants can be planted with slow-growing plants. When radishes, for example, are paired with romaine lettuce, the radishes will be harvested before the romaine grows large enough to crowd the row. Plant lettuce plants between the broccoli or kale plants—by the time the weather is hot, the taller plants will shade the lettuce. Pumpkins act as a mulch and cool the roots of tall corn plants, which in turn provide support for pole beans.

To get the greatest return on garden space, plant seeds at about half the distance indicated in the seed packet directions. It's an old trick for maximizing soil productivity and minimizing labor: As they fill out the plants grow so closely together the foliage shades out weeds. You can also grow some vegetables vertically. A tomato plant grows just as well tethered to a see-through fence as it does tied to stakes or grown in a tomato cage. In fact, shell beans, the various peas, and tomatoes tend to produce more when they are staked. They're also easier to harvest. The scarlet runner bean is a beautiful climbing vine, and varieties of climbing beans, squash, cucumbers, and melons are available too. A fence 4 feet high by 30 feet long offers 120 square feet of growing room for trellised vegetables. You need one 6 to 8 feet high for tall snow and snap peas, pole and runner beans, and other vigorous climbers.

Many plants continue producing abundantly only when the crop is picked young and often. Some notorious examples are spring peas, snap beans, zucchini, zinnias, and snapdragons. Catalogs and seed packets tell which vegetables, herbs, and flowers must be kept harvested to keep producing. The root crops (carrots, beets, and

PERENNIAL HERBS

Bay laurel
Laurus nobilis Z8

Chives and garlic chives
Allium schoenoprasum, A. tuberosum Z3

French tarragon
Artemisia dracunculus var. *sativa* Z3

Garden sage
Salvia officinalis Z5

Greek oregano
Origanum vulgare ssp. *hirtum* Z5

Lavender
Lavandula angustifolia Z5

Lemon balm
Melissa officinalis Z5

Mint: peppermint, spearmint, and more
Mentha piperita, M. spicata Z5

Rosemary
Rosmarinus officinalis Z8, 'Arp' Z6

Thyme
Thymus vulgaris, T.pulegioides Z4

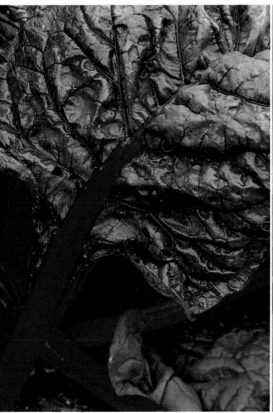

RUBY CHARD

SWEET PEPPER 'LILAC'

ZUCCHINI

Artichokes
Cynara scolymus Z6

Asparagus
Asparagus officinalis Z4

Blackberries, boysenberries,
loganberries
Rubus cultivars, variably hardy to
Z5

Currants and gooseberries
Ribes spp., cvs. Z3-7

Grapes: American and European
Vitis labrusca Z4, *V. vinifera* Z6

Jerusalem artichoke
Helianthus tuberosus Z4

Raspberries, black raspberries
Rubus idaeus, R. occidentalis Z3

Rhubarb, pie plant
Rheum cultorum Z3

Strawberries, alpine strawberries
Fragaria × *ananassa* Z4, *F. vesca*
Z5

parsnips) benefit from a longer stay in the garden, continuing to grow bigger as long as conditions are favorable. I sow many of the vegetables and the kitchen herbs thickly to have lots of thinnings to use in mesclun salad mixes and in soups and stews—spinach, for example, and kale, chard, carrots, turnips, and beets. You can harvest side leaves of the lettuces and greens such as chard, mustard, and looseleaf Chinese cabbage whenever you wish; they're delicious in salads.

PREPARING A PLANTING PLAN

Successful intensive cropping requires a planting plan. Working with a calendar, garden catalogs, and my imagination, I think through a game plan for the year that will let me get the most from the garden. It's a game, really; you always get a little more than you expected from some things, a little less from others. I begin by making a list of the vegetables my family enjoys most in each season. Beside each vegetable I write the number of days from planting to harvest for several varieties, information that I find by a patient search of trusted mail order catalogs. It sounds tedious but it's very exciting when you love fresh vegetables as much as we do. Every year something new and thrilling turns up. I still recall the pleasure of discovering yellow beets and baby white eggplants when they first appeared, the beautiful fragrant holy basil from India, which is used in Asian recipes, and most recently those elegant little miniature lettuces that serve just one person.

Once I have a list of vegetables I can't wait to plant, I use graph paper (you can also use your computer) to lay out four grids representing the garden in each of the four planting seasons. This step isn't essential, but it is an efficient way to organize all that information to get the best possible results. You can almost see the garden grow. Each line on each grid stands for a planting row. Grid One is the planting plan for very early and early spring; Grid Two is for mid- to late spring when the weather warms and warm season crops may be set out; Grid Three is for summer crops; Grid Four is for late summer and fall crops.

On the lines of Grid One enter the names of vegetables that will be sown there in very early spring. These are the hardies that handle frost, like peas, radishes, chives, hardy leaf lettuces, arugula, and corn salad. Plants that can survive the cold when set out under hot caps or plastic may be planted at the same time. Next to each plant name write the planting date, the number of days it will take to mature, and the date the harvest probably will be complete. The latter is the approximate date that row will be available for planting the next crop. On planting rows not yet occupied write the names of the second set of vegetables, those that can stand cold but are not entirely frost hardy, for example, heading lettuces, carrots, broccoli.

Grid Two is the planting plan for the period after the air warms but before the summer heat. The nights are frost free, and days are above 68° F. Transfer to this grid the dates when rows on Grid One will become available. Then fill the grid with planting dates for the flowers and warm weather crops such as tomatoes, eggplant, melons, and peppers. Record the dates the harvests will be complete.

On Grid Three pencil in the rows in Grid Two that will become available, and the dates. For the free rows plan vegetables that will grow through summer heat—beans, cucumbers, early watermelon, and bush summer squash, for instance.

For Grid Four, depending on how soon real cold will arrive, enter the names of late crops of hardy lettuces, broccoli, carrots, and other cold hardy vegetables. In regions where summer heat remains through August, it will be too hot to sow the fall

COMPANION PLANTINGS

Almost any sun-loving annual flower will do well in a kitchen garden.
The following are combinations of flowers and vegetables that are
especially attractive together:

- Ruby oakleaf lettuce growing with Iceland poppies and purple basil.
- Green frilly lettuce and pink, white, and red-centered Madagascar periwinkle (*Catharanthus roseus*) with lettuce-leaf basil.
- Green leaf lettuce between clumps of orange calendulas fronted by clumps of chives.
- Bronze lettuces in a row behind clumps of gold French marigolds, interplanted with tricolor sage.
- Eggplant on a fence behind clumps of pink cosmos 'Sensation', edged by purple alyssum.
- Red or white runner beans intertwined with cardinal vine.
- Kale interplanted with pink and lavender 'Giant Imperial' stock, and backed by bronze fennel.
- Cabbage interplanted with pink cosmos 'Sensation': tall, cactus-flowered,

hot pink zinnias; and dill.
- Purple eggplant and purple basil edged with purple alyssum.
- Colorful hot peppers with bright little Mexican zinnias.
- Yellow sweet peppers interplanted with clumps of golden coreopsis and fronted by variegated pineapple mint.
- Swiss chard interplanted with clumps of red salvia and white Madagascar periwinkle.
- White Swiss chard with orange cosmos and a silvery sage.
- Summer squash backed by tall gold African marigolds. For edger, mounds of variegated thyme.
- Tomatoes backed by multicolored hollyhocks and edged with summer savory.
- Big, bold zucchini as the backdrop to a bed of pastel snapdragons edged with moss-curled parsley.

crops directly in the garden. Sow them indoors or in a cold frame and transplant the seedlings when the temperature abates. In regions where winter temperatures fall below 25° F., limit your seed plantings to quick-maturing crops, like greens and radishes.

A New England tradition I like to follow is to plant early daffodils and tulips at the outer edges of the kitchen garden, in early spring the satiny petals fairly shine against the backdrop of moist brown earth. After the bulbs have flowered, and before you fill the garden, you can move them to another spot that needs a lift in early spring—next to the mailbox, in front of the compost pile, by the kitchen door. Or interplant herbs that will cover their yellowing leaves and till around them.

No matter how well you plan, expect to make adjustments repeatedly throughout the growing season because harvests never work out quite as expected. My goal is to have the rows planted and filled with vigorous, healthy, good looking vegetables, herbs, and flowers all season long. Where a crop comes out, another must go in. A kitchen garden is small, so keeping up isn't much of a chore, and even if the garden doesn't keep to my plan, it still will be extremely productive—always colorful, always in a fascinating state of becoming.

LEARNING FROM CATALOGS

To make a planting plan that will work, you need to find out how many days each plant you have chosen requires from sowing to harvest and how cold hardy it is. Hundreds of mail order garden catalogs supply the information; together, they form

ORNAMENTAL VEGETABLES

Alpine strawberry: Baron Solemacher

Broad bean: The Sutton, Red Epicure

Chili peppers: Fiesta, Super Chili, Thai

Chinese mustard: Green In Snow, Red Giant

Chives and garlic chives

Choy sum: Flowering Purple

Eggplant: Japanese Purple Pickling, Ichiban

Endive: Green Curled, Salad King

Florence fennel

Globe artichoke and cardoon

Hyacinth bean

Jerusalem artichoke

Kale: Russian Red, Dwarf Blue Curled Scotch

Lettuce: Red Sails, Royal Oak Leaf

Nasturtiums and pot marigolds

Okra: Burgundy

Ornamental cabbage: Dynasty Pink

Ornamental kale: Frizzy White, Peacock Pink

Purple Perilla

Radicchio: Red Treviso, Rouge De Verone

Runner beans: Scarlet Emperor, Sunset

Sunflowers: Mammoth, Sunbird Hybrid

Swiss chard: Ruby Red, Fordhook Giant

Tomatillo, purple tomatillo

Tomatoes: Golden Nugget, Red Robin, Sweet Million, Sweetie, Tumbler Hybrid

In early spring Nigel Colborn's kitchen garden is trim and tidy, but by late spring it overflows with bountiful harvests. A pair of trellised supports anchors the garden visually and offers climbing room for scarlet runner beans (*Phaseolus coccineus*) and sweet peas (*Lathyrus odoratus*), which are wonderfully fragrant old-fashioned cutting flowers you can't buy for love or money. Below, white and ruby chard, ornamental kale, thyme, and variegated sage share the earth with French marigolds (*Tagetes patula*). A pristine white cloche protects tender seedlings from late frosts.

Pebbled walks and raised beds framed by pressure-treated boards define a formal kitchen-and-herb garden laid out in squares and centered on decorative trees. The square in the foreground combines orange calendulas with white and green pineapple mint, the most decorative of this herb's forty varieties. To the left are chives spangled with purple blossoms. To the right are seedlings of yarrow surrounded by lavender. Behind are beets edged with red oakleaf lettuce.

an immense, annually revised plant encyclopedia. You'll find the big color catalogs very useful because they publish helpful color photos (take the color with a grain of salt!) of individual varieties. You will find varieties described as "early," "midseason," or "late." Midseason varieties take longer to mature than early ones; late vegetables may not take all that much longer than midseason types, but they usually stand more cold and are good winter keepers. Where the growing season is brief—in the north and in the mountains, for example—plant early vegetable varieties. Small forms of vegetables usually can be counted on to mature quickly; for example, icebox watermelons mature weeks ahead of the big football varieties. Tomatoes are an exception: 'Early Girl', a medium-sized tomato with excellent flavor, matures in 52 days, while 'Sweet Million' which produces 1-inch fruits with intoxicating sweet-tart flavor, matures in 65 to 75 days. Catalogs also describe the plant's growth habit. If your garden is small, you may choose compact bush varieties instead of sprawling vines or tall varieties to grow on a trellis.

The big color catalogs deal with well-known and popular varieties, and I often buy from them. But I find the little homespun regional catalogs a better read, and some provide growing instructions that are outstanding. Those seedsmen breed plants adapted to their local climates and growing conditions, for example, short-season mountain country, hot and dry desert regions, semi-tropical southern Florida and California, and the rainy Northwest coast. Keep in mind that your local garden centers will sell seeds and seedlings of the common varieties and often some unusual ones. Specialty catalogs from Fox Hollow Herbs, in McGrann, Pennsylvania; the Pepper Gal, in Fort Lauderdale, Florida; Ronniger's Seed Potatoes, in Moyie Springs, Idaho; Shepherd's Seeds, in Torrington, Connecticut; and The Cook's Garden, in Londonderry, Vermont, are especially good at stirring the imagination. To add romance and a sense of history to the kitchen garden, as well as interesting varieties with exceptional flavor, look to the heirloom plants. They are advertised in many general catalogs and by specialists.

A PLANTING PLAN

GRID ONE: EARLY SPRING
As soon as the ground can be worked in early spring, plant the frost hardy snow, snap, and pod peas, radishes, spinach, beets, parsnips, and carrots. In the North, force the season by planting under hot caps or plastic tents. Sow hardy herbs, such as dill, chives, and parsley. About two to three weeks before the last frost is due, set out broccoli, kale, and lettuce plants; and sow lettuce and chard.

GRID TWO: LATE SPRING
After frost is over, you can plant warm-season tomatoes, eggplant, peppers, melons, watermelons, sweet potatoes, cucumbers, zucchini and summer squash, and beans, as well as tender herbs, such as basil and coriander.

GRID THREE: SUMMER
In rows empty of spring-planted vegetables, plant vegetables that withstand heat, such as snap beans, sown in successive plantings 2 weeks apart, and squashes, and pumpkins.

GRID FOUR: LATE SUMMER/FALL
Now plant vegetables that endure the cold, such as arugula, mâche, leaf lettuces, broccoli, cabbage, and greens. Where winter temperatures rarely fall below 25° F., plant a fall crop of carrots and parsnips.

SOIL, FERTILIZERS, AND WATER

The best beginning you can give to a high-yield kitchen garden is the fertile, humus-rich, well-drained soil of a raised bed. It's a good idea to test the pH and adjust it to between 5.5 and 6.8, the range in which most vegetables thrive. Each year before you plant, spread fertilizer, such as 5-10-5, over the soil and dig it in to a depth of 4 to 6 inches. You may wish to use 10-10-10 where you plant leafy greens, such as lettuce, spinach, and chard; it's rich in nitrogen, which promotes the growth of lush, healthy leaves, and potassium, which builds strong root systems. With succession planting, repeat the treatment before every growing cycle. To improve the productivity of long-standing plants, such as tomatoes and summer squash, you can apply side dressings of fertilizer after the plants have begun to set fruit. Just scratch a handful of quick-release fertilizer into the soil 6 to 8 inches from each plant and water well, or use a complete soluble fertilizer according to the manufacturer's directions. As an alternative, dig in a complete slow-release fertilizer in the spring to keep your plants growing all season long. But, whatever method you choose, don't overdo it—too much fertilizer can cause as many problems as too little.

When the soil is prepared, install a ground watering system if you can. Soaker hoses are inexpensive and effective, less trouble to install than an emitter system, and more appropriate for a garden of annuals that will be tilled deeply every year. Sustained moisture allows sustained growth and helps you coax top performance from your vegetables, which are far less tolerant than flowers when it comes to drought conditions.

Now you are ready to plant. Seeds are best planted in humid to dry soil, about three times as deep as their width. Broadcast the finest seeds, like those of carrots, and tamp them firmly in place. Water the seedbed with a fine spray and keep it moist until the seedlings are growing well. Transplants are best planted in moist soil on a cloudy day; water them well. From then on, how often and how much you'll need to water depend on your weather, your soil, and your plants—how many, how close together, and what kind (see page 237). If you mulch the garden, leaving 3-inch gap around the stems of your seedlings and transplants, you'll cut the need to water by 30 to 50 percent, as well as keep down the weeds. Ideally, you should water in the early morning before the sun reaches the plants. It's a lovely time of day to be out in the garden—the air is fresh, the colors are brilliant, and because the sun isn't there to evaporate the water, the plants seem visibly renewed by their bath.

In warm weather, I water a container garden every day until the water begins to drain from the bottom. I include a light application of fertilizer at each watering to compensate for the nutrients that are leeched away.

I haven't touched on weeds. In a vegetable garden, they'll be with you the first few years in spite of mulching. It's best to remove weed seedlings while they are still tiny; at the least pull or hoe them before they go to seed, and eventually there will be almost none. Think of weeding as an invitation to get to know the vegetables. Early evening is a grand time to visit the garden, that moment between sunset and dusk when the air is clear as a bell and the earth is cooling. Crouch by the rows where seedlings are emerging and gently pull up anything radically different from the prevailing forms growing along the rows. You'll soon come to know the difference between the intruders and the fernlike carrot leaves, the little pairs of round leaves of the eager-beaver radishes, the slim grassy spears that are a sign of chives to come.

I go down to the garden to weed, and stay to gloat over the little green knobs on the tomato plants and the pale blossoms that will become beans. I love the earth smell that rises as I kneel by the garden, the sense of oneness with my ancestors that comes from performing this humble task. That's the special gift of the kitchen garden—a deep, satisfying sense of continuity with the past.

THE SEASONAL ROUND

WINTER. The season for the kitchen garden begins in midwinter. The catalogs arrive; draw up the planting plan.

EXTENDING THE SEASON. Where the growing season is brief, it can be extended by four to six weeks at either end. Start seed indoors, or in a cold frame or a hotbed, four to six weeks before the last frost. Set out transplants protected, if necessary, by hot caps, plastic sheets, or other devices (see page 237) that conserve the warmth available. The same protective devices can be used to extend the season as summer ends.

SPRING. As soon as the frost is out of the ground, fertilize and dig the garden. In late winter/early spring plant the frost hardy vegetables. Harvest peas as they ripen to encourage production. When the first crops have been harvested, remove the roots to the compost pile. Prepare the soil for its next planting: dig in humus and fertilizer, smooth the soil with a rake. Replant empty rows.

LATE SPRING/EARLY SUMMER. When temperatures head for 68° F. during the day and all chance of frost is past, set out seedlings of warm season vegetables such as tomatoes and sweet peppers. The earliest tomatoes are ready in about 50 days. Monitor soil moisture and water every three or four days if necessary from now until the fall rains begin. If you have any space left, plant snap beans.

SUMMER. Re-dig and replant empty rows with heat-resistant vegetables and make successive sowings every 2 weeks of more snap beans. The beans mature 7 to 8 weeks later, and continue producing for 4 weeks or so. Harvest beans as they mature to encourage continued production.

LATE SUMMER. As temperatures cool, sow seeds or start seedlings for a second round of cool season vegetables, such as hardy lettuces, broccoli, arugula, mâche (corn salad), carrots, parsnips, and Chinese greens.

EARLY FALL. In regions where fall is late and winters mild, plant seeds or seedlings of cold-hardy crops such as kale and winter radishes, and parsnips.

LATE FALL. Use covers to protect late-season crops from frost and extend your harvest. Clean up garden debris. Assess your results and start thinking about next year's kitchen garden.

SMALL
GARDENS

I know a little garden close,
Set thick with lily and red rose,
Where I would wander if I might
From dewy morn to dewy night.

WILLIAM MORRIS

he most magical garden of all is a small enclosed space, a vignette. It can be a secret garden on a large estate, a diminutive terrace garden behind a town house, or a container garden on a rooftop. It can be an alley between buildings where a wide brick path makes a long, lazy curve through the romantic tangle of cottage-garden perennials. It can be Colette's earthly paradise represented by a pear espaliered on a balcony wall and a chaise longue beside a perfumed purple heliotrope. Focused on a single theme, a small garden may appear both spacious and intimate.

Any type of garden, whether it be shade or rock, water or hillside, can be created in any of the room-sized yards typical of subdivisions and city lots. By room-sized, I mean yards that are about 20 feet by 30 feet or larger. With imaginative plantings, even the narrow, L-shaped land framing a corner property can be transformed into a little woodland or a fair-sized kitchen garden.

If your space is even smaller, I recommend that you keep the theme narrowly focused. I'm always surprised to see how well a collection of even big exotic summer-flowering bulbs like the blue lily-of-the-Nile (*Agapanthus*) and the Kaffir lily (*Clivia miniata*) work in a small space. An in-ground garden hardly larger than a carpet has plenty of room for a modest planting of such a collection, for a few varieties of fragrant herbs or flowers, or a few rose bushes grouped together in a bed bordered with a low curving brick retaining wall. The collection needn't be all the same species. It can be flowers of one color, a Victorian all-white moon garden, for example, or an all-gold garden where *Rudbeckia fulgida* 'Goldsturm' blooms for weeks on end and golden *Calamagrostis* sways in the wind beneath the saffron flowers of a golden-rain tree (*Koelreuteria paniculata*).

If the space is even smaller still, a theme can be expressed with very few plants. Two or three tubbed azaleas grouped in a corner of a condominium deck makes a shrinelike setting for a bonsai or a bower for baskets and pots of fuschias or tuberous begonias. A balcony or a small penthouse garden furnished with ice-cream parlor table and chairs, a weeping cherry, and a planter overflowing with perfumed white and purple petunias suggests an intimate little dining area. In addition to expressing a single concept, the major plantings in a small garden must bring to the design more than one brief season of beauty, and they must have more than one superb attribute. To be all it can be, the plan for a small garden must make less do, and seem like more.

MAKING THE SPACE SEEM MORE

By looking beyond the confines of your garden area, you can design a small garden as though it is a fragment of a larger whole deliberately made small because it has been enclosed to create a sense of intimacy. I like to think of a small garden as a place created so I can deadhead yesterday's petunias in my pajamas and robe. To make the transformation work, it's important to appropriate beauty that lies outside the garden. If an agreeable view is blocked by evergreen foliage, I prune it back. An evergreen that is in the way can also be replaced with a deciduous tree—the airy, layered branching of a dogwood, for example. If you have a view that is visible only when the leaves fall, your winter vistas can be framed with the wide-arching, painterly branches of a cherry tree,

PREVIOUS SPREAD:
Container plantings add immensely to the versatility of the small garden. On the left-hand page, a planter overflowing with red nasturtiums, red cabbage, and little French marigolds (*Tagetes patula*) provides bright color below a strip of pale spring flowers. On the right-hand page, red geraniums and the soft gray-green foliage and ivory flower-heads of licorice plant (*Helichrysum petiolare*) screen the entrance to a charming small garden.

OPPOSITE:
The restrained use of color bestows harmony on the lavish plantings in a pocket garden. The creamy white of the perfumed lilies repeats in a soaring spike of yucca bells and in a mound of variegated ivy; red impatiens and fuchsias provide bright, colorful accents.

ABOVE:
Climbing red and pink roses, purple clematis, and goldflame honeysuckle (*Lonicera* ✕ *heckrottii*) frame the flowers next door, effectively tieing this small garden into compatible neighboring assets.

The soaring flower-heads of blue lily-of-the-Nile (*Agapanthus*) and a cascading golden-variegated hakonechloa (*Hakonechloa macra* 'Aureola') provide focus for a porch garden at Wave Hill, an estate that is now a public garden in the Bronx, New York. Tubbed boxwood, juniper, and other evergreen shrubs frame the exotic summer-flowering bulbs. The smaller green plants include a terra-cotta strawberry jar with strawberries and the fernlike honeysuckle, *Lonicera nitida* 'Baggesen's Gold', presented here as a standard. A collection of large, bold plants can give a small space character without making it seem crowded and is easy to maintain.

Pots of spring-flowering tulips, violas, and hybrid wallflowers (*Erysimum*) make a wonderfully rich and fragrant showing in a small garden that relies primarily on potted plants for its color. The rosy reds, lavenders, coral, and soft yellows harmonize with the terra-cotta containers, which were chosen to blend with the weathered tiles. When they are spent, these plants can be replaced by others for color throughout the season. This delightful little garden was created by terracing a long narrow yard that rolled uphill away from the house.

or if you prefer, with columnar, rather than wide-spreading, evergreens. Small trees don't need a garden to grow in; they do very well growing in large tubs.

It's important to tie the design into neighboring assets. Planting flowers whose colors complement and whose bloom times coincide with a flowering crab apple on the other side of a wall will open the garden out to include the tree. Tall pink Darwin tulips would bloom with the crabapple, for example, as would fluffy pink and crimson astilbes that bloom a little later. Astilbes, with their fernlike foliage and dried seedheads, are also lovely in summer and fall. A border of tall flowers or a flowering vine, color-coded to flowers on the next property, will give your garden the appearance of greater depth. By repeating colors and species of plantings used on the common grounds of a condominium, you can make the larger picture a part of your individual condo garden.

You can also manipulate perspective to fool the eye. Paths, beds, and decks or patios that create horizontal lines cutting across the field of vision make the garden seem somewhat wider than it actually is. Paths and beds that are vertical to decks or patios, leading away into the garden, give the appearance of greater depth. You can strengthen the illusion of depth further by having the beds or paths converge a little as they approach the far end of the garden. Gradually reducing the size of plants toward the back of the garden also gives the impression of greater depth to a shallow space. When every part in a garden isn't immediately apparent, it seems that there is much more. A path to a screened-off portion of the garden works magic, even if the screened-off area is small or almost nonexistent. If the path zigzags or curves sharply back on itself between planted areas lightly screened by a trellis, bamboo, or tall grass, the glimpse of plantings beyond creates the illusion that the garden moves through ever-unfolding space. A path that curves sharply to one side and vanishes just beyond a high evergreen hedge implies a garden hidden from view. A path that disappears behind a foliage-covered trellis or one that ends just beyond a gate between shrubs produces the same effect. To complete the illusion, plant the far end of the path with paper birch, white azaleas, pieris, liriope, and lily-of-the-valley.

Another way to give the impression of a garden that has much more to it than is there is to add dimension by changing the levels. A small flat garden can be made more interesting by lowering one area and using the soil to raise the level of another portion of the yard. Raised seating, a deck at the end of the garden, a small sunken reflecting pool, or simply a lower level of emerald green grass will add interest and make the garden appear larger. Raised seating and low walls also can border narrow planting beds and double as plant stands, effectively increasing your planting space. Designs that are open-ended and incomplete increase the impression of more over there, beyond. Free-form seating, three chairs rather than two or four, asymmetrical beds and walks, and open S-curves are examples of open-ended, incomplete forms.

Small-scale furnishings and certain garden features can be exploited to gain more space for your garden. If you plan a low wall, for example, cap it and make it a planter. Broaden steps by a few inches and use them as plant stands. Gain floor space by hanging plants from wall brackets. Oddly enough, one large garden feature can often make a small space seem generous—not a large tree, of course, but a single stand of tall grasses, for example, or a 6-foot statue, a small reflecting pool with goldfish and waterlilies, or a tall jet of water falling into a small pool with goldfish and a stand of dainty little umbrella plants. (Water lilies don't bloom well when disturbed so their pool must be a quiet one.)

If you have a desire to grow a wide selection of plants, use small-scale varieties of your favorite species. Purple moor grass (*Molinia caerulea* 'Variegata'), with leaves 6 to 12 inches long and flower stalks no more than 2 to 3 feet high, is as effective in a small space as much taller grasses are in a large space. A medium-size variety of marigold on a balcony does everything a huge climax marigold does in a large garden. On a condominium deck one large clay pot containing a mid-size tomato plant, parsley, sunny French marigolds, and thyme has the impact of a whole kitchen garden in a larger setting. A single large plant, a dwarf flowering tree, perhaps, or one clump of a tall ornamental grass can become the focus of your design.

When you are choosing a theme and a style, it's best to make assets of existing permanent elements instead of crowding the garden with additions. You can often revamp dubious assets by making the color scheme more monochromatic, for example, painting walls, fences, and furniture to match, and by facing steps, edging flower borders, and redoing paths in matching brick, stone, or decking. Complementary pairs of colors, such as red and green or blue and yellow, are lively, but you should use them with caution. Such combinations can make a small space look cramped and spoil the harmony of the composition. The containers you use should also echo existing elements:

Blue and white *Browallia* 'Heavenly Bells' brightens hanging baskets and shady corners in a small garden.

RIGHT:
In late spring tall creamy lupines, purple alliums, and lavender and gold irises bloom in the morning light of this east-facing border, while the geraniums and ferns at ground level do well with less sun. In hot weather, sun in the cool morning is more beneficial than sun that reaches the plants in the heat of the day.

Redwood tubs complement redwood decking; terra-cotta pots harmonize with brick-work; curved stone pots are wonderful paired with old stone walls and with flagstone walks; ceramic pots, sculptured or rough, are handsome with weathered wood.

Where trees and shrubs crowd a garden, you can prune them back or replace them with smaller trees, vines, and shrubs. Pears, apricots, apples, flowering quince, hollies, pyracanthas, magnolias, and many other shrubs and dwarf trees can be espaliered, that is, pruned and trained on a wall or trellis. Shrubs and vines also will thrive in tubs of moderate size and have modest watering needs for the foliage produced. Vines combine beauty and practicality. Deep-rooted, vigorous growers, they are relatively drought-resistant and require little help once established. In return they bloom and fruit, give shade, soften and cover stark modern walls, beautify fences, hide unsightly posts and drains, and screen out unattractive views.

MAKING THE LIGHT DO MORE
Light changes in a small garden are apt to be swift and extreme, and you should take note of seasonal as well as daily fluctuations. A wall can put an end to morning sun-shine at ten o'clock and, by the same token, can bless late summer afternoons by

SMALL FLOWERING TREES
Chinese fringe tree
Chionanthus retusus Z6-8

Eastern redbud
Cercis canadensis Z5-9

English hawthorn
Crataegus laevigata Z5-8

Flowering cherry
Prunus 'Kwanzan' Z6-8

Goldenrain tree
Koelreuteria paniculata Z6-9

Japanese flowering crab apple
Malus floribunda Z4-7

Japanese tree lilac
Syringa reticulata Z4-7

Silk tree, mimosa
Albizia julibrissin Z7-10

Silver bell tree
Halesia tetraptera Z5-8

Sweet bay magnolia
Magnolia virginiana Z6-9

Weeping cherry
Prunus subhirtella 'Pendula' Z6-8

Crimson California poppies (*Eschscholzia californica*) and a mound of golden threadleaf coreopsis (*Coreopsis verticillata*) are the color accents in a monochromatic garden of summer-blooming flowers. Thriving together in a sunny, sheltered site are orange daylilies (*Hemerocallis* 'Prima Donna'), coral Peruvian lilies (*Alstroemeria* Ligtu Hybrids), Erysimum 'Flame', Maltese cross (*Lychnis chalcedonica*), and Transvaal daisies (*Gerbera jamesonii*.)

89

FRAGRANCE PLANTS

Cheddar pink
Dianthus gratianopolitanus Z4-8

Flowering tobacco
Nicotiana alata Tender perennial

Fragrant viburnum cultivars
V. × burkwoodii 'Mohawk' Z4-8

Heliotrope
Heliotropium arborescens Z10-11

Holly olive
Osmanthus heterophyllus Z7-9

Lavender 'Hidcote'
Lavandula angustifolia 'Hidcote'

Lily-of-the-valley
Convallaria majalis Z3-10

Mock organge
Philadelphus lemoinei Z5-8

Night-scented stock
Matthiola longipetala Annual

Sweet rocket
Hesperis matronalis Z3-9

Wallflower
Erysimum cheiri Tender perennial

Winter honeysuckle
Lonicera fragrantissima Z5-8

Golden yarrow, airy meadowsweet, bold hostas, and a golden variegated grass thrive in the shelter and light shade created by a board fence and tall evergreen shrubs. The deeper shade cast by the taller plants is just right for *Chiastophyllum oppositofolium,* the low-growing succulent in the foreground, which has covered its evergreen foliage with graceful sprays of tiny yellow flowers.

blocking out the sun's hot rays. An enclosed small garden will have a large proportion of shadow at ground level, more than is immediately apparent. The availability and intensity of light obviously governs plant choices and their locations. Also, before deciding on plants to carry out your chosen theme, sketch the garden and chart the light that reaches its various levels. Make a chart of the light received in the morning, at noon, and in late afternoon to enable you to locate suitable light for your plantings, and suitable new plants for the light. In hot regions, Zone 8 and southward, the light shade present in a small enclosed garden provides protection from direct sun in summer and makes growing most of the garden favorites possible. If you think that too much direct sun will be a problem, you can choose a theme for the garden that includes trellising, vines, and awnings that will provide relief. In the cooler northern states, Zones 3 and 4, where the growing season is short, plants need more exposure to direct sun. Shadows can be a liability, but the remedies are simple. You can prune overhanging tree branches to reduce shadows, and white walls and other reflective surfaces can be used to increase the available light. You can also give your garden annuals a head start by planting good-sized seedlings and setting them out early, protected by hot caps and similar plastic covers.

The mobility of containerized plants makes all areas of the garden potential plant sites. Where a too-sunny bed excludes shade-loving impatiens and fragrant nicotiana, you can grow these in pots and planters in a shadowed corner or grouped on shelves in the light shade of a vine-covered pergola. Where a shadowed ground-level garden is devoted to caladiums, the color in the caladiums can be repeated to charming effect in sun-loving petunias growing in hanging baskets in the sunlight above. Potted flowers that need some sun but not a lot, like the exquisite blue edging lobelia

(*Lobelia erinus*) can spend the morning in sunshine and be moved in the afternoon to the shade of a wall, or be placed strategically to receive sun only in the morning.

I also make it a point to take advantage of the special light preferences of some plants. Clematis, like many other flowering vines, does very well with its roots cooled by shade and its leaves and flowers in full sunshine. It's a great vine for small gardens. *Clematis cirrhosa* var. *balearica,* an evergreen, bears lovely, creamy white flowers flecked red or maroon within; *C. tangutica* bears nodding, golden yellow flowers in spring and fall; and the many large-flowered clematis hybrids and cultivars bear spectacular blooms in white, pink, red, purple, and blue. *Clematis flammula*, a fall-blooming shrub with fragrant white flowers, is hardy to Zone 7, and hardy *C. recta* 'Purpurea (Zone 3) is a striking shrub with bronze-red foliage and fragrant white summer blooms.

CHOOSING PLANTS THAT DO MORE

Because the space for plants in a small garden is limited, each one chosen must perform its assigned role superbly. The most desirable plants are those that are as interesting in fall and winter as they are in spring and summer, for example, flowering and fruiting trees and shrubs. A small garden needs the structure provided by woody plants; the textures and contrasts of grasses and foliage, fragrance to enhance its sense of intimacy, and color in every season. Plants with more limited talents can be combined into groups that have something to give in every season. For example, imagine planting a terraced collection of fragrant tulips and the little red silver grass, *Miscanthus sinensis* var. *purpurascens*, beneath a white bark birch tree. When spring and the tulips have gone, the grasses will be lifting silky seedheads toward the sun, and, with the first frost, the white birch will stand in a miniature meadow of golden-maroon-orange grass.

A small garden attached to a home must be attractive in fall and winter because it is so visible, so much a part of your life in every season, not just when the weather is nice. I like to outfit the garden with plants whose foliage turns crimson, vines and shrubs that produce berries, and stems that remain interesting, like the rusty brown spears of Siberian iris. The red stems of red-osier dogwood rising from a mass of variegated *Euonymus fortunei* are spectacular all winter long. When I walk alone in the garden as the leaves fall, I need evergreens, to evoke summer and the growing seasons, and starkly beautiful plant structures that will be rimed in frost and cast blue shadows in the snow.

STRUCTURE: The ideal tree for a small garden bears beautiful flowers, has foliage that colors in autumn, and branching patterns attractive in winter. Dogwoods, hawthorns, cherries and the other flowering fruit trees fulfill these requirements. *Euonymus alatus* 'Compactus', the 6-foot-tall dwarf winged euonymus, bears inconspicuous flowers, but in fall its foliage fairly flames in shades of pink to scarlet, and its graceful horizontal branches are lovely in winter. The lacy blossoms of the fringe tree (*Chionanthus retusus*) have a light, sweet scent, and the leaves turn a brilliant yellow before they fall. A superb, if messy, small tree for all seasons is the mimosa (*Albizia julibrissin*). The fluffy flowers that perfume the air for weeks in late spring are followed by long golden seedpods in winter that look as though they had been hung there by a very patient artist.

Where space is restricted, on a balcony, for instance, you can use a woody vine instead of a tree for vertical structure. The gold flame honeysuckle (*Lonicera* ✕

CLIMBERS

Black-eyed Susan vine
Thunbergia alata Annual

Boston ivy
Parthenocissus tricuspidata Z4-8

Clematis species and hybrids

Climbing hydrangea
Hydrangea petiolaris Z5-7

Honeysuckles
Lonicera sempervirens, L. ✕ *heckrottii, L. brownii* 'Dropmore Scarlet' Z4-9; *L. periclymenum* Z5-9

Japanese wisteria
Wisteria floribunda Z4-9

Memorial rose
Rosa wichuraiana Z5-8

Morninglories and moonflowers
Ipomoea spp. Grown as annuals

Trumpet vine
Campsis tagliabuana Z4-10

PLANTS FOR TEXTURE

American maidenhair fern
Adiantum pedatum Z3-8

Amethyst sea holly
Eryngium amethystinum Z5-9

Artemisia, wormwood
Artemisia cvs. Z4-8

Bear grass, Adam's needle
Yucca filamentosa Z5-10

Christmas fern
Polystichum acrostichoides Z3-8

Giant rhubarb
Gunnera manicata Z7-10

Heartleaf and hybrid bergenia
Bergenia cordifolia, B. cvs. Z3-8

Hosta, large-leaved varieties
Hosta sieboldiana, H. montana Z4-9

Japanese silver painted fern
Athyrium nipponicum 'Pictum' Z3-8

Lamb's ears
Stachys byzantina Z4-9

Russian sage
Perovskia atriplicifolia Z5/6-9

Scotch thistle
Onopordum acanthium Biennial

A small, magical garden screened from the world outside by flowering shrubs and trees. Sun-loving, fragrant roses and a lavender-flowered tree mallow (*Lavatera*) have filled the upper reaches of the garden, but careful pruning allows enough light and air to meet the needs of the irises and other perennials in the border below.

heckrottii) bears very fragrant carmine and yellow flowers from late spring to fall; its blue-green foliage is evergreen where winters are mild. *Lonicera periclymenum* 'Graham Thomas' has grayish green leaves and bears fragrant yellow-white flowers, followed by red fruits the birds love. The climbing hydrangea (*Hydrangea petiolaris*) though very slow growing, is a magnificent vine, woody and impressive in maturity, and very hardy. The small, slightly scented flowers are borne in clusters in late spring and early summer, and the leaves are dark green and lustrous.

To fill in while a young tree develops, as well as for summer screening, I like to plant several seeds of one of the fast-growing annual vines. The cup-and-saucer vine (*Cobaea scandens*) can grow 25 feet tall in a season and bears showy, dark purple or white flowers. Or try a mixed planting of morning glories and moonflowers for double the pleasure with a touch of magic—cheerful blue and red flowers during the day, followed at night by huge fragrant white flowers that open before your eyes.

To balance the tall verticals and provide greenery in winter, you should include in the mix some dwarf or slow-growing evergreens. Some shrubs I particularly like are the wonderful dwarf box (*Buxus sempervirens* 'Suffruticosa'), dwarf and pygmy varieties of Hanoki cypress (*Chamaecyparis obtusa*), and Japanese holly (*Ilex crenata* 'Tiny Tim'), which has elegant foliage. Standard hollies grow large, but they can be pruned back to dwarf size almost indefinitely. I find variegated English holly very beautiful. There are dwarf and pygmy junipers and yews to choose from as well. For contrast, add some deciduous shrubs that are interesting in the cold seasons. Barberries and cotoneaster are unbeatable for fall foliage and fruits. The brilliant spring flowering of evergreen azaleas is followed in some varieties by colorful autumn foliage. Dwarf forsythia covers itself with golden blooms early in spring, and the arching structure of the branches, interesting all winter long, is particularly delightful in snow.

TEXTURE: To make the garden sing, I like to group together plants with contrasting textures. Texture can be found in the fluffy quality of ornamental grasses and fennel foliage and in the furry silk of lamb's ears (*Stachys*). Holly has small, shiny, light-reflecting leaves that are striking in contrast when paired with the large and handsome, but dull, leaves of a giant hosta. Such contrasting textures give life to plant groups. You should strive for combinations that bring contrasting textures together, for example, candelabra primroses planted with variegated, grasslike *Carex elata* 'Aurea', feathery astilbe, and the bold leaves of rhubarb or *Gunnera manicata*. In a small garden, rhubarb and the large hostas look like exotic jungle plants. The bold and leathery, glossy evergreen leaves of *Bergenia cordifolia* are a superb addition to any plant group, and they turn a stunning bronze in the winter sun.

Spiky angular plants add yet another texture to the mix. The thistles are superb choices for this. Scotch thistle (*Onopordum acanthium*) is especially dramatic when it is used as a foil for shiny-leaved ivies and soft-leaved nicotiana. The angular branches of amethyst sea holly (*Eryngium amethystinum*) are a haze of blue when the plant blooms in summer, and the structure makes a fine tall accent in winter.

For me, flowers that are fragrant are a priority in a small garden. I love passing by perfumed flowers when they are planted close to entrances. Those that wait for moonlight to release their scent are lovely when planted close to the windows. Be sure to plant fragrant herbs, like mint and English lavender for instance, where you will brush against them. And creeping thyme can be planted between flagstones where it will be stepped on. Many of the spring-flowering shrubs are fragrant, including lilacs. The strong, sweet, spicy fragrance of blossoms of *Viburnum* × *burkwoodii* 'Mohawk' resembles the scents of cloves and lilies. Mock orange—one of my favorites is *Philadelphus* × *lemoinei* 'Innocence'—recalls orange blossoms. Honeysuckle is summer's sweetest scent, and the holly olive (*Osmanthus heterophyllus*) bears small, hauntingly fragrant flowers in the fall. With careful planning you can have fragrance throughout the season. In spring come the scents of hyacinths, wallflowers, and sweet peas—all irresistible. In summer can follow sweet garden heliotrope, valerian, perfumed stock, and lilies. The wonderfully scented little cheddar pinks (*Dianthus gratianopolitanus* 'Tiny Rubies', 'La Bourbille', and 'Warbonnet') bloom all summer long, and they make fine edgers. Some white and purple petunias release a sweet, spicy fragrance in cool evening air; they thrive in hanging baskets. Nicotiana, in shade, and sweet alyssum, in sun, are late summer's sweetest perfume plants.

For color, I plant flowers everywhere. Containers display flowering bulbs beautifully. A lilliputian drift of blue muscari and miniature daffodils is especially appealing under small trees and shrubs in a big planter. And the tall, exotic, lily-flowered tulips combine marvelously with ornamental grasses that take over as the tulips go by, which they do rather quickly. I allow daffodils and narcissus to yellow before I cut them back, but in a small garden I discard the spent tulip bulbs. I use the spaces freed to plant pansies and primroses. In mid-spring the markets offer a marvelous selection of these plants and of summer annuals already showing their colors, so designing the season's display is easy. Like vegetables, the annuals are once-only plants, new every year, and if a color or a plant doesn't live up to my expectations, I discard it. Empty spaces can be filled with geraniums, lantanas, wax begonias, dahlias, caladiums, and impatiens, and big spaces, with cannas.

When fall's failing light and cool air slow the flowering of the summer annuals, I acknowledge that it is time to haul them off to the compost pile, and I fill the

GRASSES FOR SMALL GARDENS

Autumn moor grass
Sesleria autumnalis Z5-9

Blue fescue
Festuca glauca cvs. Z4-8

Blue oat grass
Helictotrichon sempervirens Z4-9

Fountain grass
Pennisetum alopecuroides Z6-9

Golden Hakonechloa
Hakonechloa macra 'Aureola'

Golden sedge
Carex elata 'Aurea' Z5-9

Hair grass
Deschampsia caespitosa Z4-9

Japanese blood grass
Imperata cylindrica 'Red Baron' Z6-9

Variegated purple moor grass
Molinia caerulia 'Variegata' Z4-9

Wood rush
Luzula nivea Z4-8

OVERLEAF:

Converging vertical lines and a grass path that narrows as it recedes create the impression of greater depth than this small, shallow garden actually possesses. The illusion is enhanced by a daffodil border in which the taller flowers—12-inch high 'Peeping Tom' and 'February Gold'—have been planted up front, while the little 6-inch high 'Tête à Tête' has been planted farther back.

spaces with potted chrysanthemums. When the mums go by, I set out the spring flowering bulbs and plant over them an array of pansies. Pansies are amazingly cold hardy, and in my Washington, D.C. garden they live through winter's snow and ice storms and are fresh and bright in early spring.

KEEPING THE GARDEN PRODUCTIVE

Beds and containers can be kept flowering by using intercropping and companion planting methods (see pages 68-69). To sustain the unchecked growth that keeps a small garden glowing with color and filled with interesting developments all season long, provide fertile, moisture-holding soil. Creating a raised bed (see page 235), will do that, and also can solve a number of problems, such as drainage, competition from tree roots, special soil requirements for particular plants. Before you plant, you'll want to dig in plenty of compost or other organic soil amendments and to adjust the pH of your soil, if necessary. Your soil's pH should be appropriate for the plants you plan to grow. A wide variety of annual and perennial flowers and many shrubs grow best in slightly acid soils (pH 5.5 to pH 6.8); you can adjust your soil's pH to this range or to grow plants with more extreme requirements (see page 234).

To conserve moisture, as well as to keep down weeds, you'll want to mulch your beds. Mulch will also enhance your design. How often you need to water will depend on your climate, your soil, and the plants you've chosen. As you spend time with your plants, you'll learn when it's time to water. Learn the signs, and learn the feel of the soil. As the soil dries out, plants will begin to show stress—the leaves droop or become dull, the plants wilt. Watering deeply and thoroughly to encourage the roots to grow deep, will lengthen the time until you need to water again (see page 237).

SUCCESS WITH CONTAINERS

The success of plants growing in containers depends on a humus-rich planting mix that holds water well and whose fertility is maintained in spite of sustained watering. For big planters, pots, and tubs, I like to use a mix that is half garden soil and half soil-less potting mix. The soil-less mixes have a desirably high humus content, and they are light as a feather, which makes moving the big containers much easier. On a rooftop garden, I recommend using two-thirds soil-less mix to keep down the weight. I find it helpful to add water-holding gels (polymers) to soils and growing mixes used in baskets and pots. They help to retain moisture and keep the plants growing without check. Baskets and pots require frequent watering, at least once daily in hot or windy weather, and adding the gel helps to keep them from drying out between waterings. The soil in pots smaller than 14 inches in diameter should be replaced every year, as should the growing medium in baskets and planters that are less than 14 inches deep (see page 236).

Perennials and bulbs thrive in well-drained, well-fertilized soil in large containers. In cold regions they need a generous buffer of soil as protection from frost. In Zone 6 and Zone 7 a minimum container size is 14 to 16 inches in length, width, and height. In colder zones you'll need to increase the size; in warmer zones it can be less. The containers should be top-dressed with humus or fresh soil scratched into the surface along with fertilizer in late winter.

Plants growing in containers will need to be fertilized more often than those growing in the open garden. The limited amount of soil in a container dries quickly in sun and wind and requires daily, or almost daily, watering. The frequent flow of

RECIPE: A SOIL-LESS MIX FOR CONTAINERS

START WITH:
½ bushel coarse peat
   moss
½ bushel perlite

ADD:
1 cup 5-10-5
1 cup limestone (omit for
   acid-loving plants)

1 cup gypsum
Polymers according to
   label instructions

Recipe yields about 1 bushel of soil-less container mix.

water leaches nutrients from the soil, and they must be replaced to keep the plant growing vigorously. With each watering, I recommend adding a very light application of a complete soluble fertilizer. For flowering and fruiting plants I use 10-20-10. Plants grown for their foliage do well with a fertilizer richer in nitrogen.

In warm, dry weather, a container garden that includes several large planters, along with trees and shrubs growing in tubs, requires about half an hour's watering with a hose every day. I soak each container until water begins to drain from the bottom. (You can also provide the containers with a system of leaky hoses or emitters turned on and off by an electric timer.) Containers on balconies and rooftops are subject to much more wind than are containers at ground level and may need to be watered more often. You must raise large rooftop planters well off the ground even if the roof is tiled. It's the only way to be sure they will not cause water damage to the apartment below.

Monitor the moisture in small containers daily. If watering becomes a burden, consider switching to double-bottomed, self-watering planters and pots. The reservoirs built into these containers keep the soil suitably damp for several days, or even weeks, depending on the size of the planter.

Summer's end on a rooftop terrace in New York with lavender asters in full bloom and 'Autumn Joy' sedum changing from its summer jade to autumnal pink, cerise, and maroon brown. Good soil, sustained watering, and fertilization keep this garden glowing with color all season.

WATER
GARDENS

*And nearer to the river's trembling edge
There grew broad flag-flowers, purple,
    pranked with white,
And starry river buds among the sedge,
And floating water-lilies, broad and bright.*

PERCY BYSSHE SHELLEY

A water garden offers unique gifts—
sound and movement, sparkle, and a touch of the wild in the creatures that inhabit or
visit it: koi and goldfish, snails and frogs, birds and butterflies. Water spilling into a
pool, water rushing over stones, a fountain splashing in the moonlight—to have it all
is surprisingly easy. A water feature can be as majestic as the Taj Mahal or as cozy as a
bucket with a single miniature water lily in bloom. There's a pond sized and styled for
every garden and for every purse. With some help from neighbors, you can even
install a water garden of modest size over a weekend.

The living elements in a water garden work together to keep the pond clean,
controlling insects and algae. The goldfish and snails, the submerged plants, even the
ornamentals—water lilies and lotus, the little floaters, and the upright plants that
define the margins—are working members of an ecosystem, and they provide a fascinating view of the interrelationships in nature. Establishing a water garden requires
mastering some technical information that isn't part of soil-based gardening, but basic
gardening principles apply. Nearly all the aquatic plants grow in soil, respond to fertilizing, have active and dormant seasons, and are hardy or tender. Only a few hundred
aquatics are cultivated, so learning to handle them isn't demanding. Nor is maintenance a chore if you start right.

In our environmentally concerned age all nature's wet places and ponds are
under the jurisdiction of environmental protection agencies. Even if your property features a natural pond, to stock it with non-native plants and animals would be seen as
tampering with the way nature has laid out her garden—it would also be illegal: The
law protects wetlands, and the law is enforced. A home water garden is typically a
man-made excavation waterproofed by a liner. Preformed fiberglass ponds are available
up to about 14 feet long, while flexible liners are available in virtually any size. Shelves
may be included for the marginal plants. The aquatic plants are grown in shallow
pans, pails, and tubs that rest on a shelf, blocks, or the pond bottom, depending on
the water depth required by the plants.

Your water garden can be as quiet or as lively as you wish. I love to sit by a lily
pond whose mirrored surface reflects the clouds above and the flowers and foliage
nearby in an ever-changing scene; in the light of the full moon, a tranquil pond of
night-blooming water lilies is pure magic. And I delight in watching the sunlight
sparkle in the droplets of a fountain and hearing the music of a waterfall cascading
over rocks into the pool below. Moving water delights the senses and calms the soul,
and it can easily become part of your water garden design. Today's pumps and filter
systems are reliable, affordable, and easy to maintain. Bubbler, fountain, stream,
waterfall, even a triple waterfall—choose one, or choose them all.

FINDING THE RIGHT LOCATION

The first step in creating a water garden, after checking local ordinances that apply to
ponds, is to decide its location and size. A successful water garden needs an open,
sunny site. Under or near deciduous trees the pond will collect fallen leaves and will
need frequent cleaning. Most aquatic plants require at least six hours of direct sun
daily. (More may be even better in northern regions, where the growing season is relatively brief; in warm climates, too much sun can overheat the water and kill the fish.)

PREVIOUS SPREAD:
A triple waterfall brings sound
and movement to a secluded rock
garden and a touch of the wild in
the creatures—goldfish and frogs,
birds and butterflies—that
inhabit and visit it. Creamy
white bleeding heart (*Dicentra*)
and golden *Trollius* thrive in the
humid atmosphere. The green
frog (*Rana clamitans*) on mosquito patrol is one of many living
elements that help with pond
maintenance.

OPPOSITE:
The soaring aerial leaves of a
lotus (*Nelumbo nucifera*) backdrop a day-blooming tropical
water lily. Some tropicals bloom
only at night and have an extraordinary, compelling perfume.

Nymphaea 'Attraction', is one of
the hardy water lilies. It blooms
only in daylight.

If the only site you have available receives less than four hours of direct sun, I recommend, rather than a complete water garden, a water feature—for instance, a fountain or a brook ending in a waterfall.

It's tempting to believe that a marshy area is just the place to construct a water garden, but that isn't the case. Good drainage is essential; a wet spot can heave a pond in big rainstorms and in winter when the ground freezes and thaws.

You should choose a fairly level site for your pond. A moderately uneven site can be leveled by adding a few inches of packed builders' sand. A very gentle slope can be terraced to provide a level site. If you terrace a steep slope to install a water garden, you will have to reroute runoff that will otherwise carry mud, old grass clippings, and dead leaves into the water. Try to avoid sites frequented by snail-hungry raccoons and fish-eating birds. (Cats are fascinated by fish but few actually go fishing.) A steeply sloped pond side without a shelf will help discourage furry paws; if a small pond is haunted by night raiders, you can cover it at night with screening. You can also discourage marauders by stocking the pond with fast-swimming comets or with less-colorful fish. If these measures fail, sit back and enjoy the wildlife.

Your water garden will need electrical power for a pump and for night lighting, if they are planned and, in Zones 3 to 7, for a deicer. You will also want access to a water supply so you can easily fill and occasionally top up the pond. While you might think otherwise, a pond uses less water in the course of a season than a lawn the same size.

DESIGNING A WATER GARDEN

Once you have determined your site, you can begin to design your water garden and choose the equipment that will be used to create the pond. Most pond styles are either informal and natural or formal and clearly man-made. Another possibility is to choose a little of each style, which can have a really dramatic effect—the juxtaposition of a cherub fountain or a rollaway concrete garden seat and a wild-seeming waterfall has a compelling dynamic.

If you want to create an informal water garden, plan to use native materials as far as possible and mimic the design characteristic of wild ponds. Natural ponds are usually irregularly shaped—there's hardly a perfect curve or straight line anywhere. Whether your garden is to be large or quite small, choose a free-form container design. For the coping that is placed around a water garden to keep debris out of the water and to protect the pond liner, choose flat native stones. Small bodies of water naturally occur at the base of a slope and are often fed by a low waterfall. If you have a

STEPS TO A BEAUTIFUL GARDEN

PLAN THE POND	BUILD THE POND	STOCK THE POND
Find right light and site	Dig the pond	Pot the plants
Choose design, size, and liner	Install the liner	Place the plants in the pond
Choose filter and pump	Fill the pond	Wait 8 to 10 days; or
Sketch out placement of the aquatics	Check and adjust the pH of the water	Dechlorinate the water
Order plants and livestock		Loose the fish and the snails

gently sloping lawn, you could install the pond at the bottom of the grade with a waterfall spilling into it. In nature tiny pools lap against rocky ledges, fed by narrow spills of water issuing higher up. In a garden you could place the pond right against a low stone wall, a rock garden, or a fence below a waterfall. Water also collects where a stream running through nearly level ground is dammed or partially dammed by rocks before it spills downhill. You could create a pebble-strewn stream bed that ends with water flowing over a flat rock and into the pond. At the edges of a wild water garden, marsh plants will clump in asymmetrical patterns, tall and short, narrow-leaved and broad-leaved together. When you place the marginal plants in your pond, arrange them in similar groupings. You can emphasize the informal, naturalistic theme by grouping a few of the native trees and shrubs mentioned in the chapter on natural gardens a short distance from the pond.

Nature often brings grasses and meadow flowers right to the edge of the water. If you surround the pond with a meadow or lawn, always remember to aim the mower's clipping chute *away* from the pond, otherwise the mower will spit grass into the water. You can easily remove the grass with a skimmer, but it's a nuisance. Use a weedeater to cut the grass closest to the liner to avoid the possibility of damaging it.

The effect of a formal water garden is to impart a sense of elegance, order, and harmony. You can choose forms that echo graceful classical shapes or that express

In late summer the still waters of a peaceful garden pond are framed by river birches (*Betula nigra*), rudbeckia, *Lythrum,* and pink spider flowers (*Cleome*), and reflect the gracefully cascading foliage of *Miscanthus* and *Pennisetum* on the other side.

ABOVE:
Handsome in a February snowstorm and beautiful in bloom, evergreen *Skimmia japonica* thrives in the shade and humid soil under the moon bridge in the Japanese Garden in Portland, Oregon. Other beautiful flowering broad-leaved evergreens that thrive near water are rhododendrons and azaleas. The appeal of a water garden in winter depends on the selection of nearby foliage plants.

LEFT:
This formal pond is fed by a rivulet and a fountain jet, whose graceful plumes coin rainbows from sunlight. It's spring, and the irises on the far side are marking the pond boundaries while gently leading the eye from the flat, reflective plane of the water to the park and up to the sky.

Nymphaea 'Blue Beauty'
Scented, lilac blue; leaves
speckled

N. 'Daubeniana'
Lavender-tipped, creamy white

N. 'Eldorado'
Scented, lemon yellow blooms

N. 'Enchantment'
Scented, salmon-rose flowers

N. 'Jack Wood'
Scented, raspberry red flowers

N. 'Leopardus'
Cobalt blue; leaves mottled

N. 'Peach Blow'
Pink flowers with peach centers

LOTUS

Sacred lotus 'Charles Thomas'
Nelumbo nucifera 'Charles
Thomas'; small pink flowers Z8

N. 'Alba Grandiflora'; pure white

N. 'Mrs. Perry D. Slocum'
Red, changing to pink, then
white

N. 'Tulip'; dwarf, white flowers

Nelumbo lutea
American lotus, yellow lotus Z6

stark, sleek modern lines. The pond can be circular or oval, square or rectangular. Glassy sheets of water, lawns, statuesque fountains, statuary, moon gates, Greek columns, repetition of plants and forms, and similar classical elements all have the symmetry that you expect in a formal style. The coping you choose should have the same hard edge and symmetry as the pond design. Poured concrete, concrete blocks, patterned concrete blocks, glass bricks, and cemented or fitted cut stone or bricks are all suitable.

To my surprise, a classically styled water garden, one equipped with a fountain, for instance, looks equally at home in a small urban yard as it does in a corner of a suburban half acre or, viewed from a distance, in a large landscape. Even an apartment balcony can be transformed by a small fountain spilling water into a fiberglass pool outfitted with a few goldfish and a small floating-leaved plant. I find that it is most effective to provide a formal pond with plants associated with a classical landscape—boxwood topiaries, tree roses, and small-leaved ivy come to mind. Urns and ornate jars of annuals in pairs reinforce the formal mood. Italian cypress is well suited to a formal setting, as is the small, pyramidal evergreen Sawara cypress (*Chamaecyparis pisifera*); 'Boulevard' is an exquisite cultivar with fine, silvery blue foliage and a strikingly narrow shape.

Night lighting, from outside or inside the pond, is a feature that I really love to see in a water garden. To imitate the appearance of a pond lit by a full moon, try hanging a lantern or placing a spotlight in a tree so that the light creates a moonlit path across the pond. For a formal effect, place one or two small floodlights in shrubbery a short distance from the pond and focus the beams on a fountain. Light that comes from inside the pond itself gives the water a magical luminosity. The underwater glow outlines the floating pads of the lilies and hints at the flower colors of night-blooming tropicals.

You can use the electrical outlet that powers the water garden pump to power low-voltage underwater lighting equipment using a transformer. An underwater unit with three 36-watt bulbs is sufficient to light a small pond. Be sure to buy only non-corroding installations, and do not fail to use them in conjunction with a ground fault circuit interrupter. Install the longest-lasting light bulbs available because replacing them is a nuisance, and add a timer to automate the lighting.

SELECTING THE RIGHT LINER

Now that you have chosen the design and location of your pond, outline it on the site. You can outline an informal pond easily using cord or a hose; use stakes and string to outline a formal shape that includes straight lines. To determine the size of the liner, measure the outline's length and width in feet. Choose a preformed fiberglass liner of the size and shape you want, or calculate the size of the flexible liner. Its length is the length of the pond plus twice the depth plus 2 feet, and its width is the widest distance perpendicular to the length plus twice the depth plus 2 feet. To keep your fish healthy and plants thriving, the pond should be at least 15 to 30 inches deep. In ponds that are 30 to 48 inches deep, fish can live through winters even in Zone 4 and northward, but check with local authorities: Some municipalities require fencing for anything deeper than 24 to 30 inches.

You'll need the pond's dimensions to determine its surface area and volume. The manufacturer should supply these figures for a preformed pond; otherwise you'll need to calculate them. The surface area determines the number of plants, fish, and snails the pond can support, information you'll need to know to stock the pond. The area of a rectangle is length multiplied by width; the area of a circle is the square of the radius multiplied by 3.14. For a free-form pond, divide the surface into smaller rectangular and/or circular units and calculate the area of each; the sum of these is an estimate of the surface area of the pond. To select a pump and a filter appropriate for your pond, you'll need to know its volume in gallons, or gallon capacity; to determine this, multiply the surface area by the depth in feet by 7.5. The pond dealer will recommend a pump and a filter based on gallon capacity

PREFORMED LINERS: You can use a water garden in a tub, an old barrel, or a bucket that holds as little as 4 gallons of water. (If your container has held compounds that might be harmful to fish or plants, for example, weeds treated with pesticides, provide the container with a waterproof liner—even minute amounts of pesticides can be toxic.) A container this size will support the snails and the submerged plants that maintain the clarity of the water and one small water lily, such as the yellow pygmy *Nymphaea tetragona* 'Helvola'. One 2-inch fish will find it ample space and will control the mosquitoes and other insects that multiply where there is water.

There is an almost infinite number of sizes of preformed liners. Tubs 18 to 28 inches across by 12 to 19 inches deep and pans and kettles about 3 feet in diameter and 18 inches deep will accommodate submerged plants, a pair of snails, two or three goldfish, and a pair of aquatic plants, such as the pale blue tropical water lily 'Daubeniana' or the white pygmy 'Ermine' and the lovely marginal plant, sweet flag (*Acorus calamus*). A bubbler powered by a small pump will aerate the water and provide a musical dimension.

A preformed fiberglass pond liner measuring about 4 by 6 feet is the next size up. It can accommodate the submerged plants, snails, fish, and a pair of water lilies, such as white 'Gonnere' and *Marliacea* 'Albida', along with a small floating-leaved plant and one or two of the upright marginals.

RUBBER LINERS: For a larger pond, a flexible rubber liner will cost as little as a quarter the price of a preformed pond the same size. Popular dimensions for home water gardens are between 10 by 10 feet and 10 by 15 feet. Ponds in this size range will hold five water lilies, one lotus, some small-leaved floaters, and a few upright plants. Flexible liners are made of long-lasting, flexible material, typically non-toxic butyl rubber or non-toxic PVC (polyvinyl chloride). The thicker the liner the more it costs and the longer it lasts. A 20-mil PVC liner should last 7 to 10 years; a 32-mil liner, 15 to 20 years; an ultraviolet stabilized rubber liner, up to 30 years. A lifetime guarantee is provided with liners that have a bonded geotex backing, which eliminates the need for a protective layer between the rubber liner and the earth. If the liner you purchase doesn't have protective backing, you will need to purchase one.

RECIRCULATING/AERATING THE WATER

Filtration is not essential to maintain a properly stocked, well-balanced pond, but a filter and pump will help to keep the pond healthy and beautiful. The pump circulates the water through the filter, which cleanses it. Small, relatively inexpensive, combined filter-and-pump units are suited to tubs and water gardens holding up to 300 gallons. For larger water gardens the usual arrangement is a submersible pump that delivers to a filter placed outside the pond. The size of the filter and the power of the pump are dictated by the pond's volume, which is determined by its size. Firms that

OVERLEAF:
The lake and the elegant bridge dominate the park at Stourhead in Wiltshire, England, where time seems to have stopped once the temples, grotto, and cascades were built. Designed in the mid-1700s, Stourhead exemplifies the romantic English Landscape Style of William Kent, with whom "Capability" Brown was associated. Here lawns follow the land, trees frame antiquities, and water mirrors the sky, giving life to the pastoral scene. In spring magnificent banks of mature rhododendrons bloom in soft shades of pink and crimson. The gigantic leaves belong to *Gunnera*.

sell water garden equipment should be able to help you choose the pump and filter system most suited to your pond.

MECHANICAL FILTERS: If cost is a consideration and time for maintenance is plentiful, you may find that a mechanical filter meets all your needs. About 13 to 20 inches long and light in weight, it will need to be cleaned daily in summer, and as often as twice daily when you are dealing with temperatures soaring over 85 º F. If you fail to clean the filter, the pump may overheat and burn out. To keep your pond in good condition with a mechanical filter, the water must be recirculated once every two hours. A pond the size of a typical living room requires a filter and pump combination capable of handling up to 4,000 gallons of water an hour; it usually needs only weekly cleaning, but may need cleaning daily in hot weather.

BIOLOGICAL FILTERS: If you have a limited amount of time to devote to maintenance, you will be much happier with a biological filter. It will be larger and cost more, but the cost is mitigated because a biological filter works with a less-powerful, less-costly pump. With a well-designed biological filter the pump needs to recirculate the water only once every four to six hours. An even greater advantage is that maintenance consists mainly of draining it once or twice a month. A biological filter unit is always placed outside the pond, so you will need a waterfall installation, large shrubs, or decking to conceal it.

The equipment consists of a fiberglass tank 24 to 30 inches high filled with layers of coarse and fine gravel or other media. Bacteria in the filter transform toxic ammonia from fish waste into benign nitrates; submerged plants absorb the nitrates, which would otherwise promote algae growth. The most effective biological filters are those that include an aeration tower because the bacteria require oxygen. Biological filters come in sizes that can handle from 200 to 2,000 gallons of water; several units can be joined to filter larger ponds.

POWER SUPPLY AND WINTER MAINTENANCE: Any weatherproof, standard, three-prong electrical outlet with a ground fault circuit interrupter can supply power to your pump. You will need to have a licensed electrician install the power source for the pump at least 6 feet away from the edge of the pond. Pump manufacturers indicate the amps required to operate each pump. Starting a pump draws substantially more current than is used to operate the pump, so be sure to provide an electrical circuit that has sufficient reserve amp capacity. This is especially important with pumps using more than 8 amps. Otherwise overload will cause the circuit breaker to turn off the current.

Where the pond will freeze in winter, remove, drain, and clean the pump and filter when the weather cools and store them indoors. During the cold months the

ABOUT ICE IN WINTER

Water gardens in Zones 3 through 7 often freeze for more than three or four consecutive days, a critical interval for fish. A persistent ice sheet will cause the fish to die from lack of oxygen and accumulation of gas from decaying wastes. A simple, inexpensive deicer will prevent ice buildup. A deicer is a floating, 1,000- or 1500-watt heating element; it should include a thermostat so that it operates only when necessary. Use the deicer with a ground fault circuit interrupter.

warmest area is in the bottom of the pond and the fish linger there; a pump would circulate cold water to the bottom and the fish would suffer. Snails are not a concern since they are dormant in winter in cool regions.

DIGGING AND INSTALLING THE POND:

Before you install the pond, make a planting plan as you would for an in-ground garden, and order or buy the plants so that they will arrive when your pond is ready for them. You will place the plants in the pond when the water has reached air temperature. That can take a day or more after filling the pond, depending on the depth of the pond and the temperatures of the water and the air.

If possible, you should plan to dig and install the water garden in early spring or as the weather begins to cool in early fall. Heat stimulates the growth of undesirable algae during the start-up period. If a waterfall or stream bed is planned, prepare it when the pond is installed and complete it after the pump is installed and working.

INSTALLING A PREFORMED LINER: Outline the rim of the preformed liner on the site. Measure the depth of the liner, and follow the outline, but 2 to 3 inches outside of it (to allow space for backfill), excavate to the depth of the liner. Use sand to line and level the excavation. Place the liner in the excavation. Using a carpenter's level and a

A water feature can be as simple as this Zenlike composition featuring an antique pump, a seashell, and pristine snowdrops, or it can be as formal as the romantic pond garden on the overleaf.

111

The mirrorlike surface of this exquisite formal pond centers a small park surrounded by dogwoods and azaleas. Once established, flowering trees and shrubs need little attention, so the garden should require only an hour or two each month in maintenance, feeding the goldfish and removing yellowing foliage of the aquatic plants and their spent blossoms. In autumn the quiet waters will reflect the crimson-maroon foliage of the surrounding trees. To make the most of reflections, a third to half of the surface of a pond should be kept free of plants.

board, check the level at various positions around the liner rim, marking the high spots. Remove the liner and rake the sand in the bottom to level the high spots. Continue fitting and checking the liner until it is level and the rim is just above the grade. Remove the sod to make space for the coping stones, as described in the instructions below for installing a flexible liner. Recheck and adjust the level of the rim if necessary. You are now ready to fill the pond; as the water level rises, pack sand behind the sides to support them. Set the coping stones as described below.

INSTALLING A RUBBER LINER: Outline the form of the pond. On one side, the side opposite the position from which you will most often view the pond, leave a shelf 9 to 15 inches high and wide for marginal plants. If raccoons are common in your area, omit this step and raise the marginal plants on bricks or concrete blocks instead. Dig at a 75-degree angle.

Complete the excavation: For most ponds it will be 15 to 30 inches deep. Dig a depression in the center 18 inches wide and 2 inches deep. It will provide a refuge for the fish when the pond is drained, and you'll be able to scoop them up and transfer them to a bucket for the duration. Remove stones and roots sharp enough to damage the liner, and line and level the floor with an inch or two of damp sand. If you are using a protective pad, place it around the sides of the hole. Use a board and a carpenter's level to level the rims. Remove the sod a foot out from the edge of the rim for the coping stones. Then loosen, cut, and turn back another 3 to 5 inches of sod.

Open the liner out. Standing outside the pond area, spread the liner over the pond and the edges. (If the liner is too heavy, fold it up and start over, working from the floor of the excavation.) Position the edges of the liner over the rim and hold down the flap with stones 6 to 12 inches out from the rim to keep it in place while the pond is being filled. Recheck and relevel the rims. Smaller wrinkles in the bottom can be eliminated by creating a few larger folds on the walls of the excavation. It is impossible to eliminate all wrinkles, but they go unnoticed once the pond is filled and stocked.

Fill the pond to within an inch of the rim. Leaving a flap 6 to 12 inches wide all around, cut away the excess liner. To hold the flap in place while positioning the coping stones, hammer 4- to 6-inch spike nails into the liner 4 to 10 inches from the pond edge.

SETTING THE COPING STONES: To protect the liner sides from the sun's ultraviolet rays and to hide any minor flaws in leveling the pond edge, set the coping stones on the liner flap so they jut out over the pond an inch or so. You can set the stones loosely in the desired pattern, but it's probably a better idea to cement the stones so they won't fall into the pond and damage the liner. Snug the turned-back strips of sod in around the stones and clean the coping with a hose. Use the pump or siphon to empty the pond and clean it. If mortar was used for the coping, clean it with a stiff brush and a mixture of one part ordinary vinegar to five parts water, so that lime in the mortar won't kill the fish. Rinse thoroughly.

STOCKING THE POND: THE MAGIC FORMULA

A key ratio of plants to livestock to the *surface area* of the pond will maintain the balance of the pond and keep it beautiful. This "magic formula" is provided by Charles Thomas, this country's leading authority on water gardens and founder of the International Water Lily Society. You can use the formula to design your water garden and compile a shopping list.

MAGIC FORMULA FOR BALANCING POND WATER

For every 1 to 2 square feet of pond surface, assuming 18 inches or more in depth, provide:

one bunch (six stems each) of submerged plants
one black Japanese snail
2 inches of fish, for fish up to 6 inches long
$^1/_{10}$ of a small or medium-size water lily,
or one lily per 10 to 20 square feet
$^1/_3$ of a marginal or a small floating-leaved plant for every 3 to 6 square feet

These delightful little violet-blue flowers belong to the Brazilian pickerel rush (*Eichhornia paniculata*), one of the small-leaved floating plants whose frills add lace to the big round pads of the lilies and the lotus. Rooted in containers or growing free on the surface, the little floaters leaf out with the water lilies, sketching fanciful, rather busy horizontal patterns, each with its own distinct texture and form. They fill a place comparable to the niche occupied by pansies in the flower border. Brazilian pickerel rush is a relative of the beautiful, but too-prolific, water hyacinth and in some states is entirely restricted by law.

OVERLEAF:
The cupped aerial leaves, blossoms, and seed heads of lotus at Longwood Gardens in Pennsylvania. These exotically perfumed aquatic flowers bloom on stems 2 to 6 feet tall, and when fully opened are as large around as a person's head. Even where summer heat doesn't last long enough to bring a hybrid lotus into bloom, lotus is often planted just for its exotic leaves.

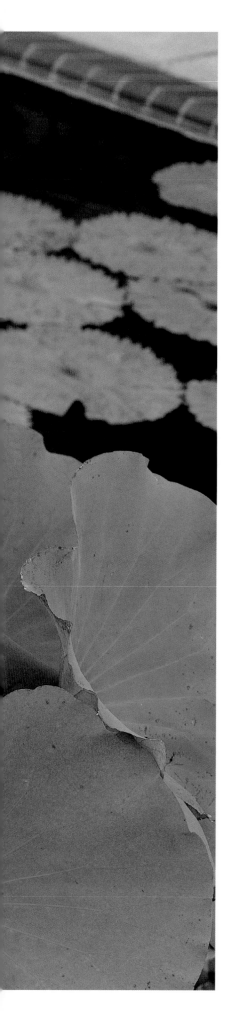

Following this formula, you would order only enough floating plants, both lilies and small-leaved floaters, to cover 30 to 50 percent of a water garden 20 by 50 feet or 60 to 70 percent of water gardens 10 by 10 square feet, but you can vary these amounts up to 50 percent depending how much foliage and open water you want to see. Catalog and nursery information about aquatics includes the area of pond surface they cover. Lilies restrict or expand their ultimate size according to the surface space available, container size, light, fertility, temperature, and movement of the water. Include containers for the aquatics in the order. Aquatics are set out in shallow pans, in pails, and in large tubs. These containers have no drainage holes. Since fish nibble submerged plants, order containers fitted with plastic mesh to protect them.

POTTING AND PLANTING THE AQUATICS

Pot the plants when you receive tham. Place no more than one to three plants of a single variety in a container: Most aquatics are aggressive and the stronger will overcome the weaker if they are grown together. You can make appealing combinations using plants of similar spreading characteristics in a single container, however. Use rinsed coarse sand to pot submerged plants. Use heavy garden soil with a pH range of 6.5 to 7.5 to pot other aquatics. Do not use commercial potting mixes, peat, vermiculite, or anything else that will float and soil the water. Push a fertilizer tablet (10-14-8) into the soil of each container, and cover the soil with an inch of *rinsed*, ½- to ¾-inch gravel. Using pond water, soak the containers thoroughly to eliminate any air pockets. Keep the plants moist and shaded, and set them in the pond as soon as possible after the pond has been filled.

Distribute the containers of the submerged plants over the floor of the pond where the sunlight will not be blocked by the wide-ranging floating foliage of the ornamentals. Most other aquatics need 4 inches of water overhead. You can raise the containers on platforms to the required depth as necessary using clean native stones, weathered bricks, weathered cement blocks, or upturned pots. Set the marginal plants on the shelf, if there is one: They grow upright, so space them a foot or two apart. Space the water lilies and other ornamental aquatics several feet apart on the shelf or on platforms on the floor of the pond. Use leftover liner scraps under the platforms to avoid damaging the pond liner.

The water may become murky about a week after the pond is filled. The hotter the season, the sooner new pond murk is likely to appear and the longer it may last due to algae growth. Turbidity occurs in spring, too, and may appear any time after a pond has been cleaned and refilled with fresh water. Unless extremely dense, the algal bloom doesn't harm anything, but many people find it unsightly. A pond stocked with submerged plants, snails, and other aquatics in the ratio given in the magic formula, together with a pump and filter, will clear up the water in six to eight weeks. A pump and a filter, while not absolutely necessary, are especially helpful if the pond is stocked with many fish. If clearing the water takes longer, resist the temptation to drain the pond and refill it with clean water. The pond (and you) will just have to go through the process again. Be patient.

Before you place snails or fish in the pond, wait a week or ten days for the chlorine in your water to dissipate, or use a dechlorinating agent suited to destroying the type of chlorine used in your public water supply. (The local public water authority can identify the type.) It's also a good idea to treat the pond this one time with a broad-spectrum fish disease remedy.

ADJUSTING THE WATER PH

The ideal pH for a water garden is about neutral, pH 7.0. Fluctuation between 6.5 and 7.5 is normal, but any reading beyond calls for observation and possible correction. Test the pH for 3 days running before putting fish or snails into a newly filled and dechlorinated pond; take the readings in the cool of the morning. After the fish have been in the pond 6 or 7 days, test the pH once more. Adding a lot of new plants or fish or liming the surrounding lawn can affect the pH. Check the pH after these changes and also if the fish become lethargic but show no signs of disease or if plants begin to yellow before normal dormancy. Products to adjust the pH of the pond water are available.

RELEASING LIVESTOCK: When the water is free of chlorine, your pond is ready for snails and fish. Pet shops and aquatic mail order houses pack fish in water or plastic bags. You should release the fish into the pond as soon as possible. Shade the bags with wet paper towels to keep them cool and float them in the water for fifteen minutes to acclimate them to the water temperature. For the first week or two after their release, feed the fish lightly with an antibiotic-medicated food. Never feed fish more than once or twice daily, and never feed them more than they can eat in ten minutes: Excess fish food stimulates the growth of algae.

Snails are shipped in water or in moist packing material. Rinse them off and slip them into the pond. If the snails are viable, they'll sink. Remove the ones that float to the surface; they're dead. After about three days the snails will become active and go to work.

Most aquatic plants are hardy or frost-tender perennials, and with care, they will return year after year. There are three main groups: the submerged, or oxygenating plants; the aquatics, or ornamentals, with large or small floating leaves; and the marginals, the narrow- or broad-leaved, upright plants that live at the edge of the pond.

SUBMERGED PLANTS: These small leafy plants are essential to the health of the pond. They grow below the surface of the water, oxygenating it by day and using up nutrients that otherwise would nourish unwanted algae. Fish like to spawn among them.

Five varieties are commonly used: wild celery (*Vallisneria americana*), anacharis (*Elodea canadensis* var. *gigantea*), various species of *Myriophyllum*, Washington grass (*Cabomba caroliniana*), and dwarf sagittaria (*Sagittaria subulata*). Wild celery and dwarf sagittaria arrive packaged as individual plants; the others are shipped in bundles of about six cuttings about 6 inches high. As they grow, take cuttings and root them in sand-filled containers in your pond to increase the supply.

FLOATING AQUATICS: Design the placement of the aquatics in the pond to feature the water lilies: They are the stars of the water garden. The floating foliage of the beautiful water lilies, the extraordinary leaves of the lotuses, and even the dainty leaves of the small floating-leaved plants provide privacy for the fish, and they also perform useful functions. By shading the water, they reduce the amount of sun reaching the algae, reducing their growth, and, by cooling the water, they increase its capacity to hold oxygen, which benefits the fish.

The exquisite flowers of the water lilies, open and close for 3 to 4 days, then their bloom is over. There are hardy water lilies and tropical water lilies and the variety

FISH AND SNAILS

Goldfish (*Carassius auratus*)

    Calico fantails
    Comets
    Japanese fantails
    Shubunkins

Golden orfe (*Leuciscus idus* f. *orfus*)

Koi
Cyprinus carpio

Black Japanese snail
Viviparus malleatus

OPPOSITE:
Surrounded by tulips and daffodils, golden koi weave enchanting serpentines in the clear water of a small, informal pond. Highly intelligent, colored carp, koi are the focus of books, societies, and competitions. On the far side of the pond *Magnolia stellata* is blooming. Weeping hemlock (*Tsuga canadensis* 'Pendula') softens the edges of the boardwalk. The grassy marginal in the pond is *Iris pseudacorus* 'Variegata'.

Creamy white calla lilies (*Zantedeschia aethiopica*) bloom among the reeds, water irises, and other narrow-leaved marginal plants growing at the edge of a pond. The most satisfying water garden designs include marginals of various heights, textures, and colors. Choose some for their blooms, others for their rich, contrasting foliage.

of sizes and colors is staggering. The smallest size of hardy lily is the charming little pygmy, a delightful water lily with flowers no more than 2½ inches across, that will cover less than 3 square feet of your pond. The next size up is the small lily, which will float out over the pond and take up 3 to 6 square feet; my favorites are the exquisite white 'Hermine' and the fascinating 'Paul Hariot', whose flowers change from canary yellow to dark red as they mature. The medium and medium-large size lilies cover 6 to 12 square feet. They float their lovely blossoms on the water, or hold them slightly above the water, and open them in the morning. In midafternoon, the water lilies slowly close. There are beautiful shades of yellow, warm apricot, pretty pinks, salmon, and even some firecracker reds. You might try at least one of the fascinating changeables, which transform their color from yellow to red over the 3-day blooming period; 'Comanche' is one of the best. The young leaves of some lilies start out beautifully mottled or flecked, turning green as they mature. Plant hardy water lilies as the weather warms in spring; they are likely to flower as pond temperatures move up into the sixties. In Zone 8 the hardy lilies flower earlier and usually bloom from April until early November, although some red varieties do not tolerate extended periods above 90° F.

Tropical water lilies lift their huge exotic flowers 5 to 10 inches above the water. Some species are day-bloomers; others bloom only as dusk arrives. The day-bloomers close in mid- to late afternoon, and the lilies that open as night falls close the following noon. The tropical lily pads typically move out over the surface of the water, covering twice as much water surface as the pads of the hardy lily. The fragrance of many of the tropical lilies is extraordinary, heavy and compelling. You can spend a whole hour watching a night-blooming tropical open. You can actually see the flower bud unfold—first one sepal pops loose, then a second slips open, then another, until the perfect flower is there before you. On a night when there is moonlight, seeing a white lily floating on the water is a magical experience. The foliage of many tropical varieties is quite exotic: sometimes mottled, often spotted on the underside, and attractively toothed and crimped.

Tropical water lilies should be set out when the pond temperature stays above 69°F. They will begin to bloom after about a month of air temperatures above 80°F. In the north, as winter approaches, they should be lifted and wintered in a greenhouse pool or their tubers should be harvested after frost and stored at 55°F. in distilled water.

The small-leaved floating plants are charming tucked in among the big round

A lovely beardless waterside iris, *Iris laevigata*, naturalized in the still waters of the pond at Brook Cottage, Oxfordshire, England. With the other narrow-leaved marginals, irises bring to the pond vertical motion and the sound of wind in tall grasses. Behind the irises, red *Euphorbia griffithii* 'Fireglow' spreads a warm glow.

121

floating pads of lilies and the lotus. They also shade and cool the water, and many have lovely, dainty flowers. The pretty little water poppies (*Hydrocleys nymphoides*), floating heart (*Nymphoides peltata*), and the white and yellow snowflakes, (*N. cristata* and *N. geminata*) are small-leaved floaters that will spread like weeds. One will probably be enough to start.

LOTUSES: I find lotuses fascinating. A lotus can take as much space as a large water lily, and for the average pond just one 'Tulip', a miniature, will be enough; it will be glorious and slightly fragrant. Lotus blossoms are immense, and they open on stems 2 to 6 feet tall. The seed pod looks to me like Spielberg's extraterrestrial ET; it is sought after for use in dried arrangements. The lotus produces two sets of leaves: The beautiful floating pads appear first, then the lovely cupped leaves rise on tall, round stems. When the aerials are established, the floating leaves come together and create a large shaded area for the fish. The cupped aerial leaves give the pond a wonderfully exotic look, and they hold raindrops for hours after a shower.

Two or three weeks after being planted in mid spring, a lotus tuber sends up a first set of floating leaves. After three or four weeks of temperatures above 80°F., the lotus will bloom. In regions warmer than Zone 7, it will bloom in June, pause as heat bears down, and resume briefly in September. Farther north, lotuses flower later, or may not bloom at all. Even where it doesn't bloom, I urge you to include a lotus in your water garden just for the beauty of its magnificent aerial leaves.

MARGINAL PLANTS: The upright marginal plants mark the boundaries of the water garden and contrast with the horizontal foliage of the floating plants. A tub or a kettle garden has space for a small, narrow-leaved marginal, such as the graceful cattail (*Typha laxmannii*), or the bamboolike horsetail (*Equisetum hyemale*). A slightly larger pond can also accommodate the beautiful variegated sweet flag (*Acorus calamus* 'Variegatus'). Next size up will also have space for the three-way sedge (*Dulichium arundinaceum*) and red-stemmed sagittaria (*Sagittaria lancifolia* f. *ruminoides*), which bears pretty little white flowers. Bright-hued Louisiana irises and majestic yellow flag (*Iris pseudacorus*) will provide the pond with spring's first color.

Some of the broad-leaved marginals are magnificent in their sculptural qualities. Black princess taro (*Colocasia affinis* var. *Jenningsii*) has immense leaves like elephant's ear. The graceful umbrella plant (*Cyperus alternifolius*) dances in a breeze. Water arum (*Peltandra virginica*), high-rising *Thalia dealbata*, and other broad-leaved marginals add form and texture to your water garden.

LIVESTOCK: Place in the pond only the number of fish "inches" recommended in the magic formula (page 115). You can feed them, or you can leave them to forage. Fed at a regular hour, they will come to expect your visit, and you will make friends. I have heard of, though I have never met, a pond owner who grew so fond of her fish that she trained them to accept kisses. You will enjoy watching the fish grow and multiply. But—excess feeding encourages ever more spawning, and that will result in overpopulation and pond pollution.

I can't recommend any particular type of fish: I love them all. Any combination of the four goldfish varieties sold for the home pond is suitable: comets, Japanese fantails, shubunkins, and calico fantails. The comet is a sturdy, streamlined little fish that barrels through the water. The double-tailed Japanese fantail is a languid beauty that turns to gold in time and may become white and opalescent. The shubunkins are silver with splashes of red, yellow, purple, black and blue, and gold. They and the calico fantails have transparent scales and seem to glisten as they weave in and out among the submerged grasses and lily stems.

These little creatures are not only charming and decorative; they also have important roles to play in the health of the water garden. They help to control mosquito larvae and other insects that abound in and on water, and their waste provides nutrients used by the aquatic plants. The activity of the goldfish indicates the health of their environment. If the fish become unaccountably languid, check the water quality, especially the pH, and the levels of nitrates and ammonia. If they come repeatedly to the surface to gulp air, the oxygen in the pond may be depleted. Turn up your pump or bubbler to circulate more oxygen-rich air through the water.

Koi (*Cyprinus carpio*) are breathtakingly beautiful fish that develop extraordinary markings. These intelligent fish readily become pets. A special breed of Japanese carp, koi's remarkable qualities and appearance have made it the focus of books, societies, and competitions. A young koi resembles a young comet, but it has little whiskers on both sides of the mouth. Koi sometimes learn to eat new leaves, which can be a problem, but they are a fascinating addition to the water garden. Submerged plants in a koi pond must be protected with plastic mesh.

The snails are the housekeepers of your water garden. They are fascinating to watch as they creep up the sides of the pond over the submerged pots, eating algae and keeping the pond clean. Be sure to stock your pond with the full number of snails indicated by the magic formula given above. The only recommended variety of snail is the black Japanese snail, *Viviparis malleatus*. Snails also work to keep the pond healthy by consuming excess fish food, fish waste, and dead leaves. They multiply once a year and do not overpopulate the pond, nor do they eat aquatics. They live for many years.

Other animals will arrive on their own. Birds will visit the pond; provide a shallow spot for them to bathe in and plant shrubs nearby for cover. Frogs and toads will come to lay their eggs. I love to watch tadpoles weaving in and out among the stems of the lily pads. They are frogs-in-waiting, of course, and, as the season advances, the tiny legs begin to emerge before the tail is quite gone. As adults they will join the mosquito patrol. They clean up excess fish food, and their chorus announces the arrival of spring. When a tadpole becomes a bullfrog, don't fret it if wanders off in rainy weather—it may come back, but more likely, a neighboring troubadour will come to take its place. You needn't worry about your frogs in winter either: They tuck up in a bed in the mud and sleep it away.

BROAD-LEAVED VERTICAL AQUATICS

Arrowhead
Sagittaria latifolia Z5-10

Arrowhead, double Old World
S. sagittifolia 'Flore Pleno' Z5-10

Bog lily
Crinum americanum Z8-10

Buckbean
Menyanthes trifoliata Z3-9

Calla lily hybrids
Zantedeschia aethiopica Z9-10

Canna lily hybrids
Canna 'Nirvana', Erebus', 'Ra' Z7-10

Chameleon plant
Houttuynia cordata 'Chameleon'

Dwarf papyrus
Cyperus haspan Z9-10

Elephant's-ear plant
Alocasia amazonica Z9-10

Giant arrowhead
Sagittaria montevidensis Z4-10

Golden club
Orontium aquaticum Z6-10

Hottuynia cultivars
H. Chameleon', *H.* 'Pleno' Z6-10

Lizard's tail
Saururus cernuus Z4-9

Marsh marigold
Caltha palustris Z4-9

Papyrus, Egyptian paper reed
Cyperus papyrus Z9-10

Pickerel weed
Pontederia cordata Z3-10

Taro hybrids
Colocasia esculenta 'Fontanesii', *C.* 'Illustris' Z9-10

Thalia
Thalia dealbata Z6-10
T. geniculata var. *ruminoides* Z9

Umbrella plant
Cyperus alternifolius Z9-10

Water arum
Peltandra virginica Z5-9

Water plantain
Alisma plantago-aquatica Z3-8

Wild calla, water dragon
Calla palustris Z3-8

SHADE
GARDENS

Oh for a lodge in some vast wilderness,
Some boundless contiguity of shade,
Where rumor of oppression and deceit,
Of unsuccessful or successful war,
Might never reach me more.

WILLIAM COWPER

In shade, the greens are deeper, cooler. An emerald lawn under tall trees appears to darken and at the far end seems to melt into the shadows, even in a quite small garden shaded by just one or two trees. Overarching branches and shadow-casting hedges and vines impart a sense of privacy and protection, as though the garden were a secret room, a special place in nature beyond the open sunniness of a flowery landscape. A shade garden invites intimacy. It seems to say, I will keep your secrets.

A wealth of beautiful plants will flourish in various degrees of shade. Some of our most cherished spring-flowering trees and shrubs originated in shaded situations. Where the high-branching deciduous trees thin out at the edge of the forest, dogwood, redbud, shadblow, and other lovely understory trees bloom from April to June. Azaleas and rhododendrons evolved in woodlands, their roots cooled by ferns and mosses and nourished by the transformation of fallen leaves into rich humus. Early spring bulbs succeed in light shade, as do primroses and violets, just two of the many flowers that need protection from direct sun. Every form of garden ornamental that makes the garden beautiful and gives a landscape "good bones" is available in species that prefer shade—shrubs, trees, and lovely flowers, as well as vines and ground covers, and grasses that dance and whisper in the wind. Combined in groups chosen for variety in height and structure, in leaf size, texture, and color, the shade-lovers create restful, livable spaces, elegant landscapes that have quiet charm.

Before you can choose plants for your shade garden, you must decide whether the overall size of the garden is to be somewhat formal or rather casual. When I am trying to make up my mind about a landscape, I try to visualize myself moving about in it. Do you picture yourself in the shade of tall trees, strolling across the lawn past the fountain and the formal border of white impatiens, caladiums, and rhododendrons to savor the enchanting perfume of the daphnes? Or is the vision that attracts you one of a woodland path bordered with mountain laurels, violets, and ferns? The light requirements of the plantings are similar, but the styles of the two gardens are quite different. After you've chosen the style, you can begin to match plants to the light your site provides, and the garden will begin to design itself in your mind.

PLANTING YOUR SHADE GARDEN

I think of a formal shade garden as a composition in green and darker greens, lightened by luminous white and pastel flowers and by the light bouncing from shiny and/or colorful foliage. If you are fortunate, your property has tall, shade-giving trees that you can embellish by planting flowering shrubs and flowers where the light permits, to create a landscape design that pleases you. The source of the shade may be just a high wall; its appearance can be softened and changed if you plant in front of it evergreens of various heights, to imitate the layered effect of a tree's branching. In a formal garden, the design of the shrubbery groups will tend to be symmetrical, with tall plants towards the center and shorter shrubs descending in an orderly scale on either side. The middle ground of the flowering borders will typically have as a backdrop clumps of tall, pastel-flowered perennials and, in front, variegated hostas and other low-growing plants with contrasting foliage, such as the maroon red *Heuchera* 'Palace Purple', accompanied by some of the pastel flowers described below.

PREVIOUS SPREAD:
Left: Golden chain trees trained on metal supports to meet overhead are caught with stately purple alliums (*Allium aflatunense*) and sunny Welsh poppies (*Meconopsis cambrica*) in an extraordinary play of light and shadow. This is the fabled laburnum walk created by Rosemary Verey, British writer and gardener, whose garden combines many classical elements and an abundance of plants in designs that are structured but not restrained.

Right: Lenten roses (*Helleborus orientalis*) growing in the dappled shade of tall *Rhododendron barbatum,* whose scarlet petals carpet the ground at their feet.

OPPOSITE:
Many beautiful cultivated flowers originated, and now thrive, in the tall shade of woodlands like this, where in spring blue forget-me-nots (*Myosotis*) bloom with *Geranium macrorrhizum* and carpets of ajuga.

OPPOSITE:
A seemingly wild border of silvery lamb's ears, ferns, and late azaleas and rhododendrons thrives in the light shade of tall trees opposite a bank of ferns and roses. This is Anne Waring's lovely woodland garden in Sussex, England.

The more casual shade landscape will have something of the look of a woodland garden. A woodland-style garden needn't be planted only with authentic woodland wildings. I love woodlands, and paths, and I also love the beautiful flowers that grow in our cultivated gardens, so I have put these elements together in my Washington, D.C., garden, which grows in shade. The ideas can be adapted to any shady yard. The garden is L-shaped; it wraps two sides of our rather long, narrow house, which occupies a corner. Though it is only five blocks from the nation's Capitol, I have landscaped this little garden as a woodland path. Our "woods" are three flowering cherry trees, two upright and one weeping, as well as several varieties of hollies planted for their pretty evergreen foliage and red berries in winter, a Chinese dogwood, a fringe tree, and a big, old, shaggy Leyland cypress. All but the Leyland cypress are understory trees, so they thrive in the dappled light of the five old maple trees that shade the sidewalk. A path winds through the pachysandra carpet, past the flowering trees and groups of evergreen shrubs and azaleas that backdrop borders of shade-loving flowers. There's a somewhat sunny spot, and it is our woodland glade (the size of a parlor rug), planted with bulbs. They bloom before the trees leaf out in spring, coming up through a mix of ground covers and low-growing herbs, such as Greek oregano, that struggle with each other for supremacy. The small-leaved ivy wins every year, and gets cut back for its pains.

UNDERSTORY TREES: Flowering understory trees and tall, flowering, broadleaf evergreen shrubs are natural focal points for both formal and informal shade gardens. Among the first to bloom are the witch hazels, followed by the little pink flowers of the plum trees and the cherries, with the beautiful white or pink star magnolias not far behind. The Florida dogwoods and the redbuds come along at about the same time as the serviceberries, or shadblows, and then the apples and the crab apples bloom. These trees will all thrive in the dappled shade of tall trees or the light shade of a building. The big, white-flowering Chinese dogwoods (*Cornus kousa*) are beautiful planted at the entrance to and marking the boundaries of a property, and I love also to see them blooming somewhere near a pair of silver birches set in a lovely lawn.

If you have a wooded area, flowering trees like the delicate little redbud, which blooms at the margins of open woodlands, will look lovely planted along the edge. Then you could plant shadblows and dogwoods, which are larger, in among the trees to lead the eye into the woodland. The small, wide-spreading crab apples are beautiful growing out in the open, almost anywhere. They need more sun. They are delightful at the ends of a long, lightly shaded flowering border fronting a wall, and I love the way they look in either big rustic tubs or formal cement urns on a shaded patio, with variegated vinca spilling over the sides of their containers.

While these trees are all showy, even spectacular, in bloom, to look good the rest of the summer the garden will need a supporting cast of evergreen shrubs. If the tree is used as a lawn specimen, you can join it visually to the shrubs by planting a flowering or evergreen ground cover, or a mix of ground covers, between them. *Vinca minor* and plumbago do well in part shade, and ajuga does well in diffuse light. The ajuga I think looks best in a shade garden is the green-leaved variety. If possible, plant the ground cover when you plant the tree, and scatter through it clumps of flowering bulbs, like little 'Hawera' daffodils and the lovely wood hyacinth, *Hyacinthoides hispanicus* (synonyms *Scilla campanulata* and *Endymion hispanicus*).

SPRING-FLOWERING PERENNIALS FOR SHADE

Bethlehem sage
Pulmonaria saccharata cvs. Z4-8

Bleeding heart
Dicentra spectabilis Z3-9

Columbines
Aquilegia canadensis, A. caerulea
cvs. Z3/4-9

Cowslip
Primula veris Z3-8

Creeping phlox
Phlox stolonifera Z4-8

Crested iris
Iris cristata Z4-9

False Solomon's seal
Smilacina racemosa Z4-9

Foamflower
Tiarella cordifolia cvs. Z3-9

Jacob's ladder
Polemonium caeruleum Z2-8

Lenten rose and Christmas rose
Helleborus orientalis Z3-9
H. niger var. *macranthus* Z3-8

Siberian bugloss
Brunnera macrophylla Z4-8

Solomon's seal
Polygonatum hybridum Z5-9
P. multiflorum cvs. Z3-9

Spotted cranesbill, wild geranium
Geranium maculatum Z4-9

Virginia bluebell
Mertensia virginica Z3-9

Wood anemone
Anemone sylvestris cvs. Z4-9

OVERLEAF:
Under a venerable apple tree, a
shade garden unfolds the seasons.
Reading clockwise from top left:
Early spring finds crocus and
snow drops (*Galanthus*); in mid-
spring come sweet woodruff
(*Galium odoratum*), white bleeding heart (*Dicentra*), and Solomon's seal (*Polygonatum*); in summer white mallow blooms with
Japanese holly fern (*Cyrtomium*)
and polygonatum foliage as backdrop; in autumn the polygonatum turns to gold.

129

SHRUBS: Tall, flowering evergreen shrubs look wonderful as the central backdrop and focal point for a formal bed. Among the tallest are mountain laurels and rhododendrons, and the flowers they bear in spring are among the loveliest of all. The rhododendrons, commonly used in formal landscapes, always remind me of estate gardens, while the laurels recall the mountain woodlands of Connecticut where I first saw them blooming in the wild. I love to see them planted with deciduous shrubs, whose naked winter structure creates off-season drama, especially in snow country. Of the deciduous shrubs, I think the viburnums have the most to offer. The branching of many varieties is attractively layered, and the strong, sweet, spicy fragrance of species such as *Viburnum* × *burkwoodii* 'Mohawk' is the early garden's most intoxicating perfume. Our viburnum is planted by the porch where the sweet scent reaches us when we are having our first (cool and brief) *al fresco* meals of the year. Another magnificent deciduous shrub is the big, oak-leaved *Hydrangea quercifolia,* of value for its handsome foliage and fall color even in climates so cold that it dies to the ground during the onset of winter.

In front of the tall plants, set flowering shrubs with contrasting structure, such as the low, wide daphnes. The leaves of *Daphne odora* 'Aureomarginata' and *D.* × *burkwoodii* 'Variegata' are edged with gold or creamy white and appear gray-silver in shade, a delightful effect when set in front of dark evergreens. The azaleas can be placed where splashes of showy color in spring will enhance the garden. Their color range even outsizzles impatiens. I find some of the Kaempferi azaleas, among them 'Armstrong's Fall' and 'Indian Summer', especially desirable because they often rebloom in fall.

For fall color, be sure to tuck into highly visible places a few dwarf hollies and barberries. The bright red berries of the barberries feed the birds, and the autumn reds of their leaves are unbeatable. For contrast, plant one or two needle-leaved evergreen shrubs. One of the most beautiful is the slow-growing weeping Canadian hemlock, *Tsuga canadensis* 'Pendula', a beautiful plant with deep green needles.

Among exquisite color plants for shade are caladiums like 'Red Flash' and 'Candidum', both cultivars of *Caladium bicolor.*

PERENNIALS: Shade-loving perennials come in a variety of shapes and sizes, and I find many uses for them in the shade garden. Some develop large, thin leaves on long, flexible stems; they are excellent fillers for the middle of the border. Astilbe's airy, fernlike foliage stays after its flowers go by; the plumelike flower clusters themselves dry quite beautifully on the plant and often remain until fall. Low-growing plants with bold foliage should be set in front. The hostas are outstanding foliage plants for shade, and they come in so many colors, forms, and sizes that you never tire of them. The big green and blue-green hostas are superb as background for small variegated forms splashed or edged with cream. For a nice effect, plant hostas in contrasting pairs, for instance, big 'Blue Wedgewood' with lower-growing 'Gold Standard', whose heart-shaped leaves are edged yellow with green. The blue hostas also are superb with clumps of spiky bugbane (*Cimicifuga simplex*) and 'Palace Purple' heuchera.

To lighten the color of the border, interplant the greens with silvery leaves and variegated foliage plants. Gorgeous together are the silvery Japanese painted fern (*Athyrium nipponicum* 'Pictum') and *Pulmonaria saccharata* 'Mrs. Moon', which is blotched with platinum, with white-variegated *Euonymus fortunei* or English holly.

In woodlands, perennials are best planted in drifts and casual clumps. Big, bold hostas can be used with ferns and *Dicentra eximia*, the little fringed bleeding heart native to Eastern forests, and with *Geranium* cultivars and hybrids, such as 'Wargrave Pink' and 'Johnson's Blue', which flower in airy pastel mounds for weeks on end in mid spring and are quite lovely.

COLOR IN THE SHADE

Perennial flowers that bloom in the shade tend toward white, pale gold, and pastels. I find that I appreciate these shades most as summer deepens the greens. Keep in mind that stronger colors tend to be swallowed by the greens, as do blue flowers without pink or light mauve nearby.

After months of fall's buffs and maroons and winter's naked branches dark and wet with rain, spring's first burst of color, like the return of warmth to the sunlight, I always feel as a personal blessing. To make the most of it, I plant drifts of spring-flowering bulbs everywhere. With no leaves yet on the trees, even sun-loving bulbs will bloom, at least the first year after planting; growing under trees that don't leaf out until after the bulb foliage has ripened, they may well return the next year. Many spring bulbs thrive under these conditions. Plant the small bulbs close together and in groups of twenty, or better yet fifty, or a hundred. The first to bloom are always the most welcome: winter aconite (*Eranthis*), snowdrops (*Galanthus*), and crocus. I love to see these blooming with the lacy foliage of *Anemone blanda* in the background, which appears early and remains after its daisylike blooms go by. The brilliant colors of tall, willowy lily-flowered tulips and *Tulipa sprengeri* can be used as dramatic accents with broad-leaved perennials, such as bronzeleaf (*Rodgersia podophylla*) and hellebores.

After the little spring bulbs have gone by, you can fill the empty spaces with annuals or tender perennials, such as primroses and pansies. In shade, they'll last until the heat comes; then you can replace them with tall and dwarf impatiens. White impatiens look wonderfully cool and fresh shining out among variegated hostas, white-veined caladiums, and feathery ferns. Combinations of pink impatiens backed by pink-veined caladiums and red impatiens with red-variegated caladiums are also delightful.

To sharpen the colors in a shade garden, double them. Plant white impatiens next to white-variegated hollies. Use container plants to move color where it is needed. Plant movable pots in the colors you desire—say, orange calendula or white snapdragons—and bring them into full bloom in the sun. Then set the pots in the shaded border; when their blooms begin to slow, return them to recuperate in the sun. Set the orange calendula near gold-edged hostas and the white snapdragons beside white-edged euonymus. When the container plants stop blooming, replace them.

ORNAMENTAL GRASSES: Some graceful, wind-catching ornamental grasses flourish in semishade at the edge of woodlands and in the shade cast by buildings and tall plants. To soften a stark masonry wall, nothing is more effective than feathery fountain grass (*Pennisetum setaceum*) flanked by the grasslike snowy wood rush (*Luzula nivea*). To brighten a bare patch at the crest of a hill, plant low-growing Japanese blood grass (*Imperata cylindrica*); catching the sun, it flames a brilliant red.

LAWNS AND GROUND COVERS: Success with a lawn in shade can be tricky, especially under tall trees. As with any kind of lawn, you will need to prepare the ground thoroughly by rototilling, amending and fertilizing the soil. Plant a grass variety recommended for shade by a local nursery. To expose more leaf surface to light, mow the grass an inch higher than the variety's recommended height for sun and fertilize three times a year. In droughts, water well with a sprinkler once a week or as needed.

Where lawn grasses fail for lack of light, ivy makes a beautiful, deep green ground cover. It's a vine and in time grows woody; as a ground cover, it grows 1 to 2 feet high. Ivy can take three to four years to become established, so if you use it as a lawn alternative, plant it thickly, keep it well fertilized, and water it during droughts. It runs, or spreads, in the fall. Don't let it climb trees. It gets into fissures in the bark and is hard to get out; left to climb, it can damage the tree. Lilyturf (*Liriope spicata*) is another excellent evergreen lawn alternative. A graceful, tough, and resistant plant, it has narrow, grasslike foliage about a foot tall. In summer or early fall thin spikes covered with grainlike lavender, blue, or white flowers rise well above the grassy tufts; shiny black fruits develop in late fall and persist into winter. The variegated liriopes at a distance appear pale green and are quite lovely when in bloom. Lily-of-the-vallcy (*Convallaria majalis*), sweet violets (*Viola odorata*), and beautiful plumbago (*Ceratostigma plumbaginoides*) are also used as ground covers, but they require four to six hours of sun to bloom well, and they're deciduous. I love plumbago; in late summer and early fall it's covered with intensely blue flowers, and, if the weather is cool enough, the foliage turns bronze red. Its only drawback is that it is deciduous and looks unattractive in winter.

In the deep shade under a low-branching tree, either grow moss or spread an attractive gravel and use pots of white or multi-colored impatiens here and there to soften the starkness.

VINES: Vines soften the landscape, whether they are covering a stump or rambling along the top of a fence. But, given the rich soil and sustained moisture that I recommend for shade plants, many vines can become invasive and soon smother everything. Even a lovely species like the small-flowering, fragrant sweet autumn clematis can be overpowering. The safe vines are slow-growing species, such as the beautiful climbing hydrangea (*Hydrangea petiolaris*). American bittersweet (*Celastrus scandens*) isn't slow-growing, but its brilliant display of berries in fall is worth the pruning needed to keep it in shape. Vines of the big-flowered hybrid clematis grow at a moderate pace and are stunning with ferns and clumps of foamflower (*Tiarella cordifolia*). But these clematis, like most, flower well only in the sun—just the roots should be shaded.

LIGHT FOR SHADE PLANTS

Before choosing plants for your shady garden, you need to assess the shade climate of your site. Is your site shaded in the middle of the day but sunny in early morning or late afternoon? Does it receive dappled sunlight filtered through an open leaf canopy throughout the day? Or is it a dark place under low, dense broad-leaved or evergreen branches or in the dark shadow of a tall fence or building? Shaded areas in a home garden typically fall into one of the following categories: Part, light, full, and dense shade. Your garden may have several of these types of shade, each one offering different opportunities. Keep in mind that these are broad terms; boundaries are often gradual, and shade conditions will vary during the season as the angle of the sun changes and the leaves expand overhead.

Part shade, or semi-shade, describes a site that alternates between direct sun and full shade, for example, the east side of a building or fence or at the edge of a tree canopy. Morning sun followed by shade in the afternoon is most desirable, especially in the South, where cool, shady mornings followed by a blast of heat at noon and a long afternoon in the summer sun can be devastating.

A plant marked "full sun" will do best if it receives at least six to eight hours of direct sun daily. But all sun-loving plants are not excluded from shady gardens. In fact, many do well in partially shaded sites, especially where summers are very hot. Herbs are surprisingly versatile: Basil and mint, for example, thrive both in direct sun and in part shade, and oregano competes with the ivy in my little woodland.

ORNAMENTAL GRASSES FOR SHADE

Autumn moor grass
Sesleria autumnalis Z5-9

Drooping sedge
Carex pendula Z5-9

Golden grass
Milium effusum 'Aureum' Z5-8

Golden variegated hakonechloa
Hakonechloa macra 'Aureola'
Z5-9

Gray's sedge
Carex grayi Z3-8

Japanese blood grass
Imperata 'Red Baron' Z6-9

Japanese silver grass
Miscanthus sinensis cvs. Z4-9

Japanese sweet flag
Acorus gramineus 'Variegatus' Z5

Miniature sedge
Carex conica 'Variegata' Z5-8

Northern sea oats
Chasmanthium latifolium Z5-8

Ribbon grass
Phalaris arundinacea 'Picta' Z4-9

Silver spike grass
Spodiopogon sibericus Z5

Snowy wood rush
Luzula nivea Z4-9

Tufted hair grass
Deschampsia caespitosa Z5-9

LEFT:
Hosta sieboldiana, a magnificent bluish gray hosta with puckered leaves, grows to 3 feet or more and is a superb ground cover for even deep shade.

OVERLEAF:
Scilla and chionodoxa carpet the woodland at Great Thurlow Hall, Suffolk, England. Small flowering bulbs thrive in the soft early-spring sunlight, before the trees begin to leaf out.

135

Lilies thrive in full sun where temperatures remain below 90°F., but they need protection from the noonday sun in hot climates. In the South, the rule of thumb for lilies is four to six hours of full sun, with shade during the hottest part of the day. Pastel lilies can handle more shade than the brighter-hued lilies can, even in the far North.

Many usually sun-loving species, even roses, have shade-tolerant varieties. The rose show will be modest in summer shade, but, before the trees leaf out and again after the leaves fall, the flowers leave nothing to be desired. 'Grüss an Aachen', a compact, sweetly fragrant, pale pink rose, is one that will bloom in light shade. I've had some luck with one gorgeous 'David Austin' rose, deep pink 'Bow Bells', which blooms in the tall shade near our porch just as though it had a full day of sunlight.

In light, or dappled, shade, sunlight is available all day filtered through small or finely divided leaves, such as those of birch or mountain ash. Little flecks of sun dance across the ground, and no single spot is exposed to direct sun for long; many shade-tolerant trees, shrubs, perennials and annuals thrive here, as well as in the high shade of deciduous trees whose canopies begin well above the ground; to mention just a few, dogwoods, viburnums, azaleas, camellias, hollies, spring-flowering bulbs, and many of the species that grow in part shade, such as foxglove and astilbe, will grow well in dappled or indirect light. Study your site carefully to see where direct hot summer sun shines through a large gap in the canopy or even from low angle near the horizon late in the afternoon. It can be enough to sizzle particularly delicate shade plants.

In full shade, north of structures and beneath the unbroken canopies of old mature trees, a garden is almost always substantially shaded during the growing season. In an open area, north of a building or tall fence, try tall plants, such as rhododendrons, azaleas, sweet pepper bush (*Clethra alnifolia*), and the lovely mountain laurel (*Kalmia latifolia*). There's usually more light than is evident, from open sky and reflected from buildings, expanses of glass, and water—even a small reflecting pool can bounce enough light to make a difference.

Plants close to the soil will receive less light in full shade, but you still have many to choose from. Under shade trees, try English ivy, epimediums, and bergenias, as well as woodland flowers, such as hauntingly fragrant mayflower (*Epigaea repens*) and graceful Solomon's seal; *Polygonatum odoratum* var. *thunbergii* 'Variegatum' is particularly lovely. Hostas and many species of ferns thrive here, and the bright foliage of both coleus and caladiums maintains its color. And faithful impatiens blooms, though not lavishly, in full shade.

In dense shade conditions can be harsh. The ground under low-branched evergreen and deciduous trees and shrubs and between tall, closely spaced buildings is often short on water, as well as light. But don't give up—if you improve the soil and provide moisture, many of the plants that grow in full shade will grow here as well. Some mosses thrive in moist soil in dense shade, and they are marvelous with ferns (see page 30).

TAKE A CHANCE: BE PATIENT

I always try to remember that, whatever I am doing in the garden, failure is information, not disaster. Plants are living organisms that have individual responses to light, heat, moisture, and soil. Many shade-loving plants succeed in a wide range of light conditions; they are surprisingly adaptable when they are growing in suitable soil and

In late winter frost-hardy snow drops, golden *Eranthis,* and rosy *Cyclamen coum* spread a fresh, bright carpet in the light shade of a wonderful old tree.

have plenty of moisture. In a site whose light may be borderline, try young plants: A seedling or a sapling may adapt to levels of shade or sun that would harm a plant that had matured in a different light environment. Often the site can be improved. Plants don't make a secret of their problems—lacking light, they stretch out and flop over. Before removing them, consider whether pruning or moving a tall shrub or a small tree will provide the needed increase in light. Just painting a fence or a wall white can help, because white reflects light onto nearby plants, adding to their store of energy and so keeping them in good condition. Shade plants exposed to light that is too intense will bleach and curl up. You can improve their situation by shading them with taller plants or a vine-covered arbor, or by installing an awning that will provide them with some shade during the hottest part of the day. Plants that stay green but wilt regularly in the heat of the day may adapt to direct sunlight if they have more moisture. Dig more humus into the soil, increase the depth of the mulch, and water well early in the morning.

Don't give up too quickly on a plant that is performing poorly. Shade plants often need two or three years to become established. Your best bet is to provide each one with optimum growing conditions tailored to its particular light, soil, and moisture requirements. Give them extra attention during the first season. And be patient. Adapting can be a slow process. Even a hosta, the foliage plant most often recommended for shade, can fuss along not doing much for a couple of seasons, then suddenly perk up, grow up, bloom, and multiply.

PREPARING YOUR SHADE GARDEN

An excellent start for a shade garden is a raised bed. In such an environment, the soil will warm earlier in the spring, giving the plants a head start so they can take better advantage of the full sunlight before the canopy leafs out. The acidic soil in many shaded wooded sites is well suited to many shade plants, but digging beyond the top inch or two of soil in the woods can be like digging into a hair mattress; digging beside a hedge is worse. Only a pickax can make a meaningful dent, and the soil next to the trunk of a well-established tree is a cross between concrete and coconut hulls. Farther out from the trunk the soil is looser, but it is filled with roots, both large and small. Often the soil is dry and impoverished; the surface roots of many species of trees are located just 6 to 8 inches below the surface, and they have voracious appetites for water and nutrients.

Rototilling can be used to initiate a raised bed, but it will damage roots and weaken the existing trees. Instead of rototilling, I recommend using earthworms to work mulch into the soil. In fall, cover the planned site with 6 to 8 inches of chopped or ground leaves. To speed decomposition of the leaves, dust the top of the mulch with compost activator or all-purpose fertilizer, and water it in. The earthworms present in the soil will begin to work the pile of organic matter and the soil below, and their castings will enrich it. The following season the site, now a mixture of several inches of compost and soil, will be ready for a raised bed (see page 235).

MAINTAINING THE SHADE GARDEN

LATE WINTER/EARLY SPRING
Fertilize with an acidic fertilizer at half the strength recommended. Clear away leaves and fallen branches.

LATE SPRING: Mulch 3 inches deep to protect the roots from summer heat and to retain moisture.

SUMMER:
Water deeply in periods of prolonged drought, as necessary.

FALL:
Maintain the mulch cover to help retain soil warmth and moisture throughout the winter.

LATE FALL:
Fertilize at half strength. Cover tender perennials with evergreen branches or other light, airy materials.

SUMMER-FLOWERING PERENNIALS FOR SHADE

Astilbe
Astilbe arendsii cvs. Z5-8

Azure monkshood
Aconitum carmichaelii Z3/4-8

Bee balm
Monarda didyma Z4-9

Black snakeroot, black cohosh
Cimicifuga racemosa Z4-7

Blue cranesbill
Geranium 'Johnson's Blue' Z4-8

Blue lobelia
Lobelia siphilitica Z5-9

Common monkshood
Aconitum napellus Z5-8

Coralbells
Heuchera sanguinea Z3-8

Daylily species and cultivars
Hemerocallis Z3/4-9

Hollyhock mallow
Malva alcea Z4-8

Heuchera 'Palace Purple'
Heuchera 'Palace Purple' Z4-8

Japanese anemone
Anemone hybrida Z6-8

Lady's mantle
Alchemilla mollis Z4-8

Ladybells
Adenophora confusa Z3-8

Queen-of-the-prairie
Filipendula rubra Z3-9

Turtlehead
Chelone lyonii Z4-9

Woodland lilies
Lilium martagon, L. spp. Z4-10

Yellow foxglove
Digitalis grandiflora Z4-9

139

Annual foxglove
Digitalis purpurea

Browallia
Browallia speciosa 'Blue Bells'

Canterbury bells
Campanula medium

Evening stock
Matthiola longipetala

Flowering tobacco
Nicotiana alata

Impatiens, busy Lizzy
Impatiens walleriana

Lobelia, edging lobelia
Lobelia erinus

Pansy
Viola × *wittrockiana*

Sweet William
Dianthus barbatus

Tuberous begonias
Begonia Tuberhybrida Hybrids

Wax begonia
B. Semperflorens-Cultorum
Hybrids

Wishbone flower
Torenia fournieri 'Clown Mix'

OPPOSITE:
The luminous blossoms of a flowering cherry frame a grassy path that winds past pink and white heathers, conical white spruce (*Picea glauca* 'Conica'), bright yellow hinoki cypress (*Chamaecyparis obtusa* 'Tetragona Aurea'), and arborvitae (*Thuja plicata*).

PLANTING SHRUBS UNDER TREES: Provide a generous hole for the small trees and the shrubs you plant under trees, but take care not to damage too many of the important tree roots. A large planting hole gives the roots of the new plants extra space to become established before the roots of the overhead trees can reclaim the entire territory. For each plant dig a hole the size of a card table and loosen the soil in the bottom with a spading fork. Use pruning shears to sever all the tree roots less than an inch in diameter, and try not to cut into larger roots. If you must get through a larger root, however, use a saw or a hatchet. Set the root ball a little high: As the soil settles the plant will sink and the crown will be at ground level.

IMPROVING THE SOIL: More shade plants fail because of lack of water and nutrients than because of too little or too much light. Their hairlike rootlets take up the nutrients that are dissolved in the moisture present in the soil: when the soil dries out the plant not only suffers from lack of water, it also starves. Competition among shade-loving plants for water and nutrients can be fierce, so for a successful shade garden the fertility of the soil and its moisture content are all important.

The ideal soil for most shade plants is rich in moisture-holding humus and is light enough to drain well. Two parts humus, one part garden soil, and one part sand create a mix that holds moisture, allows air to circulate, and drains quickly. Tender young roots grow through it easily, and plants quickly become established. If the humus is leaf mold (partially composted chopped leaves or evergreen needles) or peat moss, the soil will be on the acid side. That's all to the good because most shade plants thrive in acidic soil.

Test soil pH and adjust it if necessary, as explained on page 234. Most shade plants grow well in slightly acid soils (pH 5.5 and 6.5). Rhododendrons and azaleas prefer acid conditions (pH 4.5 to 6.0). Many woodland species thrive in these soils as well, but some natives, such as bunchberry (*Cornus canadensis*), Jack-in-the-pulpit (*Arisaema triphyllum*), and mayflower (*Epigaea repens*), do better in soils even more acidic (pH 4.0-5.0). Soil amenders and mulches of peat moss, leaf mold and lime-free compost help to lower soil pH. Some shade plants, especially those native to lime-rich soil, require alkaline soil, for example the shade-loving shield fern (*Polystichum braunii*).

Ideally, to sustain unchecked growth in the new plantings, you should install a drip irrigation system or a set of leaky hoses. Soil supplied with sufficient humus shouldn't need watering except in times of drought, but, when plants are competing for water and nutrients with massive, well-established root systems, they often need help. Monitor soil moisture, especially in sites under or among trees, beside hedges, next to walls that retain heat, and in windy places. Whether or not you install an irrigation system, cover the bed with 2 to 3 inches of mulch: Chips of pine bark, hardwood bark, or West Coast fir, cedar or cypress bark, are all suitably acid and long lasting. Peat moss, leaf mold, and lime-free compost are excellent mulches but they decompose quickly and can grow a devastating crop of weeds if neglected. Do not apply mulch more than 3 inches deep, and remember to keep the mulch 2 to 3 inches from the stems and trunks of the plants. Mulch close to the stems of trees can cause rot and rodent problems.

Most shade-loving plants need an acidic fertilizer, one labeled as suitable for azaleas and evergreens. The instructions for preparing a raised bed (page 235) also include information about fertilizing so that your plants won't need more until they have been through a complete growth cycle. Each November and again in late winter before growth begins, apply a slow-release acid fertilizer at half strength.

XERISCAPE
GARDENS

The desert shall rejoice, and blossom as the rose.

ISAIAH 35:1

Desert gardens have an austere elegance satisfying to those who love the land's sun-baked vastness, its grand silences, the clear night sky carpeted with stars. In these natural xeriscapes, sand and rocks are the backdrop for groups of great sculptural cacti, spear-shaped yuccas, jade green agaves, and other desert natives that manage without water for months at a time. For color, a few pots of brilliant heat- and drought-tolerant ornamental plants are scattered around, sedums, geraniums, and bougainvillea vines dressed in hot pink, luminous melon, and incandescent purple.

A garden composed primarily of cacti is the xeriscape typical of desert country like southwestern Texas, where the rainfall is 7 to 8 inches a year. But xeriscaping, a landscaping approach based on water conservation through the use of tough, drought-resistant plants, can be practiced anywhere. The true, or "pure," xeriscape includes only drought-tolerant plants native to the garden's geographic region to minimize damage to the environment. A related type of xeriscape includes drought-tolerant natives from other parts of the world that have a similar climate. Whether it is located in Arizona or New York, it should never, or hardly ever, need more water than that provided by rainfall.

Not all xeriscapes are planted entirely with natives, however, even in desert climates. Most of the xeriscapes I have visited in semi-arid regions like south central Texas, for example, mingle varieties of drought-tolerant ornamentals with native plants. They also convert portions of the ground to outdoor living spaces, hardscapes that won't need watering. The annual rainfall in south central Texas is up to three times that of southwestern Texas. Gardeners there once lavished tap water on water-guzzling plants and large lawns. Now many of them believe that it is wiser to reduce big lawns to manicured islands planted in drought-tolerant grasses. Some of the space is given over to drought-tolerant evergreen ground covers like Bar Harbor juniper and *Vinca minor*. The reduced lawns are bounded by lovely groves of shade trees and shrubs, native plants usually, and linked by island beds bright with flowers and fragrant herbs. Splashes of color are provided by familiar cultivars that are naturally drought-adapted, like marigolds and sedums. Roses and other favorites grow in these gardens, too, but they are usually confined to containers or beds where their special watering needs can be met without soaking the whole garden.

Some supplemental watering for the garden is usually necessary even for well-planned xeriscapes, as the plants do require more than nature provides now and then, especially if they are to look their best. But water is distributed efficiently by drip emitters or by leaky hoses. A 3-inch mulch protects the soil surface from desiccating winds and the effects of searing heat.

DESIGNING A XERISCAPE

You can use the principles followed in designing xeriscapes in Texas to create a beautiful xeriscape anywhere. The challenge is to rethink your entire property in terms of water-conservation. I know that isn't easy, but there's pleasure in being able to plan both the additional outdoor living spaces that are typical of a xeriscape and the lush gardens that require few water maintenance chores. You can minimize the dark side of a makeover, the annoyance of a torn-up yard, by thoughtful timing.

PREVIOUS SPREAD:
The Austrian black pine (*Pinus nigra*), on the left-hand page, and the agaves and the aloes in the desert xeriscape on the right-hand page, thrive in regions whose rainfall resembles that of their native habitats.

OPPOSITE:
South American cacti in Huntington Botanical Garden, Los Angeles, California, include the 4-foot golden barrel cactus (*Echinocactus grusonii*) and *Echinopsis pasacana*, which grows to 35 feet. Whether in Arizona or New York, true xeriscapes include only natives adapted to the local climate and aliens from similar climates, and they rarely need extra watering.

ABOVE:
Woolly lamb's ears (*Stachys byzantina*) and *Veronica* 'True Blue' are among many beautiful drought-tolerant ornamentals used in xeriscapes.

It's a good idea to schedule major work for early spring or late fall when your activities are mainly indoors. The makeover can be planned in phases that span two or three years, or whatever is comfortable to your life and your body. A postponable dream will make it panic-free, and the extra time will encourage your creative imagination to soar. Limit the financial outlay and the hard-work projects planned for each year. Pine bark chips will do as temporary flooring for areas where decking or paved paths are planned, and annual vines can be trained to shade areas that later will be covered with awnings. Hedges of quick-growing annuals can be planted to mark the place planned for a wall or a fence—dwarf burning bush (*Bassia scoparia trichophylla*) is perfect for this purpose: In a single season it develops from seed into what appears to be a full-grown dwarf evergreen 24 to 36 inches high. With cold weather the 2-inch leaves turn purplish to bright red.

You can minimize costs by buying moderately priced plants in 1-gallon containers rather than expensive mature specimens. A miniature yaupon holly in a 10-inch pot costs much less than one in a 5-gallon container and is easier to establish. Two or three years after planting they will be about the same size. To establish the more mature plant would require more water, so starting out with younger material is just part of good xeriscaping practice.

There are other benefits to spacing out the remodeling timetable. A multi-year plan provides experience in moving large plants and allows for trial and error. Almost always in large-scale conversions some plants are moved more than once, particularly shrubs that transplant easily, like shallow-rooted azaleas and hemlocks.

DEVELOPING A PLAN

The first step in the transformation of your garden is to develop a comprehensive plan. Whether the goal is to redesign water-wasting features or a complete make-over, evaluate the whole yard in light of its water needs.

Prepare a sketch of the property to scale. Working either with a computer landscaping program or with ruled graph paper, draw in the immovable components: the house, the garage, rocky outcroppings, stone walls, big shade trees. Next, make and cut out scale drawings of the movable elements—existing walks, hedges, fences, driveways, parking spaces, lawns, flower borders, vegetable beds, shrubs, specimen trees, hedges, everything. Position the cutouts loosely on the graph in their present locations. Remove water-wasting features like beds of drought-sensitive annuals that often wilt at midday, and shrubs that are constantly drying out. Trim back and reposition a water-hungry lawn. Consider terracing or regrading slopes that spill precious rain water and soil down to the street or into your neighbor's yard.

Study the spaces newly available. Daydream. Design.

The most effective changes, though often the most costly, involve converting water-hungry garden spaces to agreeable outdoor features, or hardscapes, that need no watering at all. Adding new hardscapes or enlarging old ones, such as the driveway, paths, a patio, will be among your first major decisions. Then ask yourself what other replacements and changes will both reduce watering and enhance the family's pleasure in the garden.

Is there a view that could be better enjoyed from a wide flagstoned terrace furnished with deck chairs? How about an awninged, pebbled breakfast nook near the kitchen door? Would a greenhouse, a potting shed, or a compost bin make your life as a gardener more fulfilling? If you have young children, consider a generous sand

OPPOSITE:
Bright summer bedding plants growing in raised beds and containers provide a maximum of color with a minimum of watering. Petunias, geraniums, heliotrope, marigolds, and lilies are among many beautiful ornamentals that do as well in pots as in the ground.

ABOVE:
Rose campion, or mullein pink, (*Lychnis coronaria*), and its white cultivar (*L. c.* 'Alba'), with *Lavandula* 'Hidcote', thrive in full sun and can withstand drought.

OVERLEAF:
Ice plant (*Mesembryanthemum*) carpets a walled, stepped xeriscape planted in flowers and ornamental grasses. *Helictotrichon* occupies the foreground, with *Pennisetum* behind: Trumpet vine (*Campsis*) is blooming on the low wall.

box, as well as swings, a slide, and a jungle gym with a resilient floor or shredded pine bark or pine needles.

Don't feel constrained by limited space. A small urban yard becomes a great big playground if it is entirely given over to a swimming pool with wide coping, chairs and tables with gaily striped umbrellas, and raised beds all around. A minuscule town house garden outfitted with a musical fountain, comfortable patio furniture, and island beds invites moonlit reveries. Oddly enough, pools and water gardens require less water to maintain than do lawns and flower beds, so they definitely have a place in a xeriscape.

You should also try to free yourself from being hemmed in by what always has been. Consider changing your front yard by redesigning the entrance to accommodate a sheet of still, dark water reflecting the sky, or a waterfall splashing over rocks. A front yard can be given the privacy of a back yard if you enclose it with a high and handsome hedge of drought-tolerant rugosa roses or a stone wall. Screened from the street it can become a Japanese sand garden for meditation, a decked nook, a tea room, or a play yard for children. When your decisions about additional landscaping are final, make scale drawings that represent the new features. Cut out the hardscape sketches and accommodate them on the graph of your property by eliminating or moving plants and garden features now there. Except for mature shade, little is sacrosanct when you are undertaking a xeriscape makeover.

CHOOSING TREES AND SHRUBS
A xeriscape takes advantage of the height, texture, and sculptural form of shade trees for practical as well as for aesthetic reasons. Magnificent old trees can't be moved and

shouldn't be removed. I find great beauty in a monumental trunk with deeply fissured bark. Wide-spreading, gnarled branches are arresting sculptural elements in winter, as well as in summer. Work around older trees and, if necessary, reshape the hardscapes to accommodate them. If the present shade trees are so old you can't count on their longevity, plant young shade trees nearby as replacements.

When the hardscapes have been worked into the landscape, consider whether more trees are needed. Trees contribute cool, green spaces and their shadows have an aura of mystery. They can also screen out unattractive views and create private areas. The most valuable position for shade trees is on the south and the west sides of the grounds. There they afford protection from the worst of the sun and create wonderful deep green shadows in late afternoon. While there are many excellent shade trees to recommend, I am especially fond of the various disease-resistant elms and the beautiful sugar maple.

In places where you want to add new trees, choose drought-tolerant ones. Set them in pairs combining less desirable but fast-growing trees, such as Austrian pine

OPPOSITE:
A xeriscape designed to complement a property with a Spanish flavor features *Helleborus* in the foreground, backed by allium's pink spheres, red-hot poker and King's-spear (*Asphodeline lutea*).

LEFT:
Marigolds make an elegant, drought-tolerant ground cover under a windmill palm (*Trachycarpus fortunei*). A frost-hardy evergreen grown for its form and foliage, in summer the windmill palm bears sprays of fragrant, creamy yellow flowers.

OVERLEAF:
Left: Plants with the look of the desert that can grow in somewhat cooler climates include spearlike Spanish bayonet, (*Yucca aloifolia*), Adam's needle (*Y. filamentosa*), low-growing rock rose (*Helianthemum*), and the evergreen *Euphorbia characias* ssp. *wulfenii*.

Right: Drought-tolerant plants used as tall ground cover are, above, shrubby cinquefoil (*Potentilla fruticosa*), which blooms all summer, and below, Carolina jasmine (*Gelsemium sempervirens*), which flowers in the spring.

TALL DROUGHT-TOLERANT SHADE TREES

American yellowwood
Cladastris lutea Z3-8

Black gum, sour gum
Nyssa sylvatica Z3-9

Bull bay, southern magnolia
Magnolia grandiflora cvs. Z6-9

Bur oak, mossy-cup oak
Quercus macrocarpa Z2-8

Chinese elm, lacebark elm
Ulmus parvifolia Z4-9

Fruitless white mulberry
Morus alba 'Fruitless' Z4-8

Golden rain tree
Koelreuteria paniculata Z5-9

Gray birch
Betula populifolia Z3-6/7

Green ash, red ash
Fraxinus pennsylvanica Z3-9

Hackberry
Celtis occidentalis Z2-9

Japanese zelkova
Zelkova serrata cvs. Z5-8

Littleleaf linden
Tilia cordata Z3-7

London plane tree
Platanus acerifolia Z4-8/9

Maidenhair tree, gingko
Gingko biloba Z3-8/9

Northen catalpa
Catalpa bignonioides Z4-8

Norway maple
Acer platanoides Z3-7

Pin oak
Quercus palustris Z4-8/9

Red maple
Acer rubrum Z3-9

Red oak
Quercus rubra Z4-8

Red pine
Pinus resinosa Z2-7

Scarlet oak
Quercus coccinea Z4-9

Thornless honey locust
Gleditsia triacanthos f. *inermis*
Z3-9

White pine
Pinus strobus Z3-8

LOW-GROWING DROUGHT-TOLERANT SHRUBS

Bluebeard, blue spirea
Caryopteris clandonensis Z5-10

Bumald spiraea
Spiraea japonica 'Bumalda' Z3-8

Carolina rhododendron
Rhododendron minus Z4/5-8

Dwarf yaupon holly
Ilex vomitoria cvs. Z7-10

Euonymus
Euonymus spp. Variably hardy

Heavenly bamboo, dwarf cultivars
Nandina domestica Z6-9

Indian hawthorn
Rhaphiolepis umbellata Z7-10

Japanese barberry
Berberis thunbergii cvs. Z4-8

Juniper species and cultivars
Juniperus spp. Hardiness variable

Northern bayberry
Myrica pensylvanica Z3-9

Rugosa rose
Rosa rugosa Z2-7

Sargent crabapple
Malus sargentii Z4-8

Shrubby St. Johnswort
Hypericum prolificum Z3-8

Spreading cotoneaster
Cotoneaster divaricatus Z4-7

Wintercreeper 'Emerald 'n Gold'
Euonymus fortunei 'Emerald 'n Gold' Z4-8

153

Photinia ✕ *fraseri* 'Red Robin' Z7

154

or honey locust, with more desirable but slower-growing species. When the slower-growing trees begin to provide sufficient shade, you can remove the less desirable trees to make space. I recommend buying the fast-growing species in 5- to 10-gallon containers and buying the largest size available for slower-growing species. Dig the hole for trees three times the size of the rootballs and dig the planting hole for the permanent trees the size of a card table. Make the holes square to encourage the roots to grow outwards. Grade the soil so that water will not flow away from the trees, cover the soil in a 4- to 8-foot radius around the trees with mulch 3 inches deep, and water thoroughly. For the first two seasons check the soil moisture regularly, especially during drought, and water thoroughly if necessary.

UNDERSTORY TREES: Healthy, young understory trees, such as flowering plums or cherries and crape myrtles, that are in the way of your evolving xeriscape can be moved to more desirable locations when they are dormant. You'll find many of your favorites will thrive under the new regime if the water you supply is gradually reduced over several seasons. Plants growing in a xeriscape become more drought tolerant as they become established. Many gardeners expect to change their watering ways abruptly and just walk away, when actually even natives may need two or three years to adjust before they can be turned loose on their own. But you should plan to replace flowering trees that require a lot of watering or chemical support with cultivars of hardy natives, such as mountain laurel, redbud, or serviceberry (*Amelanchier alnifolia* is the most drought resistant). For the warm areas of the West Coast there are many lovely flowering trees, among them the charming strawberry tree (*Arbutus unedo*), a lovely little evergreen whose foliage is tinted amber that bears masses of white flowers in fall, followed by long-lasting fruits, orange red as strawberries. In cooler regions the shrub-size cultivar 'Compacta' is often grown in containers and moved to shelter during cold weather.

Native plants may not always be the showiest, but they thrive in local conditions and introduce an interesting diversity into the landscape. There are often different species of the most popular natives in cultivation, and it is a good idea to

Croton (*Codiaeum variegatum* var. *pietum* 'Miss Peter')

Photinia serrulata

learn about the origins of the species you are bringing home. The amelanchier native to western Canada and the northwestern United States is the Saskatoon serviceberry (*A. alnifolia*); the juneberry (*A. arborea*) is the one that belongs in a garden in New England. Another serviceberry, known also as the shadblow (*A. canadensis*), is found in boggy areas along the East Coast down to the Carolinas and is ideal only for a naturally wet area in the garden.

If native plants don't meet your needs, you can use drought-tolerant garden ornamentals that are pest- and disease-resistant. Older forms of crab apples and the beautiful Florida dogwood have been greatly overused and are prone to disease, but many new and beautiful cultivars have been introduced, such as the Sargent crab apple (*Malus sargentii*); and *M.* 'Narragansett'. The lovely Chinese dogwood (*Cornus kousa* var. *chinensis*) and the Rutgers Hybrid dogwoods resist the problems attacking the Florida dogwoods and are available in pink as well as white varieties.

When you have decided what trees you want to add, sketch and cut out forms that represent them, and position them on your property graph.

SHRUBS: Shrubs are easier than trees to move and less costly to replace. Assess the value of existing shrubbery to the developing xeriscape. Remove from the plan plants that aren't in great condition and replace them with natives or more desirable flowering and fruiting species, such as dwarf yaupon holly and heavenly bamboo (*Nandina domestica*), cotoneaster and Indian hawthorn (*Raphiolepis indica*). Most healthy, well-established shrubs on your property have proven they can live with the regional rainfall. They are good candidates for your xeriscape and should be removed only if absolutely necessary. Valuable mature shrubs can be moved when they are dormant or semi-dormant and will recover if you follow sound transplanting procedures and the new location is suitable. To transplant a large shrub you need to know how to move it and where it grows best. (One of the best books on the subject that I know is Michael A. Dirr's *Manual of Woody Landscape Plants*.)

For example, the common lilac adjusts to a move if the new soil is well supplied with lime, but the trouble-free, white-flowered Japanese tree lilac (*Syringa reticulata*,

DROUGHT-TOLERANT
ANNUALS

Sweet alyssum
Lobularia maritima

California poppy
Eschscholzia californica

Corn poppy
Papaver rhoeas

Cornflower, bachelor's buttons
Centaurea cyanus

Cosmos cultivars
Cosmos bipinnatus, C. sulphureus

Garden geraniums
Pelargonium hortorum

Honesty
Lunaria annua

Iceland poppy
Papaver nudicaule

Blanket flower
Gaillardia pulchella

Marigolds
Tagetes spp., cvs.

Love-in-a-mist
Nigella damascena

Mexican sunflower
Tithonia rotundifolia

Moss rose
Portulaca grandiflora

Nasturtium
Tropaeolum majus

Straw flower
Helichrysum bracteatum

Madegascar periwinkle
Catharanthus roseus

Spider flower
Cleome hassleriana

Salvia
Salvia splendens, S. farinacea

Sweet William
Dianthus barbatus

ustrian Black Pine (*Pinus nigra* 'Hornibrookiana')

Coreopsis verticillata 'Moonbeam' with Lamb's ears

155

LEFT:
Pretty 'Vera Jameson', a hybrid of *Hylotelephium* (syn. *Sedum*), is a small cultivar of the showy stonecrop clan, succulent perennials that bloom in summer and color beautifully in the fall. 'Vera Jameson' has darkish foliage and thrives in hot sun.

OPPOSITE:
'Autumn Joy', a larger sedum (*Hylotelephium*) hybrid, is about 20 inches high and has beautiful gray green foliage. As summer wanes the apple green flowerheads that it bears early in the season change to deep pink. The velvety leaves are *Stachys* 'Silver Carpet'.

BELOW:
Golden trumpet (*Allamanda cathartica* 'Hendersonii'), a colorful, heat-resistant climber, is used in xeriscaping as a container plant so that its special watering needs can be met without wasting water on the rest of the plants in the garden.

syn. *S. amurensis* var. *japonica*), needs slightly acid soil. Large evergreen rhododendrons and azaleas have shallow, wide-spreading roots that are easy to dig up. They transplant successfully if the new site is moderately acid, shady, well-drained, and has humus-rich soil. Mature needled evergreens with carrotlike tap roots, such as the spruces, are almost impossible to dig up intact; these you should replace with young plants.

Whether designing islands for shrubbery or replacing existing shrubs, keep in mind that in a xeriscape, less is more. Competing root systems need extra water. Be sure that you allow for the height and the width the *mature* plants will reach. On the graph, set the shrubs in a zigzag pattern about 3 feet apart. As they mature they will overlap. The young shrubs will look skimpy, but you can easily fill gaps with tall annuals, such as climax marigolds and burning bush.

A water-conserving shrub border that always gives me pleasure combines colorful deciduous shrubs against a background of broadleaf evergreens, such as Japanese holly or oleander, and includes narrow-leaved, extraordinarily durable yews and junipers in various heights, forms, and colors. The columnar junipers, especially the green and blue varieties, are very effective, and you will find dwarfs in every imaginable shape and height. Pfitzer junipers have a wonderful feathery texture, whether large, medium, or dwarf. For color, you might use viburnum, which bears beautiful flowers in early spring and whose foliage turns crimson-maroon in fall and the dwarf winged spindle tree (*Euonymus alatus* 'Compacta'), whose fall colors are brilliant crimson and coral. When, with the coming of cool weather, your garden has gone all buff and beige, a show of berries is a welcome mat to the birds and cheering to the gardener. Many lovely shrubs follow their spring flowers with fall berries. The beautiful fragrant flowers of the viburnums develop colorful berries, and pyracantha and barberry stage a berry spectacular.

It's a good design technique to repeat shrub species here and there on the plan to harmonize and connect the disparate elements. For example, you might repeat species of shrubs that you have used at the driveway entrance farther along the walk that leads to the front door. Then you could carry the species around the house to the back yard with repeat plantings of taller, smaller, and dwarf varieties, and/or variegated forms. There are tall and small rhododendrons and hollies, for example, and some species have small leaves while others have large ones. Some forms of juniper are solid green, others are blue-green or black-green, and some are yellow-tipped. Repeating a color scheme has the same unifying effect. You might use by the front walk one or two of the white-variegated *Euonymus fortunei*, for example, and elsewhere plant a variegated holly or the variegated Chinese dogwood 'Snowboy'.

As before, arrange the shrubs on your property graph.

Ideally, you should plan to equip the new shrub border with a leaky hose watering system topped by a 3-inch mulch. Keep the soil moderately damp for the first two years, or until the shrubs are well established. Before growth begins in early spring, apply a slow-release, high-nitrogen fertilizer, such as 20-5-10. If you are planting flowering shrubs, you might want something a little more balanced, such as 10-10-10.

ADDING LAWN AND GROUND COVERS

Does your property require a lawn? To grow, grass needs watering after the rainy season has gone by, but there are drought-tolerant grasses for every area of the country. Grass also is the most enduring of the ground covers, the only one that stands up to real wear and tear. You should consider including a grass lawn if it will be used as a carpeted playground, or if it is desirable as a design feature, a horizontal plane of emerald green. Most lawn grasses need to receive six hours or more of sun daily, though there are a few that grow in light shade. Be sure to plant a grass suited to your region.

For warm regions like Texas and for sites that will see hard wear, I recommend choosing St. Augustine grass (*Stenotaphrum secundatum*). It is somewhat drought-tolerant in the shade. For full sun, choose cultivars of Bermuda grass (*Cynodon dactylon*) or buffalo grass (*Buchloe dactyloides*), which remain bright green with less water. Zoysia can stand about the same amount of shade as St. Augustine grass, but it is also disease-resistant and tolerates warm summers coupled with cold winters. Cold turns zoysia a golden beige color. It doesn't green again until warm weather returns, so I don't recommend it for the north, although it is hardy there. Once established, zoysia is almost impossible to remove. In cooler regions, choose grasses that are mixtures of Kentucky blue grass (*Poa pratensis*), quick-growing perennial rye grass (*Lolium perenne*), and red fescue (*Festuca rubra* var. *rubra*). Perennial rye grass mixed with red fescue makes the hardest-wearing lawn. Some of the new varieties of tall fescue (*Festuca elatior*, syn. *F. arundinacacea*) can tolerate a lot of traffic, too. In full shade where grass is difficult to grow, if there is enough moisture in the soil, plant moss. It looks cool and green, but it won't tolerate much traffic. In shady areas too dry for moss, a nonliving ground cover, such as rounded pebbles or bark chips, may be the answer.

Water grass only when it needs it. When your footsteps show on the lawn, it may be because the grass is limp and needs watering. Set the sprinkler to lay down an inch of water. Fertilize the xeriscape lawn only three times a year. Apply a slow-

A stone wall, the ripe seedheads of an ornamental grass, and sedum 'Autumn Joy' make a beautiful composition. With cooler weather 'Autumn Joy' colors a rich pink, then changes to salmon bronze, and finally to a rosy russet that remains through winter. Sedums are among the best providers of color in the garden in autumn. They are used in xeriscapes everywhere because the thick fleshy leaves store water, as do aloes, agaves, cacti, and other succulent natives of dry places.

OPPOSITE:

Above: This beautiful xeriscape combines drought-tolerant annuals and perennials. Low-growing 'Vera Jameson', tall 'Autumn Joy', and related sedums show their deepening fall colors as daisies, yellow kniphofia, and pink hollyhocks reach the end of their flowering cycles. With cold weather, the ornamental grasses come into their own—rustling, tossing in the wind, changing from green to buff and beige, and in the North eventually binding snow at their feet.

Below: Kniphofia and Oriental poppies occupy the foreground in a colorful xeriscape that includes drought-resistant natives and garden ornamentals. The dainty white flowers belong to a cultivar of chamomile (*Chamaemelum nobile*), which is sometimes used as an alternative to lawn.

RIGHT:

Rosy 'Autumn Joy' sedum, alliums, and torch lily (*Kniphofia* 'Little Maid') in early autumn. The exotic, showy spikes of kniphofia cultivars range from white and yellow to orange, red, bicolor, and even green.

DROUGHT-TOLERANT
ORNAMENTAL GRASSES

Australian Fountain grass
Pennisetum alopecuroides Z4-9

Big bluestem
Andropogon gerardii Z4-9

Blue oat grass
Helictotrichon sempervirens Z4-8

Feather grass
Stipa gigantea Z5-9

Fescue species and cultivars
Festuca glauca, F. amethystina
Z4-9

Japanese silver grass
Miscanthus sinensis cvs. Z5-9

Little bluestem
Schizachyrium scoparium Z4-9

Oriental fountain grass
Pennisetum orientale Z7-9

Pampas grass
Cortaderia selloana Z8-10

Prairie cord grass
Spartina pectinata Z5-9

Purple love grass
Eragrostis spectabilis Z5-9

Red switch grass
Panicum virgatum cv. Z4-9

Ribbon grass
Phalaris arundinacea 'Picta' Z4-8

release, high nitrogen lawn fertilizer before growth in early spring and before high heat in midsummer, and, when cool weather arrives, apply a quick-release (chemical) lawn fertilizer formulated for fall application.

Cut the grass an inch higher than recommended for the variety you are planting to shade the soil and to reduce the need for water. Consider investing in a mulching mower, a rotary mower equipped with a special blade that kicks the clippings up into the air and cuts them two or three times so they're very fine when they land on the lawn. The clippings act as a fine mulch.

Planting one species of ground cover throughout the property ties disparate features and levels together in a very pleasant way. For small sunny or lightly shaded expanses close to the house, you could choose low-growing, creeping evergreen ground covers, such as blue-flowered myrtle, common ajuga (*Ajuga reptans*), which bears a spring crop of blazing blue spikes, or the fresh-looking, pretty, green-leaved ajuga cultivar 'Pink Beauty'. For difficult sites in shade or sun, I find that the evergreen ivies are indestructible, and where winters are warm Asiatic jasmine makes a lovely ground cover. Where you want a low screen rather than a flat ground cover, on a small slope, for example, and at corners, choose shrubby ground covers, such as the fluffy Pfitzer junipers or cotoneaster (*Cotoneaster horzontalis*). A few plants will cover a considerable area. You will find many other ground covers for slopes in the chapter called "Hillside Gardens."

Ground covers tend to spread easily once established. I find them tedious to plant, and they must be weeded until they fill in enough to take over the area, but they're very attractive and rarely require watering once established. To keep ground covers from spreading to adjacent beds, plan to install railroad ties or other edgers. You'll need to provide a 3-inch mulch around newly planted ground covers. In early spring before growth begins apply a slow-release, high-nitrogen fertilizer, then replenish the mulch cover. Water newly planted ground cover beds twice a week if necessary to keep the soil moist during drought for the first six weeks after planting; in the absence of rain, water them weekly thereafter throughout the first season and twice monthly the second season.

CREATING ISLAND BEDS

The hardscapes, trees and shrubs, the horizontal planes of lawn and ground covers will provide your xeriscape with structure, order, and harmony. With most of your garden a xeriscape, you can plan for flowers and specialty gardens to suit your fancy—a collector's garden of roses, peonies, or lilies; a kitchen garden of succulent vegetables; a rock garden (it's almost a xeriscape, anyway), a water garden—knowing that they take up only a small portion of your site and that even they can be designed to use water-saving plants and techniques. Raised beds, humus-rich soils, a thick mulch, and an efficient irrigation system all make even the more conventional gardens water-thrifty and easier to maintain. A xeriscape can accommodate any planting that pleases you as long as all together no more than 25 percent of the garden is given over to plants that will require regular watering in all seasons. A clump of flowers in a well-tended island bed with evergreens and tall shade trees behind, and a scrap of emerald lawn in front, can be as beautiful as a 40-foot perennial border.

But the xeriscape landscape need not exclude beds of well-loved perennials. Many perennials, and especially herbs and shade-loving woodland species, are more tolerant of drought than you would expect. A bright perennial border that is very

MAINTAINING A XERISCAPE

SOIL: Provide raised beds.

WATER: Water early in the morning or in the evening. Use a drip system that puts the water where it is needed.

TREES AND SHRUBS: Soak new plantings thoroughly every two weeks for the first season. Check the soil weekly, and if necessary, water thoroughly. The second season water once a month if needed. After that water only during droughts.

LAWN AREAS: Keep the soil moist (not wet) until lawn is established, and water weekly during the dry season.

GROUND COVERS: Keep the soil moist for the first six weeks after planting. Water weekly as needed during the first season, and often enough during the second to avoid summer stress. Water ground covers during severe droughts. Lay down 1 inch of water each time.

FLOWERING BORDERS, HERBS, VEGETABLES, AND SPECIAL PLANTINGS, SUCH AS A ROCK GARDEN: Water deeply as needed during the growing season.

MULCH: Maintain a 3-inch mulch on all plantings, renewed yearly in spring before summer heat arrives.

drought tolerant might include orange butterfly weed (*Asclepias tuberosa*), feathery yellow *Achillea* 'Moonshine', cheerful red-and-yellow blanket flower (*Gaillardia × grandiflora*), and lance coreopsis (*Coreopsis lanceolata*), bordered by red or pink *Sedum spurium* and white rock cress (*Arabis procurrens*), with colorful annuals, for example, moss rose (*Portulaca grandiflora*) and California poppy (*Eschscholzia californica*). Many of the rock garden plants described in the last chapter would be at home here as well. For a more restful perennial border, how about pinks and whites mixed with cooling blues and soft gray-green foliage? Try pink and white mallows (*Malva alcea* and *M. moschata*), white Mediterranean eryngo (*Eryngium bourgatii*), silver horehound (*Marrubium incanum*), with the fragrant blue flowers and soft green foliage of lavender. If you choose plants that require a little more water, the possibilities seem endless: yarrows, bellflowers, daisies, asters, pinks, coneflowers, sedums—the list goes on and on. And don't forget the flowering bulbs: Many are native to regions that experience seasonal drought. For spring flowers, plant narcissus, fritillaria, crocus, scilla, even the delicate windflower (*Anemone blanda*), and for summer, try beautiful white peacock orchid (*Gladiolus callianthus*) and bright red, orange, and yellow montbretia. The shade of your xeriscape trees opens up new possibilities: A surprising number of woodland wildflowers are at least moderately tolerant of drought, including Solomon's seal, columbine, and wild ginger, and many of the more familiar garden ornamentals will require less water when they are planted in partial or light shade.

The secret to success with xeriscape perennials is to select drought-tolerant varieties and to use water-saving culture and maintenance techniques. Before you plant your xeriscape perennials, learn about their soil requirements. The more drought-tolerant species may actually prefer poor, dry soils. The others will do better if you start them off right, in a bed enriched with moisture-holding humus or compost (see page 237). Some successful xeriscape gardeners dig a large hole for each plant; they line the hole and fill in around the roots with pure compost, to provide each with a water-holding reservoir. Water them as necessary the first year, until they are well established. Then, except for long periods of drought, they'll be on their own.

DROUGHT-TOLERANT PERENNIALS

Adam's needle
Yucca filamentosa cvs. Z5-10

Bearded iris
Iris cultivars Z4-10

Bellflowers
Campanula spp., cvs. Z4/5-10

Blanket flower
Gaillardia × grandiflora Z4-10

Butterfly weed
Asclepias tuberosa 'Gay Butterflies' Z4-9

Coreopsis
Coreopsis spp. Z4-10

Daylilies
Hemerocallis spp. Z4-10

Hollyhock mallow
Malva alcea Z4-9

King's spear, asphodel
Asphodeline lutea Z6-9

Lavender cotton
Santolina chamaecyparissus Z6-9

Perennial flax
Linum perenne Z5-10

Purple coneflower
Echinacea purpurea Z3-10

Sea hollies
Eryngium spp. Z5-10

Sedum 'Autumn Joy', others
Hylotelephium hybrids Z4-10

Silver horehound
Marrubium incanum Z4-10

Sun drops
Oenothera fruticosa Z5-9

Torch lilies, red-hot poker
Kniphofia spp., cvs. Z5/7-10

Yarrows
Achillea spp., cvs. Z3/4-10

163

HILLSIDE
GARDENS

Breathless, we flung us on the windy hill,
Laughed in the sun, and kissed the lovely grass.

RUPERT BROOKE

I have never seen a hillside garden that I found ordinary. The terrain lends itself to landscaping that is beautiful, powerful, and touched with mystery and drama, even in something as simple as a precipitous incline landscaped with rugged stone steps, a waterfall, ferns, and flowers. A long slope terraced with stone retaining walls evokes the stepped gardens of the beautiful old hilltop towns of Provence and Italy. A softly rolling hill carpeted with wildflowers or flowering apple trees sets me to thinking that soon sheep will be quietly grazing in a meadow, and I long to be there when the mists come up from the valley at dusk. Whether your hillside encompasses acres, or just a fraction of an acre, the hill itself, a dynamic wave of earth and stone, an immense arrested motion, will reward your landscaping efforts with an exceptional, exciting garden.

One of the most beautiful and complex hillside gardens in America combines naturalism with formality in a design composed of the elements used in landscaping any hillside garden: terraces, meadows, steps, and paths. On the hilly, 16-acre Dumbarton Oaks estate in Washington, D.C., a now-public legacy from the 1930s, the late, great American landscaper and artist Beatrix Farrand created two dozen terrace gardens. The terraces at the top of the hill are outlined by azaleas and have views of slopes planted with flowering fruit trees and forsythia. You would love to entertain there, and that is what Farrand intended. These terraces were conceived as outdoor living rooms for family affairs, the Star Garden for dining and the Green Garden for partying. Leading from these terraces are mossy bricked paths; steps up, steps down, steps sideways, jogs, turns, allées, and lanes that take you to two dozen terrace gardens farther down the hill, including the Rose Garden, a favorite place for contemplation, and the Fountain Terrace, the Arbor Terrace, the Ellipse, and Melissande's Allee. Only in winter when the leaves are gone do you realize that following Farrand's labyrinth is a cozy experience in summer because shrubs and the tops of trees on terraces below create a sense of enclosed space. So many steps could be a nuisance, but Farrand zigzagged them and broke them up with interesting little resting places—four steps and then a landing, five or six steps, then a landing, and at each landing a new view of other terraces or of the meadows. The longest set of steps, seventeen in all, belongs to the Rose Garden. As you move through the gardens, nine fountains fill the air with the sounds of moving water. The lower reaches of the hill are occupied by the hidden Growing Garden, which supplies the flower beds and, off to the right near the little river at the bottom of the garden, there's a Lover's Lane and a magical oval pool reflecting the overarching trees and the sky.

A lesson brought home to me at Dumbarton Oaks is that native plants can become spectacular garden ornaments. Native trees growing on the property may have been Farrand's starting point. One tree that has recently gone was a massive black oak (*Quercus velutina*) that was 18 feet around. When it spread its first branches three hundred years ago, the property was part of a land grant belonging to Ninian Beall, a Scott, who named it Rock of Dumbarton for a historic fortified hill overlooking the River Clyde near Glasgow. Another very beautiful native tree, still in place, is an immense, silver-barked American beech encircled at its base by a sinuous swirl of silky gray roots interplanted with small flowering bulbs that bloom in late

PREVIOUS SPREAD:
Left: At La Casella in the Alpes Maritimes, a long, gentle slope terraced with stone retaining walls, evokes the stepped gardens of the old hilltop towns of Provence and Italy. The purple spikes in the foreground are *Echium* cultivars.

Right: A weathered garden ornament and dainty flowering perennials blooming between the steps add an appealing touch of romance to a grassy hillside garden. The flowers are growing in planting pockets created when the stone risers were built.

OPPOSITE:
An orchard of flowering cherry trees blooming on a terrace cut into a gently sloping hill covers the ground below with a blizzard of petals. The ornamental fruit trees flower here in pastel waves, and follow their spring displays of exquisite flowers with tiny fruits that attract birds.

winter and early spring. Each of these great trees was given a terrace of its own. The flat plane of the terrace with a great tree rising in its midst is truly dramatic.

LANDSCAPING WITH TERRACES AND MEADOWS

Despite the grandeur of Dumbarton Oaks, it's important to realize that Farrand's combination of garden rooms, flat planes, gently rolling meadows, and dynamic diagonals can transform any hillside property. I remember an attractive revamping of a typical suburban half-acre of lawn behind a modest home in a housing development in Westport, Connecticut. Two broad terraces were created by cutting across the yard with a low dry-stone wall that had four rugged stone steps up to the second level. The second level was raised slightly and leveled using the land cut out of the slope as fill. Ajuga, that pretty, very low-growing ground cover, carpeted the soil over the top level of stones, ivy crept down over the rock wall, and nooks and crannies in the steps were planted with sedums and hen and chickens (*Sempervivum tectorum*). Suddenly the property had the charm of an old farmstead. A kitchen garden planted to one side of the upper terrace was screened by a grove that included a white pine, a lovely little maple tree, a flowering pear, rhododendrons, azaleas, daphne, and forsythia. The two broad terraces were joined visually by a long, narrow, S-shaped flowering border angling diagonally up and across one side of the yard, a dynamic line that gave fluidity and motion to planes that might otherwise have appeared static or rigid. A staggered row of white pines was planted to screen the house from the neighbors, and to provide balance for the grove on the other side. By cutting deeply into the slopes at Dumbarton Oaks, Farrand provided the garden rooms with fairly high walls at their backs. The Westport terrace, with the house behind it, and the grove and the row of white pines flanking it, had the same aura of protection and privacy you feel in the garden rooms at Dumbarton Oaks, yet it was a fraction of the size.

The two-terrace landscape design is as effective on a large hillside property, a rounded one or two acres or more sloping gently away from the dwelling. Everything will be on a much larger scale, of course. Next to the house create a long, wide terrace

A sloping bank between terraces is planted with colorful thyme cultivars. Common thyme (*Thymus vulgaris*) and mother-of-thyme (*T. praecox* ssp. *arcticus,*) are fast-spreading, trailing plants that in early summer bear tiny pale pink, white, or lilac flowers. Shearing in late winter keeps thyme in good condition.

overlooking the terrace below and the large view beyond. Provide shade and privacy for groupings of chairs and tables by planting trees and shrubs in big tubs. For the containers I recommend using small varieties of plants that are prominent in the landscape below. Flights of steps broken by landings zigzag down to the second terrace. The location of that terrace depends on the slope of the hill: where the drop is sharp, to have enough width for the second terrace, you will need to locate it farther down the slope.

Consider landscaping the second terrace in a rather formal style, by planting a rose garden, for example, centered on an antique sundial. Or install a reflecting pool and edge the terrace with beds of colorful perennials. An even more elegant treatment is to plant an allée of trees growing in a carpet of emerald green grass, with a statuary fountain tumbling water into a reflecting pool at one end. An allée of flowering pears (*Pyrus calleryana*) would be magnificent. The callery pear is the tallest of the flowering fruit trees, and in early spring the branches are covered with clusters of airy little white blossoms. In fall the foliage colors various shades of red, plum, and purple, and, as with most ornamental fruit trees, it provides food for the birds. Choose the cultivars 'Whitehouse' or 'Capitol', which have strong central stems, rather than 'Bradford', the beautiful spreading form, which has an unfortunate tendency to split as it gets older.

In late winter chionodoxas bloom among the silken gray roots of the American beech tree that centers the Beech Terrace at Dumbarton Oaks, in Washington, D.C. The magnolias blooming on the other side of the stone wall are growing in the terrace below.

OVERLEAF:
At the Filoli gardens at Woodside, south of San Francisco, the precise horizontals of stepped lawns converge in an allée of verticals created by weeping trees and mature Irish yews. The red cascade is Virginia creeper in its fall colors.

ORCHARD TREES

Apples
Malus pumila cvs. Z4-8

Apricots
Prunus armeniaca cvs. Z4-8

Flowering pear, callery pear
Pyrus calleryana 'Bradford' Z5-8

Japanese flowering crab apple
Malus floribunda Z4-8

Japanese plums and hybrids
Prunus salicina, hybrids Z4-9

Peaches and nectarines
Prunus persica cvs. Z5-9

Pears
Pyrus communis cvs. Z4-9

Purple-leaf plum, cherry plum
Prunus cerasifera cvs. Z4-9

Red mulberry
Morus rubra Z5-9

Siberian crab apple
Malus baccata Z2-7

Sour cherry, sweet cherry
Prunus cerasus, P. avium Z4-7

Tea crab apple
Malus hupehensis Z4-8

Washington hawthorn
Crataegus phaenopyrum Z4-8

Weeping Higan cherry, *Prunus sub-hirtella* 'Pendula' Z6-8

Weeping Yoshino cherry
Prunus × yedoensis 'Shidare Yoshino' Z5-8

Yoshino cherry cultivars
Prunus × yedoensis 'Akebono', 'Ivensii', 'Pink Shell' Z5-8

A winding path and steps descend to a beach through a massed planting of ivy geraniums, nasturtiums, marguerite daisies, carnations, red-hot pokers, and Siberian wallflowers. The garden is planted on sand dunes that are fully exposed to the winds coming in from the Pacific Ocean. Topsoil was hauled in and held in place by terracing with up-ended boards.

173

OPPOSITE:
Raised beds of annuals and perennials create a shallow stepped garden as colorful as a Persian carpet. The hot colors are interspersed with white candytuft and daisies. Soft, cool snow-in-summer (*Cerastium*), are the low-growing, silvery green plants seen on the right.

A less formal landscape plan, and one requiring less maintenance, eliminates the second terrace and plants the entire slope in fruit trees. You may enjoy having orchard fruits: apples, peaches, or citrus, or you may decide to avoid the mess that dropped fruits create and plant only flowering, or ornamental, fruit trees that have been bred primarily for their flowers. Both types do well in such well-drained sites, especially if there is plenty of sunlight. Viewed from above, an apple orchard in bloom is one of the loveliest sights I know. The small, crisp, cup-shaped blossoms have a pure, quiet beauty that stills the senses and a perfume as soft as mist, yet as fragrant as wild roses. I love to visit an apple tree towards noon when the fragrance fills the air, and I try to remember that the buzzing pollen-drunk bees can't hurt me. The ornamental crab apple trees are smaller and have more interesting forms than young fruit-bearing apple trees; some varieties are scented. The fragrant violet-scented Siberian flowering crab apple (*Malus baccata*) has a fine reputation, and its spreading branches bear masses of small, pure white flowers, followed by bright fruits the birds love. They say the best cultivar for scent is 'Dolgo', a wide-spreading tree that can stand some shade and is cold hardy. The fragrant, picturesque tea crab (*M. hupehensis*) has long, wandlike branches that rise to 20 feet or more and spread in a vase shape. *M. floribunda,* a small, beautiful Japanese flowering crab, has spectacular fragrant flowers, deep pink to red in bud, and pink fading to white as they open. These trees are all disease-resistant, a point you should keep in mind when you are shopping for an ornamental crab apple tree.

If you prefer the more naturalistic aspects of the Dumbarton Oaks design, you may decide to divide the space around the house into two or three garden rooms, one flowing into the next and each having a different perspective on the garden. To separate the terraces and to screen them from neighboring properties, you can plant groups of shrubs and a tree in positions that won't interfere with the view nor with the foot traffic between the terraces. I love to begin the day on a cozy breakfast terrace sipping a hot drink and watching the sunrise. A second terrace, perhaps the luncheon terrace, should be protected from the noon sun by a shade tree or a vine-covered pergola, and a third terrace face west and the setting sun. If there's only a narrow strip of land on a level with the house, create three terraces on different levels, each overlooking some aspect of the garden you will create on the lower slope.

For the lower part of the slope, you might combine a meadow garden and a planting of ornamental fruit trees set off by a decorative split-rail fence and reached by a curving path rather than steps. The flowering plums, cherries, and peaches come into bloom in pastel waves; they follow their spring displays of exquisite flowers with tiny fruits attracting birds. Make this an orchard for the birds and enjoy their beauty and their song. A very decorative but underused little native is the Washington thorn (*Crataegus phaenopyrum*) , which bears clusters of white flowers in late spring; in fall it has bright red fruits and the foliage colors scarlet orange. If you were to plant only one tree for birds, it should be the red mulberry (*Morus rubra*), which has beautiful spreading branches, lovely flowers in spring, and red purple, juicy fruits. That mulberry trees are messy matters only when the fruits drop on a walk or a terrace. If the property is small, a bird orchard can consist of just two or three ornamental cherry trees. You might combine the large spreading cherry (*Prunus* × *yedoensis*), which can reach a height of 40 to 50 feet, with a pair of the smaller 'Shidare Yoshino' weeping cherries. The Yoshino cherry is the Japanese tree famous for the early spring display at the Tidal Basin in Washington, D.C. The fragrant blossoms open light pink and

GROUND COVERS WITH DECIDUOUS FOLIAGE

Blumald Spiraea
Spiraea japonica 'Blumalda' Z3-8

Cranberry cotoneaster
Cotoneaster apiculatus Z5-8

Deciduous azaleas
Rhododendron spp., cvs.Z3-6

Forsythia cultivars
Forsythia 'Arnold Dwarf' Z5-9

Fragrant sumac
Rhus aromatica Z3-9

Lowbush blueberry
Vaccinium angustifolium Z2-7

Memorial rose (semi-evergreen)
Rosa wichuraiana Z5-8

Prostrate broom
Cytisus decumbens Z5-8

Red osier
Cornus stolonifera Z2-8

Rock cotoneaster
Cotoneaster horizontalis Z4-8

Rose acacia
Robinia hispida Z5-10

Shrubby cinquefoil
Potentilla fruticosa Z3/5-8

Winged euonymus
Euonymus alatus 'Compacta' Z3-8

Golden Star (*Chrysogonum virginianum*)

Japanese Spurge (*Pachysandra terminalis*)   Hylotelephium (syn. *Sedum*) *sieboldii* 'Variegatum'

PRECEDING SPREAD:
At the Dingle, a valley garden in Wales, winding wooden steps cut into a gentle slope through beds of heather and other low-growing ground covers. The beautiful, bushy, bluish green evergreen behind the pink heather is a sabin juniper (*Juniperus sabina* 'Tamariscifolia').

PLANTING GROUND COVERS

Remove the turf and the weeds, and mix into the soil a third humus, or rotted leaves, and compost, along with a slow-release fertilizer. Dig a row of evenly spaced planting pockets across the top of the bed. Set the plants in their holes and firm them into place, pressing the back of the planting hole down a little more than the front. Move down the hill and dig a second row of holes, each one positioned *between* the planting pockets of the row above. When the planting is complete, spread a 3-inch layer of mulch in around the plants; maintain the mulch until the planting has grown dense enough to

shade out weeds. On a steep incline, to avoid having to replenish the mulch continually lost to rain runoff, plant through a porous landscape fabric. Dig and improve the soil, then cover the soil with the fabric. With a spade, push the ends of the fabric into the ground and weight it with rocks. Make rows of X-shaped slits in the fabric for planting holes, and use a trowel to insert the plants through the slits and into the soil. Firm the plants into their holes, and water them in.

Fertilize ground covers annually in late winter.

fade to white, and the foliage turns yellow in the fall. The cultivar 'Akebono' has true pink flowers. The 'Shidare Yoshino' weeping cherry in our garden opens its flowers later and holds them longer than the species; in October it paints its branches with leaf strokes of gold so evenly distributed that if you saw it in an illustration you'd think the symmetry was the artist's invention.

If the incline slopes rather steeply, plant a trailing, shrubby flowering ground cover, such as forsythia, instead of an orchard. *Forsythia × intermedia* 'Arnold Dwarf' is a trailing deciduous shrub whose arching branches are covered with small golden flowers early in spring. Forsythia roots where it touches the ground, it can stand drought, and the only maintenance it will require is a periodic trimming. An easy and lovely complement for a forsythia hill is a planting of groups of naturalized narcissus and lemon yellow daylilies. Another attractive plant often used for sheathing a steep grade is the little ground-hugging memorial rose (*Rosa wichuraiana*). The white flowers, which are 2 inches across and typical of wild roses, appear in late summer and are succeeded by modest reddish fruits. The branches trail and, like forsythia, they root when they touch moist soil, producing thick mats of glossy foliage that is evergreen in mild regions. A new series of ground-cover roses, 1996 Gold Medal winners in Australia, Britain, and America, bloom continuously, are immune to pests and diseases, and do not need deadheading; just a monthly fertilizing and a yearly pruning will keep the roses growing and blooming. The plants are 2 to 2 1/2 feet tall by 5 feet across. The star of the clan is 'Flower Carpet', whose flowers are lavender pink and spicily perfumed; 'Jeeper's Creepers' is a white-flowered variety, and 'Baby Blanket' is a light pink.

LANDSCAPING WITH WATERFALLS AND STEPS

A hill that drops sharply away from the house at the front entrance seems difficult to landscape at first glance, but you will find that it can be a wonderful stimulus to your creativity. Dramatic changes of level make exciting gardens. One of the most welcoming entrances I have seen belonged to a rather large house set on a lot that butted hard against a neighbor's land at the back and had only a few hundred yards of sloping land at the front entrance. The owners built a flight of wide, shallow steps—wide steps look so inviting—curving up through three small terraced gardens to a flagstoned terrace at the front door. The terraces on one side of the steps were planted with dwarf azaleas, blue salvia, fragrant white stock, jade green sedums, pink and white petunias, and pink ageratum. On the other side of the steps a small waterfall cascaded down to the bottom level and gurgled off into a thicket of dwarf Japanese hollies. (I assume the hollies screened the electric pump that moved the water back up to the top terrace.) The holly was the low-growing *Ilex crenata* 'Helleri', an elegant, black-berried, evergreen species that grows slowly to 4 feet and is excellent for edgings, rock gardens, driveway borders, or foundation plantings. One or two 'Golden Helleri' were planted with the green variety for contrast.

Falling water is always fascinating, and I have seen it used to great effect in landscaping a small, rather shaded property. The site was long and narrow, and it sloped up from the terrace next to the house. The waterfall began at almost the top of the property and fell straight down to a reflecting pool butted against one side of the terrace. A pot of lotus and a few aquatic plants were growing in the pool—I love the horizontal of the huge cupped aerial leaves of lotus even where there isn't enough sun to bring it into bloom. A wall seat had been built around the terrace, and the

GROUND COVERS WITH EVERGREEN FOLIAGE

LOW
Bearberry cotoneaster
Cotoneaster dammeri Z5-8

Bergenia species and cultivars
Bergenia cordifolia, B.crassifolia Z3-8

Blue rug juniper, 'Wiltonii' juniper
Juniperus horizontalis cv. Z3-9

Japanese pachysandra
Pachysandra terminalis Z4-8

Mountain cranberry
Vaccinium vitis-idaea minus Z2-6

Periwinkle
Vinca minor Z4-8, *V. major* Z7-9

Rat-stripper, Canby paxistima
Paxistima canbyi Z3-8

Spring heath
Erica carnea Z5-8

Stonecrops, sedums
Hylotelephium, Sedum spp. Z4-9

TALL
Coast leucothoe
Leucothoe axiliaris Z5/6-9

Cushion Japanese yew
Taxus cuspidata cvs. Z4-7

Evergreen azaleas
Rhododendron spp., cvs. Z5-9

Evergreen barberries
Berberis candidula, others Z5-8

Japanese holly
Ilex crenata 'Helleri', cvs. Z5-8

Juniper cultivars
Juniperus spp., cvs. Z3-8

Wintercreeper
Euonymus fortunei cvs. Z4-8

179

Variegated English Ivy 'Luzir'
(*Hedera helix* 'Luzir') Z5-9

OPPOSITE:
A stream cascades downhill past drifts of narcissus, *Anemone dichotoma*, and *Ranunculus ficaria,* a European buttercup now naturalized in the U.S. A hill that drops sharply away offers the opportunity to create an interesting water feature. Dramatic changes of level invite compelling garden designs.

garden behind it was planted with variegated hostas and fragrant white nicotiana. Behind these the owner had installed plantings that are most beautiful in the fall: fountain grass, which turns a soft orange gold; *Euonymus alatus* 'Compacta', backed by the taller *E. alatus*; and little maples and young red oak. At the top of the waterfall, crossing the slope above it, a set of steps led up in a long diagonal and disappeared into a grove of shrubs and small flowering trees planted at the boundary of the property. A stand of skyrocketing purple-pink gayfeather (*Liatris spicata*) was blooming by the bottom step, along with a sprawl of pale gold coreopsis and clumps of grassy liriope.

Where a waterfall is inappropriate, you can mimic its dramatic lines by planting a stepped series of ornamental grasses that cascade forward, such as drooping sedge (*Carex pendula*), or fountain grass (*Pennisetum alopecuroides*), which will seed itself in moist conditions. Or you might enjoy creating a waterfall of vines by planting vines at the top of the slope and training the runners to grow downward. I think you would enjoy having near your terrace sweet autumn clematis (*Clematis terniflora*, syn. *maximowicziana*) is a dainty-leaved deciduous vine that grows like a tidal wave all summer and then covers itself with a foam of small, sweetly fragrant white flowers in the fall. A combination of evergreen English ivy (*Hedera helix*) and the beautiful, deciduous Virginia creeper (*Parthenocissus quinquefolia*) is also attractive. English ivy is a solid, rich green all year round, and Virginia creeper has reddish new growth in spring that turns to brilliant scarlet in autumn; its clusters of small greenish flowers are followed by blue-black berries the birds love. Another deciduous vine with berries for birds that does well on rocky slopes and in wild places is bittersweet (*Celastrus*). The fruits are red-orange, and there are masses of them. Plant several, and include a male among them to ensure maximum fruiting. Pruning back the old wood in early spring will also increase the amount of fruit the plants bear. The vigorous Oriental bittersweet (*C. orbiculatus*) grows 30 to 40 feet and is considered better than the hardier American bittersweet (*C. scandens*) for erosion control, slope plantings, and dry places.

Another landscape plan for a long, narrow, precipitous incline is a step garden leading down, or up, the hill. I think you will find the steps much friendlier and much more interesting if you have them zigzag over the hill and break them up, as Beatrix Farrand did, with many small landings. Diagonal lines create a sense of ever-unfolding space. You will find the garden has much more mystery when you can't see everything that's there at a glance. The steps should disappear and reappear behind and around clumps of shrubs leading the eye to glimpses of other colorful plants, and unfolding the garden layer after layer as it leads towards the trees and shrubs screening your boundaries. Each new set of plants that comes into view should include colors and foliage that recall some of the plants just seen but should also include new and interesting colors and forms. To give yourself a reason to pause and catch your breath at the landings, plant them with unusual varieties. Along with azaleas and other flowering shrubs, plant surprising varieties like the little yellow-tipped Chinese juniper (*Juniperus chinensis* 'Gold Coast') or the lemon-yellow *Spiraea* × *bumalda* 'Limemound'. 'Limemound' foliage becomes orange red on red stems in autumn. Variegated foliage always attracts attention: A small variegated tree that always catches my eye is 'Snowboy', a form of Chinese dogwood that has white-margined foliage to go with its white flowers. Pretty gold-veined euonymus (*Euonymus fortunei* 'Emerald 'n Gold') also catches the eye.

MEETING THE CHALLENGES

Before you decide on plants for the hillside, spend some time getting to know your domain. Since a thriving garden depends on meeting the light requirements of the plants, you'll need to know how and where sunlight falls at various times of the day and seasons of the year. You may be surprised at the variations in light caused by even rather shallow dips and rises on your property. You will quickly learn that a site that faces east gets plenty of sun from early morning through early afternoon, but that as the sun moves westward, the shoulder of the hill or nearby trees can take away the garden's mid- and late-afternoon light. In the South, escaping some of the heat of late afternoon can be helpful. In the North, losing part of the day's warmth in early spring and fall may mean that you will need to protect early plantings with hot caps and other warmth-preserving covers.

A south-facing hill with its back to icy blasts from the north creates a wonderfully warm microclimate for plants whose tops are well below the crest and out of the wind. Here, lovely flowering fruit trees will come into bloom early, with less danger of their blossoms being blasted by icy winds during cold snaps. Protected by a hill, the exquisite star magnolia (*Magnolia stellata*) holds its white or pale pink flowers for several weeks even as far north as Connecticut and southern Massachusetts. A beautiful tree with silvery bark, the plant is hardy this far north, but in an open site the flowers are often ruined by late cold.

In the South, north- and east-facing slopes protect heat-sensitive plants from the burning afternoon sun. Lilacs, which usually cannot be grown south of Zone 7, may succeed when they are protected from the noon and late afternoon sun by the slope of a hill, and forsythia, which is approaching the limit of its southern hardiness in Zone 7, does better on a north-facing hill.

Walking the land may lead you to discover another, less friendly type of microclimate. Cold air naturally flows down a slope and collects in low pockets and ditches. Go barefoot to a ditchlike dip at the bottom of the hill as the day cools and your cold ankles will help you locate the cold spots. In early fall, and even in mid spring, cold air can put an unseasonable end to perennials growing there. The solution is to plant hardier species and varieties. If you were planning to use cotoneaster as a ground cover for the base of the hill, for example, I would recommend that you plant creeping cotoneaster (*Cotoneaster adpressus*), which is hardy in Zone 4, rather than bearberry cotoneaster (*C. dammeri*), which is considered hardy only as far north as Zone 5. These species are both about a foot high and have white flowers in summer, red berries in fall, and beautiful glossy foliage.

The base of the hill may present you with yet another challenge, an area that is wet, as well as cold. This problem is often encountered at a building site where a

PLANTING ON A HILL

Create planting pockets that are terraced: Remove the turf, dig the hole and mix into the soil in the hole, and into the soil taken from the hole, a third peat moss, or rotted leaves, and compost. Place the turf stripped from the hole upside down on the lip of the downside edge of the hole, creating a small raised shelf to direct water into the planting hole and prevent it from running off down the hillside. Maintain a 3-inch layer of mulch around the planting.

lot of earth has been moved. If the place is wet or moist all year, stands of marsh plants will be growing there; cattails, for example, or equisetum, a jointed, green reedlike plant. Leave them where they are: The Environmental Protection Agency protects wetlands, even from owners. But some places that appear dry may have standing water during and after rainy weather. Most garden plants grow best in well-drained soil. Even short periods of saturated soils kill many species: The flowering bulbs are especially susceptible. (Suggestions for drying out poorly drained areas are given on page 234.) But in a marshy area that is the result of the contour of the site, I recommend that you set out plants that are naturally adapted to wet soils.

GROUND COVERS FOR WET CONDITIONS

Creeping Jennie
Lysimachia nummuleria 'Aurea'
Z4-8

Daylilies
Hemerocallis spp.,cvs. Z3-9

Galax
Galax urceolata Z5-8

Lady's mantle
Alchemilla mollis Z4-8

Marsh marigold
Caltha palustris Z4-9

Mazus
Mazus reptans Z4-8

Narrow-leaved cattail
Typha angustifolia Z3-10

Pussy willows
Salix discolor, Z2-7, *S. caprea* Z5-8

Red turtlehead
Chelone obliqua Z5-9

Sweet flag
Acorus spp., cvs. Z4-10

True forget-me-not
Myosotis scorpioides Z4-10

Yellow flag
Iris pseudacorus Z4-9

Yellow loosestrife
Lysimachia punctata Z5-8

Landscaped with rugged stones, ferns, flowers, falling water, and a pool where the land levels out, a precipitous incline becomes a small Eden. The purple-pink flowering jacaranda, a tropical tree that is native to South America, blooms before its feathery foliage appears. The reddish flowers in the foreground are *Phygelius*.

A damp area, or one that is periodically wet for days at a time, is almost worth creating, just for the pleasure of having a place to grow a willow. An old way to dry out a damp spot was to cut young willow branches in early spring before the buds opened and stick them by the dozen into wet ground. They rooted and grew, and pretty soon the water was gone. The weeping willow is an elegant tree, golden in spring and romantic in summer, when the long, slim weeping branches sway in the wind. If you think a more upright tree would be attractive, plant the white willow (*Salix alba*). It's an airy, graceful tree of modest height that is easily rooted and fast-growing, and some cultivars have yellow or red twigs that are beautiful in winter. The silky gray catkins, or pussy willows, of the male trees are attractive; for more decorative catkins, plant the shrubby native pussy willow (*S. discolor*), the French pussy willow (*S. caprea*) or the rosegold pussy willow (*S. gracilistylis*). The handsome black alder (*Alnus glutinosa*), a fairly big tree used in parks and along highways,

Railroad ties and bricks make handsome steps in this terraced garden. The cascading plants include a red fuchsia, ferns, and spiky *Dasylirion*.

RIGHT:
Borders that converge until they screen off the continuation of this allée of rhododendrons add a hint of mystery to the garden. A pair of clipped yews guards the entrance.

grows well in cool wet places, and the river birch (*Betula nigra*) also profits from moist soil: Be sure to plant 'Heritage', a variety that resists the birch borer, a dangerous pest. If you need a big tree for the spot, there are many handsome natives to choose from, among them the very hardy red or green ash (*Fraxinus pensylvanica*), a great tree for the Plains; the fragrant sweet bay (*Magnolia virginiana*); and the magnificent bald cypress (*Taxodium distichum*), which is found in the southeastern United State and Mexico. Some trees that have beautiful fall color succeed in wet places: The lovely little swamp maple 'Red Sunset' (*Acer rubrum*) and the beautiful Chinese dogwood 'Summer Stars' can stand a little dampness. The American hornbeam (*Carpinus caroliniana*) has colorful fall foliage and thrives in wet places.

To carpet the soil under a tree in a damp spot, you can choose from among several lovely ground covers that thrive in shade and tolerate or even prefer moisture. Turtlehead (*Chelone obliqua*) is a native perennial that grows wild in moist woodlands and marshes. In late summer and autumn the 2-foot tall spikes bear rosy purple flowers shaped like a turtle's head; the dark green basal foliage extends up the stems and sets the flowers off beautifully. Golden star (*Chrysogonum virginianum*), a fast-spreading, low-growing plant, has scalloped bright green foliage and is covered with bright golden yellow, star-shaped flowers from early spring until autumn. It is native to the eastern United States and succeeds in full sun as well as part shade; you could extend this ground cover beyond the shade line and on up the hill. *Galax urceolata* is a cold-hardy evergreen perennial about a foot high with beautiful thick, heart-shaped basal leaves and little spikes of tiny white flowers. You'll recognize it as the plant used by florists in low arrangements and wedding bouquets. It's most successful in moist, peaty loams. One of the most beautiful of all ground covers for warm regions is *Dichondra micrantha,* the tiny-leaved, emerald green plant you may know as the houseplant baby's tears. It covers shaded moist ground with a velvety green mantle that can stand a little foot traffic.

Ornamental grasses are another attractive way to landscape wet places. Low-growing palm sedge (*Carex muskingumensis*) is hardy and will grow in wet soil and shade. It arches over gracefully and whips around in a breeze in a delightful fashion. Of the tall grasses that tolerate damp soil, my personal favorites are the silver grasses. I never tire of their wonderful, warm rusty gold fall color, and I love the sound of their dried reeds rustling in the wind. *Miscanthus sinensis* 'Variegatus' is a beauty that grows 6 to 12 feet high; the variety 'Zebrinus' is a little smaller, and the leaves are banded in gold. If the area is small and somewhat shaded by the hill, a pretty grasslike species to try is the 8-inch-high variegated sweet flag (*Acorus gramineus* 'Variegatus'). A native of marshy, somewhat shady places, it has irislike leaves and is an ancient fragrance herb valued for its sweet, lemony scent. In a place that has standing water most of the year, you might try narrow-leaved cattails (*Typha angustifolia*) or the tall yellow water iris (*Iris pseudacorus*). The big, exotic flowers of the water iris are magnificent in early summer, and I love to pick cattails to make dried arrangements in late summer and early fall.

HANDLING EROSION

The most serious challenge common to hillside gardens is erosion. I hope you like to walk in the rain as much as I do, because that's when you can best spot areas where in a long, steady downpour rivulets become torrents washing away the soil. One of the best defenses against erosion is to dig a lot of organic matter into the soil. Water that would be easily absorbed and held by humus-rich soil just washes everything away when the soil is deficient in humus. Consider terracing places that show a tendency to erode; protect those places in the meantime with shredded bark, wood chips, or mulch 4 to 5 inches deep. When landscaping is underway and you have removed the turf, a little erosion can become a big mud slide. You can prevent this temporarily by covering the soil with plastic sheeting or a layer of straw several inches deep.

If you need to plant a large expanse of naked soil on a sharp grade, I think you will find the best solution in the fast-spreading ground covers classed as bank holders and soil binders. Though their primary purpose is erosion control, some are quite beautiful. One that does well in some shade is the hardy native sweet fern (*Comptonia peregrina*). It's a fast-growing deciduous shrub up to 5 feet high with dark green leaves that have a spicy scent. It's often combined with low-growing sedges to protect exposed, infertile, somewhat acid soil. You may find it listed in catalogs as *Myrica asplenifolia*. Bearberry cotoneaster, forsythia, and the gracefully arching, pea-flowered broom (*Genista pilosa*) are all attractive, fast-spreading soil binders. The little tufting shrub called Aaron's beard (*Hypericum calycinum*) turns hillsides to gold in spring and early summer. On the West Coast hypericum is used as ground cover under eucalyptus trees. In climates like that of southern Florida, Mexican bluebell (*Ruellia brittoniana*) and oyster plant (*Tradescantia spathacea*) are naturalized as bank holders. *Tradescantia* has long narrow leaves that are purple underneath; in the North it is known as Moses-on-a-raft or two-men-in-a-boat, for the white flowers that sit in a pair of boat-shaped bracts. A variegated, non-flowering dwarf, *T.s.* 'Vittata' is recommended as a ground cover under trees, on banks and slopes, and in open areas. The Mexican bluebell is a small shrub with attractive leaves and showy, bluish lavender flowers spring and summer.

A much softer effect is created by a carpet of the dainty little crown vetch (*Coronilla varia*). You see it cascading down the sides of banks along highways, for it is one of our most valuable soil binders. It's 1 to 2 feet high, grows very thickly, and has dainty soft green foliage reminiscent of maidenhair fern. I especially like the masses of pretty pealike, pink-and-white flowers that decorate the greenery through summer and fall. Crown vetch is vigorous and invasive. You will need to isolate its plantings using barriers of edging sunk deep into the ground; otherwise it will spread and take over everything. If it shows up beyond its bed, root it out mercilessly. The species prefers full sun, but the variety 'Penngift' succeeds in sun or shade; crown vetch should be mowed or trimmed annually to maintain its neat appearance.

SHRUBS FOR EROSION CONTROL

Chenault coralberry
Symphoricarpos × *chenaultii* Z4-8

Drooping Leucothoe 'Rainbow'
Leucothoe fontanesiana Z5-9

Dwarf forsythia
Forsythia 'Arnold Dwarf' Z5-9

Fragrant sumac
Rhus aromatica Z3-9

Japanese yew
Taxus cuspidata cvs. Z4-7

Junipers
Juniperus spp, cvs. Z3-9

Red osier
Cornus stolonifera cvs. Z2-8

Sweetfern
Comptonia peregrina Z2-7

Virginia rose
Rosa virginiana Z3-10

VINES FOR SCREENING

Bittersweet
Celastrus spp. Z3/4-8

Carolina jasmine
Gelsemium sempervirens Z6-9

Cross vine
Bignonia capreolata Z7-9

English ivy
Hedera helix Z5-9

Japanese honeysuckle
Lonicera japonica Z4-9

Memorial rose
Rosa wichuraiana Z5-8

Perennial pea
Lathyrus latifolius Z5-9

Sweet autumn clematis
Clematis terniflora Z5

Virginia creeper
Parthenocissus quinquefolia Z3-9

SEASHORE

GARDENS

I must down to the seas again, for the call of
*   the running tide*
Is a wild call and a clear call that may not be
*   denied.*

JOHN MASEFIELD

Waves curling up the beach, wind-carved dunes, night fogs, and morning mists—everything about the shore that delights the senses helps to make a shore garden special. Salt sea spray brings out the fragrance of cottage pinks and pines. Cool nights give flower colors an incomparable brilliance and reduce the need to water. The wind performs hourly dances with grasses and in its more dramatic moods makes magnificent life-size bonsai of the trees.

To create a little Eden by the sea, you can harness the elements. The wind and waves that move sand about and, on occasion tear up plants, also build dunes. Beach grasses and often seashore wetlands stabilize the sand and shore up wind-breaks. The superb drainage provided by sandy soil can be used to your advantage to grow many plants that thrive in well-drained locations. Sand's open structure allows easy passage of the oxygen required by plant roots. Modified by the addition of moisture-holding humus, as suggested on page 234, and enriched with complete slow-release fertilizers, sandy soil becomes a welcoming environment.

Because of the drama of your setting, the plantings you make in a seashore garden can be bold and romantic. Wetlands and salt marshes are striking as back-drops to ornamental grasses, and together they will wed your garden to the beach and the water. You can interplant the grasses with naturalized perennials and lead the eye to the ocean with long casual sweeps of colors that change with the seasons—from early summer's mauve alliums and bear's-breech (*Acanthus baleanicus*), golden fernleaf yarrow (*Achillea filipendulina*), and daylilies, to midsummer and early autumn, when drifts of tall blue Russian sage (*Perovskia atriplicifolia*) appear to float above grassy stands of moor grass (*Molinia caerulea* ssp. *arundinacea*) and Japanese silver grass (*Miscanthus sinensis*).

You will find it wonderfully rewarding to grow fragrant flowers close to your house. Lavender and roses thrive by the sea, as do many of the aromatic herbs native to the Mediterranean shore, including thyme, oregano, and rosemary. Rosemary's botanical name, *Rosmarinus,* means "dew of the sea." Perfume and a glimpse of moonlight on the water on nights when the surf is just a whisper are among the shore garden's great gifts.

ANCHORING THE SAND

For even native plants to succeed, a garden on a sandy coast usually needs some pro-tection from drifting sand, shifting dunes, and erosion from exceptional storms. You can protect the garden, stabilize the sand, and strengthen the dunes by planting or augmenting beach grasses.

A variety of beach grasses is native to American shores. The most common is American beach grass (*Ammophila breviligulata*). Native to the dunes of the Atlantic Coast and the Great Lakes region, the plant reaches 2 to 3 feet in height, has leathery leaves about a foot long, and produces a spiky inflorescence. It's an excellent sand binder that multiplies by creeping rhizomes, and is used to anchor dunes and stop the erosion of beaches. Ammophila can stand any amount of salt spray. The European beach grass, *A. arenaria,* a smaller species, is used to stabilize dunes on the West Coast, from northern California to Washington.

PREVIOUS SPREAD:
Left: By a sun-splashed path to the sea, naturalized daisies (*Dendranthema*), bluebells (*Campanula*), and mixed garden perennials thrive in the well-drained soil and moist air of the shore environment.

Right: A clump of glowing *Kniphofia* 'Shining Sceptor' stands out in a carefree garden of evergreens and ornamental grass-es. Once established, these plants rarely need dividing.

OPPOSITE:
Native shrubs and ornamental grasses make an easy transition from the sea to a Long Island property planted in daisies, daylilies, sedum, and Russian sage (*Perovskia*).

OPPOSITE:
Lawns, flowering borders, and a rose-covered pergola flourish in a garden sheltered from sea winds and high tides by a vine-clothed wall. The soft pink pokers in the foreground are bistort (*Polygonum bistorta*), a shade-lover that thrives in the sun in cool maritime climates.

Beach grasses are easily propagated by root division at any time when the plant is dormant, from late fall until growth begins in spring. Dig up good-sized clumps, separate them into very small clumps, and plant them 8 inches deep about 18 inches apart in zigzag rows. Before planting you should dig into the sand both a slow-release 10-10-10 fertilizer (like Osmocote in a 12-month formulation, for example) and a quick release 10-10-10 non-organic lawn fertilizer. Watered in thoroughly after planting, the quick-release nutrients will give the plants a good start. When growth starts, be sure to continue to water as needed until the clumps are growing vigorously and plan to fertilize the plantings again in mid summer.

A mixed planting of beach grass with beach plum (*Prunus maritima*), seaside goldenrod (*Solidago sempervirens*), and other natives provides seasonal variations in color and texture to the dune landscape and, according to coastal ecologists, may hold the sand more tenaciously than a pure stand of beach grass alone. In warm regions, Zone 9 and south, a variety of sand binders can be used. Beach morning glory (*Ipomoea pes-caprae*) is a fast-growing creeper with vines up to 60 feet long; in summer and fall it bears showy flowers in purple, white, blue, pink, or red. Sea purslane (*Sesuvium portulacastrum*) is another star sand binder. A mat-forming sea strand plant of Florida, it grows moderately quickly to about a foot and a half and has showy pink flowers year round. *Myoporum* × 'Pacifica', an extraordinarily fast-spreading shrubby hybrid with branches to 30 feet across, is used in California and other dry, warm regions to tie down sandy slopes. The branches root where they touch the soil. It has interesting evergreen foliage dotted with translucent spots visible when the leaf stands against the light.

A dune lost to storms can be rebuilt using snow fencing, with the help of the wind and the tides. Snow fence usually consists of wooden pickets held in place by wires. Buy snow fencing twice as long as you want your dune to be, and install it in two rows about 40 feet apart and parallel to the shoreline, or at right angles to the prevailing wind. Blown sand will accumulate in drifts along the bottom of the fence,

DAMAGE CONTROL

HEAVY SALT SPRAY FROM HIGH WINDS:
Spray plants thoroughly with a hose to wash off as much salt as possible.

GARDENS FLOODED BY HIGH TIDE:
Temporary flooding doesn't cause permanent damage unless there's a real flood that remains for many hours. Use a hose to rinse as much of the salt off the plants as possible.

FLOODED LAWN:
If a dangerously high tide is expected, flood the lawn with fresh water; the damage may be reduced if the soil is so saturated that it can't absorb much of the sea water that comes in on the tide. To repair a flooded lawn, after the water has drained off apply ground limestone at the rate of 20 to 50 pounds per 1,000 square feet. Water it in thoroughly.

In the exposed areas of a seaside property, in the places reached by salt spray and regularly invaded by storms off the ocean, the most carefree plants are those native to the seashore. They can take salt spray and invasive tides. Some are American natives, and some come from other parts of the world, primarily Japan, continental Europe, and England. These native beach plants thrive and are right at home; they need no special help or protection, and they look right. They are what your eye expects.

Waves curling up the beach, night fogs and morning mists, and a few enduring yellow horned poppies (*Glaucium flavum*) invite contemplation in this serene seashore garden. The horned poppy succeeds in poor, well-drained soil and has naturalized in parts of the U.S.

In an intimate corner, golden yarrow, lavender, blonde astilbe, a climbing rose, and woolly white lamb's ears backed by purple loosestrife (*Lythrum salicaria*) give an extravagant show. Cool, humid nights at the shore reduce the need to water and impart brilliance to flower colors.

just as snow drifts form in an open field, and eventually grow into a dune. When the dune reaches the height you desire, plant beach grass and other sand binders in order to stabilize the sand.

PLANT A WINDBREAK: Where a dune is undesirable or impractical, you can install a windbreak, either a living windbreak or a fence. A windbreak provides protection on its leeward side to a distance of up to 5 times its height. To create a living windbreak, plant rows of young trees or tall shrubs in a zigzag pattern so that the branching will overlap. If you have space enough for a double row, plant the first row so that the branches touch, then plant the second row so that the trunks stand between the plants of the first row. If your property is too small to plant rows of trees, you can create a pocket windbreak by planting a single evergreen tree flanked by tall and small shrubs.

On the shore, evergreens are the best plants for the windbreaks. Your choices

are varied: broad-leaved evergreens, such as American holly; small-leaved evergreens, such as privet; and needled evergreens, such as Japanese black pine, as well as cedars and junipers. The fast-growing Leyland cypress (× *Cupressocyparis leylandii*) makes a great windbreak and makes great hedges and screening. It grows 3 feet a year, and, once established, can stand heavy pruning. The bluish green foliage is feathery and graceful, and the scaly reddish brown bark is handsome. The colorful cultivars 'Naylor's Blue', which has soft grayish blue foliage accents, and 'Castlewellan Gold', whose new growth is yellow, are among my favorites.

BUILD A FENCE: Trees and shrubs need at least a few years to grow into effective barriers. If you want immediate protection, you can install a fence and mask it with shrubs. You will be sorry if you put up a solid fence: The wind will eventually break it down. Fencing made of horizontal louvers tilted up and away from the wind or of vertical laths spaced about half an inch apart will last longer and do a better job.

PLANTS FOR THE SHORE
Exposure to wind, salt spray, and exceptional tides will dictate the choice of plants for a coastal property. For areas open to salt spray, high tides, and brine-laden wind, your choice of plants is limited to those that tolerate salt. For land protected by natural or man-made barriers or that is well back from the open beach, you can consider any garden ornamental that grows well in light, sandy soil.

ORNAMENTAL GRASSES: No garden plants appear more at home at the shore than do the ornamental grasses. Between early spring and late summer they grow up and lift exquisite light-catching inflorescences to the wind. A trim and some fertilizer in the spring is all the annual maintenance required.

Ornamental grasses seem especially at home when there are marsh grasses in the background. If your property includes brackish marshes, you will more than likely be blessed with dramatic stands of the common reed (*Phragmites australis*), which plants itself on both our coasts and in wet places almost everywhere. This extraordinarily tall plant can reach 14 feet. Reeds can be used as a natural design element, but don't tamper with wetlands: They are protected by the Environmental Protection Agency, even from you. You can plant ornamental grasses on the garden side of the marsh so that the reeds stand in the background, and they will unite the garden visually to the shore grasses, the sea, and the sky.

Ornamental grasses edging a swatch of lawn grass that curves gracefully towards the shore makes a simple, lovely, low-maintenance landscape for a small property. If you want to inject more dramatic color, you can interplant the ornamental grasses with a few naturalized perennials. The flowers can be left to ripen seeds after the blooms go by and there will be banquets and nesting materials for birds. I think it is also nice to add comfortable stopping places that invite meditation and have interest in all four seasons.

For a small property, moderately sized grasses work best. Blue wild rye (*Leymus secalinus*, syn. *Elymus glaucus*), a rapid-spreading, bold dune binder is only knee-high; the leaves are a marvelous blue-green. Prairie cord grass (*Spartina pectinata*) is a spreading grass with a graceful drooping habit that makes it seem less tall than its 4- to 6-foot height. It shows off wonderfully when it is massed on a slight incline or tumbling down towards the water's edge. The leaves of its somewhat taller

ORNAMENTAL GRASSES FOR THE SHORE

Blue fescue cultivars
Festuca glauca 'Sea Urchin', 'Spring Blue' Z4-9

Blue lyme grass, blue wild rye
Leymus secalinus Z4-9

Fountain grass
Pennisetum alopecuroides Z6-9

Japanese silver grass
Miscanthus sinensis Z5-9

Large blue fescue
Festuca amethystina Z4-9

Maiden grass
Miscanthus sinensis 'Gracillimus' Z6-9

Pampas grass
Cortaderia selloana 'Pumila', 'Sunningdale Silver' Z6-10

Prairie cord grass
Spartina pectinata Z5-9

Sea oats
Uniola paniculata Z6-9

Switch grass 'Heavy Metal'
Panicum virgatum Z4-10

Tall purple moor grass
Molinia caerulea ssp. *arundinacea* Z4-8

Variegated purple moor grass
Molinia caerulea 'Variegata' Z4-8

Zebra grass
Miscanthus sinensis 'Zebrinus' Z5-9

The cup-shaped blossom of Mexican ivy, or cup-and-saucer vine (*Cobaea scandens*), is a tender perennial that grows rapidly to 25 feet and produces masses of foliage. Vines grow quickly at the shore and are wonderfully useful for screening, shading, and softening harsh contours.

Euphorbia polychroma, a near relative of the showy poinsettia, grows 15 to 18 inches high and is topped all spring with bright yellow bracts. The leaves turn reddish in fall. In humus-improved sandy soil, euphorbias and other perennials that require good drainage do extremely well.

'Purple Wave' petunia is one of many brilliant cultivars of this beautiful but tender bedding plant. Window boxes and hanging baskets of petunias succeed at the shore in sheltered locations where they are protected from the searing winds and salt spray.

Like a great sculpture framed by an azure pool and the serene blue surface of a salt water bay, a manzanita tree (*Arctostaphylos*) raises its shapely arms to the sky. Native to North America, the manzanitas are evergreens of the heath family.

variegated cultivar ('Aureomarginata') have an interesting yellow edge.

On a large property, you can easily use tall grasses massed in drifts. You plan to anchor key points, as nature does, with small trees or tall shrubs, such as Japanese black pine or holly. The grasses can be interplanted with perennials that go wild with ease, for example, daylilies and fernleaf yarrow (*Achillea filipendulina* 'Coronation Gold'), and border these with smaller grass species and sweeps of jade green sedum 'Autumn Joy'. In early fall the grasses turn various shades of gold, and the sedum colors russet-pink-coral, then fades to a rich red-brown. Clumps of ornamental grasses standing tall and golden in snow make exquisite winter vignettes.

A tall grass excellent in mass plantings is the 8-foot-high sea oats (*Uniola paniculata*). It matures exceptionally beautiful panicles of nodding, flat, oatlike seedheads an inch wide and 2 inches long. Big bold species of gorgeous Japanese silver grass (*Miscanthus* spp.) also excel at filling large spaces. I find the broad, gracefully arching leaves of the variegated eulalia grass (*M. sinensis* 'Variegatus') delightful against a background of common reed. The silky, foot-long seedheads are pale pink to red, opening to silvery white. For contrast you could include the upright zebra grass (*M. sinensis* 'Zebrinus') in plantings of the arching species; its leaves have horizontal yellow bands.

I think it is difficult to keep a lawn beautiful on a sandy seaside property, so why not continue the ornamental grasses to the entrance of the property? You might want to use some of the midsize and low-growing grasses, along with the taller ones, in mixed groups combining contrasts in height, growth habit, and color and form. To watch tall purple moor grass (*Molinia caerulea* ssp. *arundinacea* 'Windspiel') tossing in the breeze next to the soft brushes of *Pennisetum alopecuroides* and the frothy plumes of *Miscanthus sinensis* 'Gracillimus' is a delight. For fall color, include switchgrass (*Panicum virgatum*), a narrow, upright plant 3 to 4 feet tall that produces clouds of buff-brown spikelets on open panicles up to 2 feet long. With the cold, the finely cut leaves turn bright yellow. Several cultivars have richly colored red, purple, or brown seedheads and autumn foliage.

TREES: A variety of beautiful trees live and even prosper in the teeth of coastal winds, growing more weathered, more interesting, and more beautiful with time. There are evergreens, deciduous shade trees, and even flowering trees to choose from. If you search your local nurseries for beautiful improved varieties of the shore's own

VINES FOR THE SHORE

Bittersweet
Celastrus scandens Z3-8

Clematis hybrids
Clematis cvs. Variably hardy

Climbing roses
Rosa spp, cvs. Variably hardy

Cup-and-saucer vine
Cobaea scandens Annual

Hyacinth bean,
Lablab purpureus Annual

Morning glory and moonflower
Ipomoea spp. Annual

Perennial pea
Lathyrus latifolius Z5-9

Silver lace vine
Polygonum aubertii Z4-7

Sweet autumn clematis
Clematis terniflora Z4-9

Trumpet vine
Campsis radicans Z4-10

Virginia creeper
Parthenocissus quinquefolia Z3-9

In late summer silver lace vine (*Polygonum aubertii*) covers a shoreside arbor with a fleece of small white flowers. Fast-growing and vigorous, the plant is capable of growing 20 to 30 feet in a single season. The ornamental grass is *miscanthus*.

199

The dainty brownish seedheads of purple moor grass (*Molinia caerulea* 'Altissima'), mauve alliums on their tall, slender stems, with white and purple lavender, golden yarrow, and Japanese silver grass (*Miscanthus sinensis*) all bend to breezes from the sea in a garden designed to wed the property to the beach and the water. Wetlands and salt marshes make striking backdrops for ornamental grasses, and the drama of the setting invites plantings that are bold and romantic. No garden ornamentals appear more natural at the shore than the ornamental grasses. Interplanted with naturalized perennials, the grasses lead the eye to the ocean with long, casual sweeps of color that change with the seasons. Between early spring and late summer the grasses grow up and lift exquisite light-catching inflorescences to the wind; a haircut and fertilization in January are the only annual maintenance required.

trees and shrubs, your garden will be colorful, healthy, and easy to care for.

If you have space for only one tree, make it an evergreen. Many narrow-leaved evergreens thrive in sandy soil, including handsome varieties of yew and pine. One of the best evergreens for landscaping shore properties that I know of is the Japanese black pine (*Pinus thunbergii*). It's a smallish tree with lots of character and stiff, dark green needles. The candles in spring and the cones in summer are handsome. Japanese black pine has outstanding salt tolerance and succeeds right at the edge of the beach. In time it grows wonderfully gnarled.

If you have additional space, plant a big deciduous tree for summer shade and seasonal change. The London plane tree (*Platanus × acerifolia*) withstands saline environments and high winds. Long-lived and beautiful, with attractive mottled bark, it can be pruned repeatedly. 'Columbia' and 'Liberty' are disease-resistant cultivars. Another good shade tree is the medium-tall sycamore maple, or plane tree maple (*Acer pseudoplatanus*), which flourishes in conditions other maples do not tolerate. The leaves of the colorful cultivar 'Brilliantissimum' unfold shrimp pink, change to yellow, then to green. In warm regions the holly oak (*Quercus ilex*) is commonly the preferred shade tree at the shore. Round-headed with wide spreading branches, for centuries it has provided cool shade for European gardeners contemplating the shining sea on hot summer days.

Some small flowering trees do well at the shore if you can protect the blossoms from the wind by planting the trees in the lee of a building, a fence, or a larger tree. One of the best-loved is the pretty little serviceberry (*Amelanchier canadensis*), which grows wild in open woodlands, bogs, and swamps along the East Coast to the Carolinas. Clusters of delicate white flowers appear in early spring, followed by berries that attract the birds. In fall the foliage turns yellow, orange, or dark red. Another little beauty, Japanese clethra (*Clethra barbinervis*), is covered with large clusters of fragrant white flowers in midsummer and has beautiful bark. It may be hard to find but is worth a search. The pink-flowered Lavalle hawthorn (*Crataegus × lavallei*) is gorgeous in bloom, and birds love the bright orange-red berries that follow. The foliage is glossy and turns bronze or copper red with the cold.

Other small trees that do well near the shore and will add to the charm of your garden are tamarisk (*Tamarix ramosissima*) and sour gum (*Nyssa sylvatica*). Tamarisk bears feathery, pink flower clusters, and it is an excellent sand binder. Sour gum, although difficult to transplant, is worth trying for the incomparable scarlet of its fall color.

SHRUBS: For exposed locations, you can choose improved varieties of native coastal shrubs, and you should. These cultivars are tough and handsome, they withstand the elements, and they can turn aside the wind and shelter more tender species. One of the most salt tolerant is bayberry (*Myrica pensylvanica*), a beautiful semi-evergreen. I like to see it paired with the smaller, rounded beach plum (*Prunus maritima*), whose branches are covered with white flowers in spring, followed by colorful fruit in the fall. Both shrubs grow wild along the Atlantic coast, bloom modestly, and have historic interest: Scented, waxy bayberry was used by early settlers to make candles, and beach plum was, and still is, used in jellies. Though more beautiful than the original species plants, the improved varieties are still at home next to the ocean. On the West Coast broom is used as a windbreak, and salal (*Gaultheria shallon*), which is native from Alaska to California, makes a fine ground cover. Salal

TREES FOR THE SHORE

American holly
Ilex opaca Z5-9

Austrian Black Pine,
Pinus nigra Z4-7/8

Japanese black pine
Pinus thunbergii Z4-8

Lavalle hawthorn
Crataegus × lavallei Z4-8

Leyland cypress
× Cupressocyparis leylandii Z6-10

London plane tree
Platanus × acerifolia Z4-8/9

Red maple
Acer rubrum Z3-9

Shawblow, serviceberry
Amelanchier canadensis Z4-8

Sour gum, black gum
Nyssa sylvatica Z3-9

Sweet bay magnolia
Magnolia virginiana Z6-9

Sycamore maple
Acer pseudoplatanus Z4-7

OPPOSITE:
With tall trees as a living windbreak, stately hollyhocks and bee balm (*Monarda*) grow lush in a coastal Rhode Island garden by the sea. The garden is planted in well-mulched raised beds.

203

OPPOSITE:
Protected by the dunes from frequent sea winds and salt spray, little blue kingfisher daisies (*Felicia bergeriana*), tall, daisylike *Osteospermum,* golden freesias, stands of red-hot poker (*Kniphofia*), and other perennials and annuals display a breathtaking array of colors.

RIGHT:
Rose campion (*Lychnis coronaria*), daisies, and bright orange pot marigolds (*Calendula officinalis*) carpet a sloping bank with vibrant color. The rose campion and the daisies are perennials that have naturalized; calendula is an annual that self-sows under good conditions.

has dark, leathery, evergreen leaves, clusters of pink, urn-shaped flowers, and edible purple-black fruits. Sand myrtle (*Leiophyllum buxifolium*) is often used in exposed positions in southeastern coastal areas. It's a broadly spreading, fine-textured shrub, whose summer green turns to bronze in cool weather. In spring through early summer it is covered with a froth of dainty, waxy buds that open to white flowers. Sand myrtle isn't easy to establish, but it does well in sandy, moist soil and, once established, flourishes without care.

Many of the familiar evergreen shrubs succeed very close to salt water, especially the junipers. They come in all sizes and thrive in sandy soil. Among many that I consider excellent ground covers are the salt-tolerant Sargent juniper (*Juniperus sargentii*) and shore juniper (*J. conferta*). Both are about a foot high with a very wide spread. I recommend *J. chinensis* 'Sea Spray' where winter temperatures fall well below zero. It has beautiful blue-green foliage, and is hardy to -20°F.

For diversity, you can plant broom (*Cytisus*), a carefree, rounded shrub that flourishes by the shore on both East and West Coasts, and in dry, sandy soils in between. Its long, graceful, weeping stems are nearly leafless, but they are covered with small, pealike flowers in spring or summer. The usual flower color is yellow, but there are rose pink, red, and even deep reddish purple varieties. Another interesting and very different plant for sandy places is Adam's needle (*Yucca filamentosa*). It forms a huge evergreen rosette of silvery, sword-shaped leaves and puts up an astonishing creamy white flower spike in early summer.

For fall color and brilliant displays of foliage or fruits, intersperse among the shore-lovers rugosa roses, barberry, rock cotoneaster, the bittersweets (*Celastrus*), and red osier dogwood (*Cornus stolonifera*), a multi-stemmed, vase-shaped deciduous shrub whose bark turns a vivid coral red in winter. Another colorful native is shining sumac (*Rhus copallina*), a tall shrub or small tree that bears greenish flowers in dense clusters, followed by red fruit and glossy red foliage in fall. You can also count on brilliant fall color from the Virginia creeper (*Parthenocissus quinquefolia*), a handsome deciduous vine.

Many flowering shrubs thrive in sandy soils and at the shore as long as you plant them, like the flowering trees, in an area sheltered from the wind. In the cooler regions, the graceful fountain buddleja (*Buddleja alternifolia*) does very well, as do lavender, tamarisk, and the exquisite, hardy *Fuchsia magellanica,* but the great flowering shrub for summer color at the shore is the hydrangea (*H. macrophylla*). Both the lacecap types and the round-headed Hortensias thrive in this atmosphere. The big, showy, long-lasting flowers appear in mid-to-late summer. Lacecap flowerheads are composed of small fertile flowers surrounded by rings of much larger sterile flowers; Hortensias bear big globe-shaped flowerheads composed entirely of fertile florets. Color ranges from cream through rose to dark blue and depends on soil pH: In acid soil the flowers are blue; as the soil becomes less acidic, the flowers become lavender, and then pink. To maintain the blue color every year or two apply to the soil a gallon of water in which has been dissolved a tablespoon of alum. To maintain the pink color, keep the soil pH in the range of 6.0 to 6.5, or slightly higher, by adding lime (see page 234).

In warm climates many showy flowering shrubs succeed in coastal gardens. *Pittosporum tobira* and the lovely oleander (*Nerium oleander*) are among the most successful. *Elaeagnus angustifolia* and *E. multiflora,* tall shrubs with willowlike leaves often used in high hedges, open fragrant, cream-yellow flowers in spring followed by sweet, mealy, orange fruit appealing to birds. Myrtle (*Myrtus communis*) thrives in sandy beach soil or in a pot and flowers for five or six weeks in summer. The beautiful creamy white fluff balls are followed by bluish black berries.

ROSES: Roses flourish by the sea on both coasts, in both cool and warm climates. Planted beyond the reach of salt spray, even some of the difficult hybrids thrive, and a climber will cover a cottage with ravishing blooms in just a few years. In exposed locations good choices are the sprawling Virginia rose (*Rosa virginiana*), an excellent ground cover and soil binder, and the tall, stiff, but gorgeous *Rosa rugosa*. The Virginia rose is one of the most beautiful of all native roses and an excellent performer in sandy soils, particularly by the sea. The flowers, which appear in June and July, are 2 inches across and fragrant, pale pink, and single. White and double pink cultivars are available. In autumn the foliage changes to orange red, crimson, then yellow. The rose hips ripen to a glistening red and persist in winter. Though it has

GROUND COVERS FOR THE SHORE

Aaron's beard, Creeping St. Johnswort
Hypericum calycinum Z5-9

Arrow broom, winged broom
Genista sagittalis Z5-9

Bearberry
Arctostaphylos uva-ursi Z2-7

Black chokeberry
Aronia melanocarpa Z4-9

Dusty miller
Artemisia stelleriana Z3-9

Heather
Calluna vulgaris Z4-7

Low-growing stonecrops, sedums
Hylotelephium, Sedum spp. Z4-9

Rat-stripper, Canby paxistima
Paxistima canbyi Z3-8

Sand myrtle
Leiophyllum buxifolium Z5-8

Sea thrift
Armeria maritima Z4-7

Virginia rose
Rosa virginiana Z3-10

Woolly thyme
Thymus pseudolanuginosus Z4-7

Wormwood, artemisia
Artemisia spp, cvs. Z3/5-9

On Oregon's coast, dahlia cultivar 'Julliard' blooms in the shelter of a tall wooden fence and a house. With sedums, mums, and asters, dahlias are the major source of color for the garden in the autumn.

207

Sheltered by tall trees, irises and roses bloom together in a garden of perennials.

been named for a mid-Atlantic state, it grows wild as far north as Newfoundland and flourishes on both coasts.

Rugosa roses are so trouble-free they have become the darlings of hybridizers. Rugged plants with spiny canes, superb hedge material, and handsome planted in clumps, they are so salt-tolerant they are used to hold oceanside slopes. Luscious new varieties come on line in the nursery catalogs every year. Some are fragrant, and there are now many doubles. Rugosas flower in the spring and summer, and, if they are deadheaded, many hybrids bloom again. One that can be counted on for a second showing in the fall is 'Sir Thomas Lipton', which produces masses of large, fragrant, double white flowers.

PERENNIALS: In a protected location, in humus-improved soil, you can grow any number of the perennial flowers that prefer well-drained or sandy soils and withstand wind, sun, and spells of drought. Japanese anemones, daylilies, mums, euphorbias, tall bearded irises, coreopsis, gaillardia, heuchera, lupines, valarian, and veronicas are just a few of such shore-worthy plants.

In salty marshes, statice, or sea lavender (*Limonium latifolium*), thrives. It's about 30 inches tall and bears large feathery panicles of small, bright mauve flowers. Feathery yarrow (*Achillea* spp.) grows exuberantly to 3 feet in a sunny spot. The showy, flat-topped yellow, pink, or off-white flowerheads are several inches across. For yellow accents I recommend 'Coronation Gold' and 'Moonshine'; for rosy colors, plant 'Cerise Queen', 'Paprika', and the spicy rose red 'Fire King'. For contrasting form and texture use sea holly (*Eryngium maritimum*), a dramatic thistlelike plant about a foot high. The flowerheads are bright blue and the spiny foliage, silver to blue-gray. Of the perennials that will naturalize in exposed locations, Russian sage (*Perovskia atriplicifolia*) is one of the tallest and most attractive. This 3-foot, silver-stemmed plant covers itself in summer with airy spikes of tiny, powder blue flowers. At a distance a drift of Russian sage looks like lavender blue mist.

Naturalized sweeps of perennials and grasses are especially lovely if you edge them with silver and white accents. Dusty miller (*Artemisia stelleriana*), a native to the northeastern coast, has thick, woolly white leaves, and thrives on beaches above the high-tide line. Clouds of white 'Silver King', 'Silver Queen', and 'Silver Mount' artemisia look exquisite next to flowers in shades of pink, purple, and light blue. Dwarf lavender cotton (*Santolina chamaecyparissus* 'Nana') is a half-shrubby evergreen with aromatic foliage that is white underneath and silvery in the moonlight.

For fall flower color, you should plant the tough-but-beautiful sedums. One to 3 feet tall, their summer color is a soft jade green, which changes late in the season. 'Autumn Joy' turns from pink in summer to salmon in late summer, then to rosy russet in fall; the slightly smaller 'Ruby Glow' turns ruby red.

ADDING VIBRANT COLOR

In a moderately exposed sandy site the everlastings and some of the brilliantly colored and tough annual flowers will do well. African daisies (*Arctotis venusta*), daisy-like gazanias, various species of sunflowers (*Helianthus*), and Madagascar periwinkle (*Catharanthus roseus*) all succeed. With shelter from the wind and salt, ageratum, calendula, globe amaranth, marigolds, cosmos, and even petunias bloom over a long season. For edgers, sweet alyssum and cottage pinks will do very well in sandy soil.

If you lack a suitable in-ground location, you always can plant annuals in containers. Plants in hanging baskets, window boxes, and planters thrive in a humid shore atmosphere. Geraniums bloom as they do nowhere else, petunias seem all to be fragrant, and portulaca, verbena, and lantana are brilliantly colored and quickly overflow their containers. In a location out of the wind and direct sun, planters filled with tuberous begonias and fuchsias will make a fantastic showing.

You should fill the containers with commercial potting soil rather than with the local sandy soil. As with all container plants, check their moisture needs often, but, with all the humidity, container plants at the shore usually do not need to be watered as often as when they are growing inland.

African daisy, 'Wine'
Arctotis × *hybrida*

African daisies
Arctotis venusta, hybrids

California poppy
Eschscholzia californica

Cosmos
Cosmos bipinnatus, C. sulphureus

Dahlias
Dahlia species and hybrids

Garden geraniums
Pelargonium × *domesticum*

Gazania, treasure flower
Gazania rigens

Globe amaranth
gomphrena globosa

Madagascar periwinkle
*Catharanthus roseus*t

Marigolds
Tagetes erecta, T. patula

Sage, salvia
Salvia spp., cvs.

Spider flower
cleome hasslerana

Strawflower
Helichrysum bracteatum

Sunflower
Helianthus spp.

Sweet alyssum
Lobularia maritima

Zinnia
Zinnia elegans

SPECIAL MAINTENANCE CONSIDERATIONS

Plants that succeed at the shore tend to grow marvelously well, and in a few years they outgrow their settings. Almost as soon as the garden looks full, it will begin to seem overgrown. Prune the plants back annually to keep new young shoots coming and to keep them in bounds. Periodic trimming will work marvels.

ROCK
GARDENS

I took a day to search for God,
And found Him not. But as I trod
By rocky ledge, through woods untamed,
Just where one scarlet lily flamed,
I saw His footprint in the sod.

WILLIAM BLISS CARMAN

A rock garden recreates in miniature the romance of a flowering meadow in the high mountains where the water is snow-melt, the air is thin, and great winds dwarf the trees and the shrubs. Blue-green rock cress, silvery lady's mantle, purple blue anemones, buttercup yellow hypericum, and other lovely little alpine plants cling to the stony earth and bloom as soon as they can in the short summer season. Most often the slope is littered with stones covered with gray-green lichen, patches of rocky scree, charming little shrubs, and trailing, creeping, and tufted perennials. At the bottom of the incline there may be a cool little pond lined with gravel.

To be authentic, an alpine rock garden should be planted with natives of cold, high mountainous regions. Since most alpines flourish only at high altitudes, collectors at lower altitudes grow many of them in containers in cool greenhouses. The landscapes of the highland wilds have a strong appeal for many gardeners, however, and so rock garden design has come to include, along with the easiest of the alpines, diminutive species and brightly flowered creeping plants that succeed in other climates. Instead of ending naturally at a pond, a rock garden often slopes to a low stone wall whose rugged contours are softened by creeping phlox, blazing blue gentians (*Gentiana scabra*), sedums, and the feathery foliage of *Corydalis lutea*.

Nature's design of the highland landscape can be used to make a bald, stony, and otherwise uninviting slope into an evocative, colorful, and fascinating garden. I consider the most dramatic natural site for a rock garden to be a series of bedrock outcroppings streaked with crevices that can be made to simulate pools or a stream. Other beautiful settings are a ridge that drops away to a rocky slope and an open, stone-strewn mound rising from a low point. A sharp change in grade between two

The rock garden at Babbacombe Model Village in Devon mimics a flowering meadow in the high mountains with plantings of trees and shrubs that might have been dwarfed by strong winds, a slope littered with stones and patches of rocky scree and, at the bottom of the incline, a stream spilling over rocks into a cool little pond. The golden *Chamaecyparis*, the red and the white tuberous begonias, and many other of these plantings are garden ornamentals, not the alpine plants used in authentic rock gardens. Alpine natives grow best in cold, high regions, so rock garden design has come to include diminutive species and brightly flowered creeping plants that succeed in many other environments.

relatively level areas will provide you with excellent possibilities. I have even seen a barren slope without significant rock formations transformed by hauling in native boulders and rocks.

If there's a choice, the most desirable exposure for many of the rock garden plants is east, west, or northwest. Usually shallow-rooted, they are likely to suffer in the intense summer sun and heat of a southern exposure. The design and terrain of a rock garden are such that with careful planning, however, light conditions can be created to meet the needs of a variety of plants. Shade lovers will thrive in the shadow of large rocks and of taller, sun-seeking plants.

DESIGNING A ROCK GARDEN

The plan for a rock garden develops in two directions: the placement of the rocks and the placement of the plants. An ideal way to begin is to take photographs of the site. Working on graph paper and from the photographs, make a rough sketch defining the garden's boundaries. Indicate the positions of stone outcrops or immovable

Low-growing alpine-type plants imitate the variegated patterns of an alpine meadow amid rugged native rock formations at Ohme Gardens in Wenatchee, Washington. Stone pathways connect the various levels, and soaring evergreens point to the sky.

boulders, and of plants that are perfect just where they are. I would try to design around any healthy shrub under 2 feet tall and tufts of grasses whose fall gold will burnish the late garden. Then make and cut out drawings made to scale of features that are attractive and that *can* be moved or removed. All stones, large and small, should be retained, especially stones colored by lichen and mosses.

The cutouts of these movable elements can be positioned on the graph in their present locations. I find it helpful to try them in various other places, seeking to develop a rough concept of a satisfying arrangement of stones and open planting places. Your goal is to design a planting bed strewn artlessly, as though by nature, with sculptural boulders, interesting stones, and attractive open areas. The largest movable rocks, for instance, should be positioned at the base of the slope and set at angles that follow the natural stratification of rock formations in your garden or region. In places on the slope where the incline is steep, arrange a lot of rocks as they might be in nature and to keep the soil from eroding.

Where the slope is gentler, leave the land more open. Here and there near large rocks, plan to have scree beds, patches of stone chips that will be home to plants requiring especially good drainage. Smaller rocks can be set singly and in twos and threes here and there as though they had fallen down the slope. Where material for balance and harmony is lacking, add cutouts of the missing elements to your plan and include them on your running list of materials you'll have to acquire.

It is a good idea to leave small, gently rounded spaces open. These can be planted as miniature mountain meadows that will soften your rock garden. On slopes that seem too steep for planting, you can level off sections as terraces every 2 or 3 feet. Rocks can then be rearranged so that once planted, the terracing will seem natural. Above all, you should eliminate anything movable that doesn't enhance the scene.

CHOOSING THE PLANTS

The sides of the rock garden will be defined by its dwarf shrubs and trees. The most attractive base you can devise for a rock garden is water sheeting over rocks into a small pool, but I have seen beautiful rock gardens that end in a wall garden or a lawn. The decision may already have been made for you by the location of your rock garden. Whatever the boundaries are, you should indicate these on your plan as well.

Now that you have defined the rock garden's boundaries, emphasize and enhance them with plants. Again, use cutouts as models for your choices, and shift the cutouts around on the graph paper until you are satisfied with your garden artistry. If you would like screening at the top of the site, one or two standard-size trees can be planted there. For a dense screen, fill in around the trees with shrubs. If you don't need or want screening at all, a stand of tall grasses can be planted to point to an attractive view or to the sky and the clouds.

In addition to dwarf shrubs and trees, a rock garden needs ground covers to carpet and green some of the barren areas and tufts of grasses to soften its rocky out-line. Flowering perennials, the garden's chief ornaments, should be positioned after the foundation plantings are in place. Annuals can provide quick and easy color and can be placed in spaces that you will later give to elegant little rockery plants that may be hard to find, such as alpine lady's mantle (*Alchemilla alpina*), which has silver-edged leaves and sprays of small yellow-green flowers in spring; evergreen rock jasmine (*Androsace sarmentosa*), with its showy, bright pink flowers; and trailing gray-green *Anacyclus pyrethrum* var. *depressus,* whose yellow-centered, daisylike flowers are

crimson beneath. Edelweiss (*Leontopodium alpinum*), scarcely 8 inches high even in bloom, looks as though it is made of white flannel; it is for many the symbol of the alpine meadows. At its heart, a rock garden is a collector's garden, even when its plantings aren't exclusively alpines. Acquiring new species that refine and enhance the composition of your rock garden adds to your joy year after year. The American Rock Garden Society, organized in 1934, is a great help in locating alpines and other wildflowers, and a lot can be learned about the rock garden from the quarterly bulletin included in the annual dues.

FOUNDATION PLANTS: The dwarf shrubs and trees and the small columnar evergreens that mark the side boundaries of a rock garden look best planted on larger terraces and set among big rocks. Arrange them in twos or threes chosen for contrast in height, form, and foliage. Many familiar landscape evergreens are available in dwarf varieties well suited to a rock garden. I look for upright evergreens like the conical dwarf Alberta spruce (*Picea glauca* var. *albertiana* 'Conica') and for interesting low-growing varieties of cedar, cypress, and yew. The elegant dark green weeping hemlock (*Tsuga canadensis* var. *pendula*) makes a handsome anchor when set toward the base of the rock garden. One of the most beautiful of the vertical evergreens is the dwarf Hinoki cypress (*Chamaecyparis obtusa* 'Intermedia'); I find especially appealing the combination of a tall and a smaller Hinoki cypress grouped with sprawling flowering shrubs, such as fragrant, pink-flowered *Daphne cneorum* and yellow-flowered potentilla. The variegated daphne is a particularly beautiful specimen that I love to feature; potentilla, which flowers all season, and barberry, whose foliage and berries are aflame in autumn, are wonderful used together in zigzag patches of gold and red up through the rocks and terraces. Rockspray cotoneaster (*Cotoneaster horizontalis*), with its brilliant fall display of red berries, is also delightful spaced throughout the garden.

On the smaller terraces, interspersed among the clumps of shrubbery, I find that the dwarf heaths and brooms add a graceful line. Some flower beautifully: Spike heath (*Bruckenthalia spiculifolia*), a low shrub related to heather, bears delightful little pink flowers in late spring, and *Genista pilosa* 'Vancouver Gold', a member of the pea family, produces fountains of small yellow blooms. I like to see tufts of low ornamental grasses here and there, bending and tossing with the wind. Buff, tan, sea green, gold, and blue—the ornamental grasses are perfect foils for the bright horizontal planes that will be created throughout the garden by the creeping and trailing flowering plant. The fescues form pretty clumps of fine-textured grass that shade from bright green to silver blue; blue fescue (*Festuca glauca*) is one of the easy alpines to cultivate. And small islands of spiky Japanese blood grass (*Imperata cylindrica* 'Rubra') planted where the light catches the leaves fully justify the plant's common name.

GROUND COVERS: Evergreen ground covers that flower do double duty in your rock garden. A charming plant for miniature meadows and terraces is mat-forming bearberry (*Arctostaphylos uva-ursi*). The glossy green foliage turns bronze or plum in winter, and the pink-tinted, urn-shaped flowers that appear in late spring and early summer are followed in the fall by lustrous red fruit attractive to birds. The dainty, shiny, dark green foliage of myrtle, *Vinca minor,* looks wonderful cascading between rocks, and its modest spring display of small lavender blue flowers is lovely; it will thrive in the shadier parts of your rock garden as well. Be sure to include lots of sedums, which hold their colorful foliage—soft jade, red, purple, bronze—all winter

The feathery panicles of crimson and ivory astilbes glow in the last rays of the setting sun as dusk creeps over beds of achillea, lavender, and other perennials in a rock garden located in Singer, Massachusetts.

long, and set other succulents, such as hen and chickens (*Sempervivum tectorum*), to creep over their rocky surroundings.

Many aromatic herbs make handsome ground covers; in fact, many of the most pungent thrive in the gravely soil of rock gardens. Heatherlike lavenders look well standing before evergreen shrubs, and they are amazingly fragrant growing on a sunny slope. Add a patch of catmint (*Nepeta cataria*) for the mist of dainty lavender blossoms that hover over it in late spring. The standard rosemaries look like little pine trees and are delightful paired with creeping rosemary (*Rosmarinus officinalis* var. *prostratus*), an excellent soil binder.

If you search the herb specialists' catalogs, you will find unusual varieties to add to your garden. Beside the larger catalogs, I make a point of checking out what Fox Hollow Herbs of McGrann, Pennsylvania, and Nichols Garden Nursery of Albany, Oregon, are offering when I am looking for new varieties. I have been intrigued by some of the new-to-me oreganos and thymes. *Origanum rotundifolium,* for example, has chartreuse bracts that show off beautifully against rocks. And there's gold for the garden in *O. vulgare* 'Aureum', *Thymus vulgaris* 'Golden Edge', and *T. serpyllum* 'Aureus', which creeps irrepressibly up hill, down dale, over, and among rocks. *Artemisia caucasica* looks like flowing silver, and gray-blue A. 'Powis Castle' is very attractive next to tufts of ornamental grass. The leaves of golden lamb's ears, (*Stachys byzantina*) 'Aureus', are so softly furred they make stroking irresistible.

FLOWERING CREEPERS, TRAILERS, AND TUFTS: The stars of rockeries and wall gardens are little flowering perennials that creep, trail, tuft, and mound. For a spring-long show of luscious pastels, plant lots of the creeping phloxes. In early to midspring, the lovely moss pink (*Phlox subulata*) covers itself with clusters of tiny starry flowers that are blue, purple, white, or bright pink with a darker eye. It can stand partial or full sun and quickly carpets banks and slopes and cascades down rock walls; it is semi-evergreen in warm regions. Sand phlox (*Phlox bifida*) is a honey-scented little mound 6 inches high. Tiny trailing phlox (*P. nivalis* 'Camla') has rich pink flowers in late spring or early summer. For color contrast, set basket-of-gold (*Aurinia saxatilis*) to ramble over steep banks. Plants whose foliage contrasts with the dainty spreading phloxes are invaluable: *Armeria maritima* 'Dusseldorf Pride', for example, forms little pincushions of foliage covered with tight heads of pink-to-carmine red flowers. It begins to bloom as the phloxes go by.

While there are many colorful flowers that bloom in the rock garden in spring, keeping color in the garden in summer takes a little more thought. But it is the colors of the flowers that make the garden exciting and soften the monochromatic landscape of the rocks. Planting lots of little pinks and several bellflower varieties is a good beginning for a satisfying summer display. Some choice bellflowers for the rock garden are the little tussock bellflower (*Campanula carpatica*), a small form with gossamer blue cups spangled on a canopy of green; *C. glomerata* var. *acaulis,* a dwarf

SHRUBS FOR ROCK
GARDENS

Bearberry
Arctostaphylos uva-ursi Z2-7

Dwarf common juniper
Juniperus communis 'Compressa'
Z3-7

Dwarf Hinoki cypress
Chamaecyparis obtusa 'Nana
Pyramidalis', 'Intermedia' Z4-8

Dwarf Japanese holly
Ilex crenata cvs. Z6-9

Dwarf Japanese spiraea
Spiraea japonica 'Anthony Waterer'
Z4-9

Dwarf Japanese yew
Taxus cuspidata 'Minima' Z4-7

Dwarf white spruce
Picea glauca 'Conica', Z2-6

Heather and heaths
Calluna vulgaris, Erica spp. Z3/5-8

Rock cotoneaster
Cotoneaster horizontalis Z4-8

Rose daphne
Daphne cneorum Z4-7

Shrubby cinquefoil
Potentilla fruticosa cvs. Z3/5-8

Spike heath
Bruckenthalia spiculifolia Z6-8

Winged broom
Genista sagittalis Z4-8

Wilson barberry
Berberis wilsoniae cvs. Z5-9

222

summer bloomer, is violet-blue or white; and *C. rotundifolia* is the graceful harebell that bears blue flowers on slender, 6-to-18-inch stems in late spring and summer. Where more color is needed, annuals can fill in the gaps. I am particularly fond of *Fragaria* 'Improved Rugens', an unexpected, charming little alpine strawberry that is runnerless, stays neat, and has fruits that are edible, if not prolific. Sweet alyssum will carpet the fairy meadows and soften rocks with masses of tiny flowers in shades from snowy white to pink, mauve, or lavender. It blooms all summer and haunts early fall evenings with its sweet scent. For more vibrant color, plant miniature Fantasy petunias by the dozen in mixed shades. Tiny planting pockets can be planted with small wax begonias, Thumbelina zinnias, and *Zinnia angustifolia* (syn. *linearis*), a compact 8-inch plant that bears masses of single, golden orange, daisy-shaped flowers.

In late summer plant autumn crocuses for a fall show. *Colchicum autumnale* is big and blooms in shades of amethyst, purple, rose, violet, mauve, pink, and white. It's magnificent planted in drifts of twenty or more. Romantic 'Waterlily' has large, lilac pink, many-petaled double flowers that last for weeks. 'The Giant', with showy lavender-pink flowers that are white at the base, blooms first, followed by 'Album', a luminous white. For a later fall show, I love the dwarf asters (dependable *Aster alpinus* has flowers in white and shades of pink and purple), as well as *Dendranthema weyrichii* 'White Bomb' and its pink variety. These are creeping clump-forming mums with shiny green leaves that flower after most everything else is gone. *Gentiana scabra* var. *saxatilis,* a lovely low-growing plant that covers itself with remarkably blue flowers, blooms just before the garden shuts down for the year.

Since all, or many, of the flowers in a rock garden are low-growing, just a few beautiful tall perennials will create contrast and a little drama. The spring bulb flowers are very much at home in a rock garden. I love to see a scattering of bright

MAINTAINING A ROCK GARDEN

EARLY SPRING: Walk through the garden and the soil around the plants that have been heaved during the winter. Replace plants that have died. Add a top dressing of compost combined with sharp sand, or, around nonalpine plants, apply a light application of a slow-release fertilizer, such as 5-10-5. Remove dead growth. Prune partially dead branches back to healthy growth.

SUMMER: Trim back plants that have grown rampant, like gold alyssum and arabis. Allow them to trail over the nearby rocks or ground but prune back when they encroach on neighbors. Don't attempt to shape the plants into mounds: they should creep as in nature.

LATE SUMMER: During droughts water

thoroughly as necessary. Lift and divide plants to increase the supply of plants for the garden.

EARLY AUTUMN: When the cool air and *early* rains of autumn come, discard failing plants. Set out fresh material.

AFTER THE GROUND FREEZES: If there is no snow cover, apply a layer of evergreen branches, salt or marsh hay, or other light, airy material.

WALL GARDEN: In early spring and once during the summer, check the planting pockets. Repack planting pockets that need it with humus and soil, and replant loose roots and crowns. Feed heavy bloomers early in the growing season with a liquid houseplant fertilizer.

Darwin tulips winding their way up the terraces among miniature drifts of early spring-flowering bulbs, such as *Narcissus* 'Baby Moon' and *Iris cristata*. Wild bleeding heart (*Dicentra eximia*) and dwarf columbine (*Aquilegia flabellata* 'Nana') should be planted where they will have some shade in summer, but their showy display in late spring is worth the effort. Consider setting out two or three pairs of stately dwarf foxgloves as well. In bloom in the middle of the garden, they have immense presence. For summer color, woolly yarrow (*Achillea tomentosa*) is unbeatable.

You can next use cutouts to place some of the plants suggested, shifting them around on the graph until an outline emerges that satisfies your artistic sense. The planting plan should be finalized only after the rocks are in place and the site has been readied for planting. When you are satisfied with the arrangements of rocks and plants, create a path that will lead you through the garden. Its purpose is in part practical; it will allow you to plant and to maintain the garden without stepping on the plants or the soil or hopping from rock to rock. I appreciate the practical value of a path, but to me there are more important reasons. A path is the garden beckoning to you to run in for a visit, even if it is only for a moment. A path winding its way through your plantings also symbolizes the partnership between you and the

A field of heathers and heaths (*Calluna* and *Erica* spp.) in bloom includes whites and shades of pink and red; they combine well with many of the small alpines used in rock gardens.

OVERLEAF:
Masses of white sweet alyssum (*Lobularia maritima*) soften a composition of silvery rocks and sculptural succulents. Sweet alyssum blooms all summer and haunts early fall evenings with its sweet scent.

garden: It humanizes, makes the little plants more appealing, more yours, declares that this rocky place is tended with love. It can zigzag, or it can curve gracefully. You can cover it with shredded bark, pea-size gravel, or whatever material makes it blend best with your garden. If the garden is too small to accommodate a path, a series of flat stepping stones can be arranged so they lead invitingly through the garden.

PREPARING THE SITE

For most sites you will want to reposition some of the materials already there, and you may also need to buy additional rocks and other materials. You'll need stone chips, coarse sand, gravel, and yards of the prepared planting mix described below. The mix can be made from garden soil amended with coarse sand and humus or compost. If you need to bring in a lot of material, and especially if you plan to regrade the site to change the slope or to improve the drainage, you should seriously consider professional help.

Your driest season is the best time to undertake the makeover of a rock garden site. It's a good idea to schedule the work and the planting so that the garden will be ready to benefit from autumn rainfall. You should work from the plan on the graph, but, as rocks are moved and before they are dug into the soil, try to step back often and study the effect of the changes already made. A large rock moved a foot or two can make a difference in the balance and the harmony of the composition. Don't be in a hurry to get through this phase: Be sure the arrangement is satisfying before taking the next step.

Large boulders should be set on their broadest faces and dug far enough into the ground to secure their positions. Try to angle each rock slightly backward so that rain runs off towards the roots of the plants that will be set there. Slant the terraces you build downward and backward to the same degree. When you prepare pockets for plants that require very good drainage, as many alpines and rock garden plants do, try to give a slight forward pitch to the soil, to spill excess water. Around the rocks and at each planting site place a layer of coarse gravel or small rocks. Top this with enough prepared soil to bury half of each rock, or follow the Japanese style and bury each rock to the depth of its widest point.

The soil required by most rock garden plants is gritty and slightly acid (pH of 5.5 to 6.5). A good basic soil mix is half pea-sized gravel and coarse sand, and half humus or compost and garden loam. Adjust the pH if necessary as described on page 234. If rock formations in your garden are limestone, a pH test is important because the soil is almost sure to be too alkaline for some of the alpine plants. Since a rock garden consists of individual planting pockets and areas, rather than one continuous bed of soil, providing customized soil mixes that meet the needs of individual plants is easy. For plants requiring extra moisture, you should add to the prepared mix a larger proportion of humus or compost. For plants designated as needing very good drainage and for those that will be planted in scree, add to the basic mix a third small stone chips. For plants requiring more alkalinity, adjust the pH with limestone. It may be best to limit plants preferring alkaline soils to one area, so you can more easily control soil conditions, rather than to scatter them throughout the garden.

Most rock garden plants are adapted to poor, rocky soils and do not need to be fertilized; a top dressing of sand mixed with compost, or with acidic leaf mold for acid-loving types, applied each spring should be sufficient to keep them growing well all year. Gentians and primroses may benefit from a side dressing of compost or

FOLIAGE PLANTS FOR ROCK GARDENS

Corydalis, persistent species
Corydalis cheilanthifolia Z5-7
C. wilsonii Z6-7

Golden creeping thyme
Thymus serpyllum 'Aureus' Z4-10

Golden oreganot
Origanum vulgare 'Aureum' Z4-8

Hen and chickens, houseleeks
Sempervivum spp., cvs. Z4-9
Jovibarba spp., cvs. Z5-9

Lamb's ears
Stachys byzantina cvs. Z4-9

Oconee bells
Shortia galacifolia Z5-8

Pussytoes
Antennaria dioica 'Rosea' Z4-8

Silver tanacetum
Tanacetum argenteum Z5-7

Silvermound artemisia
Artemsia schmidtiana 'Nana' Z4-8

Snow-in-summer
Cerastium tomentosum Z4-7

Stonecrops, sedums
Sedum kamtschaticum cvs. Z4-9
S. lineare 'Variegatum' Z5-9
S. spathulifolium cvs. Z5-9
S. spurium 'Dragon's Blood', 'Tricolor', 'Purple Carpet' Z3-9

Variegated basket-of-gold
Aurinia saxatilis 'Variegata' Z3-7

Variegated wall rock cress
Arabis caucasica 'Variegata' Z4-8

Wintergreen
Gaultheria procumbens Z3-8

Woolly thyme
Thymus pseudolanuginosus Z4-7

OPPOSITE:
Lichen-covered rocks edge a semi-shaded path curving through beds of ferns, golden Asiatic poppies (*Meconopsis*), and coral bells (*Heuchera sanguinea*) nodding on wiry pink wands. A maroon red Japanese maple lends strength to the pastel composition.

composted manure. If you choose to fertilize some of the plantings, be restrained. Fertilizer should be applied lightly and only in early spring: Plants fertilized late in the season may not survive the winter.

PLANTING A ROCK GARDEN

When the rock garden site is ready for planting, rework the planting plan. Before you begin planting, make sure all the miniature meadows, planting terraces, and spaces between and around the rocks are packed with soil. Air pockets that roots can creep into and dry out will kill plants in short order. It is a good practice to gather in one place the seedlings and potted plants destined for a particular area, and to put them, or as many as you have available, in at the same time. Some planting pockets are bound to be so small they can hold only one plant. These you should consider filling with showy species, such as bright red pinks or golden yarrow. Midsize plants can be set out in groups of three or four of each variety, while very small plants and bulbs should be massed in drifts of twenty, fifty, or more. Plants that spread aggressively, like arabis and ajuga, should be confined to planting pockets between fairly large rocks. Set trailers like creeping phlox just above rocks so they can trail down over the stones. Shelter small, sensitive alpine plants from direct sun in the shadow of bigger rocks and taller plants. Set plants that require very good drainage in pockets of scree.

Water each planting hole thoroughly before setting the rootball into it. As you complete the planting for each area, use a sprinkler to apply another inch of water. Mulch around the plants (tuck it in well under the stems) and over the entire garden with at least an inch of coarse gravel, pebbles, or stone chips to discourage weeds and to keep the soil cool and protected from drying winds. A stone mulch selected to blend with the garden rocks will visually unite the elements of the garden in harmony. No additional mulch will be needed in winter if the climate provides a soft, thick blanket of snow from shortly after the ground freezes until danger of frost is past.

Where and when there is no snow cover, cover the plants with a light, airy mulch after the ground freezes hard. Evergreen branches are suitable, as is salt or marsh hay, straw, and leafy branches from an oak tree. Remove the mulch in spring when the plants show signs of vigorous growth. Be aware that such a mulch may prove to be winter quarters for chipmunks and mice, however; some rock gardeners prefer losing a few plants to winterkill to losing all of them to hungry rodents.

BUILDING A WALL GARDEN

A low, rocky wall garden equipped with rough stone steps is a charming approach to the rock garden. For me the stone façade evokes the mountains that lead to real gardens in the sky. I love the contrast between the enduring strength of ancient, weathered stones and the freshness and vulnerability of the flowers; it touches the poet within.

The first step in the building of a dry stone wall is to acquire a large supply of native quarry stones flat enough to lay one on another, as bricks are laid. Lay a footing of pea-sized gravel under the first course of stones at the base of the wall. Place a row of the longest, widest, and thickest stones over the gravel, straight edges facing away from the bank. Dig the stones into the earth of the bank about 10 inches, and angle them downward a little on the bank side. As it rises, the wall should tilt downward on the inside about 1 inch per foot of height. That's just enough to direct rainwater into the soil pockets and to the roots of the plants that will be growing there, and to prevent the soil from washing out.

Pack prepared rock garden soil mix behind and around each stone, and set 2 or 3 inches of soil on top. Place the next course of stones so they span the gaps between the first course of stones. As before, be sure to pack soil behind, around, and on top of the stones. Continue in this manner until the wall reaches the height you desire. For the last course save wide, flat, attractive stones, and set them flat side up so that pots, planters, and people can rest on the wall. It's a wonderful place to sit after you have been working in the garden on a hot summer day. The stone is cool against your skin, and invites you to be still and listen to the garden growing.

I am always amazed and charmed at how brightly the creeping, trailing rock garden plants bloom in a rock wall and in crevices in stone steps. Plant as many as you can while you actually are building the wall, but if you don't get them all in, you can plant them after the wall is completed. As you raise each course of stones, create soil pockets between and behind the rocks; place the plants in them, and pack improved soil in and around the roots and rootballs. When the wall is finished, complete the planting. Using a narrow trowel or a stick, dig out the soil between and behind the rocks that have not been planted to make space for roots. Work the roots into the space, pack the space half full with soil, wet the soil, then add more soil. Repeat until the surface of the soil is level with the crown of the plant. The crown mustn't project beyond the face of the wall. When you are finished planting, spray the wall garden with an inch or so of water from a sprinkler.

To help keep plants from drying out, try pressing moss over the soil. With luck, and a little extra watering now and then, the moss will grow and spread, and it will make the wall look as though it has been there for years and years.

LOW GROWING GRASSES
FOR ROCKERIES

Autumn moor grass
Sesleria autumnalis Z5-9

Blue hair grass
Koeleria glauca Z4-9

Blue oat grass
Helictotrichon sempervirens Z4-8

Fescue
Festuca glauca cvs. Z4-9
F. amethystina Z4-9

Japanese blood grass
Imperata cylindrica 'Rubra' Z5-9

Japanese sedge grass
Carex morrowii 'Variegata' Z6-9

Miniature variegated sedge
Carex conica 'Variegata' Z5-8

Mosquito grass, blue grama
Bouteloua gracilis Z3-10

Quaking grass
Briza media Z4-8

Tuber oat grass
Arrhenatherum elatius ssp.
bulbosum 'Variegatum' Z4-9

LEFT:
Purple false rockcress (*Aubrieta deltoidea*) forms a dense mat and blooms through spring and into early summer. A choice plant for a well-drained spot in a rock garden, it does especially well on the Pacific Coast.

OVERLEAF:
Drifts of sky blue forget-me-nots (*Myosotis sylvatica*) blend the colors in a patchwork quilt featuring deep pink false rockcress (*Aubretia deltoidea*), oxeye daisies, and marigolds. An endearing shade-loving flower 6 to 8 inches high, myosotis is grown as an annual or a biennial.

BASIC GARDENING TECHNIQUES

Throughout this book I refer to procedures that may not be familiar to you.
The following information is a quick course in the design,
preparation, and maintenance of your own glorious garden.

DESIGN

Some of the happiest moments in the creation of a new garden come in the early planning stages. To enjoy that time to the fullest, install yourself in a comfortable chair out in the yard with note pads, graph paper, pencil, eraser, and your favorite garden catalogs and books, and dream. In your mind's eye superimpose beautiful new trees and shrubs over the existing foundation plants until you find those you really like. Imagine yourself in the cool of early morning visiting the new flower beds and at night opening certain windows to breathe in the perfume of the roses and jasmine planted below. Walk around the property and consider how the new plantings will look from various perspectives outside and inside the house, from upstairs and downstairs. As your dreams become desires, list the plants you have in mind, first the foundation plants, trees, shrubs, ground covers, and vines, then the perennials, the bulbs, and the other flowers. Number the plants, and on a rough-scale outline of the property mark the position of each with a circle about the size you expect it to be. As you plan, decide how much of the work you want to do yourself and how much you will want help with. Most garden centers will deliver and plant your purchases, and provide a replacement warranty for an additional cost per plant. Many employ specialists in landscaping and design who can help you to draw up plans, often without charge.

About professional help: I think it's a good idea to call in a licensed landscape architect if you are planning to engineer important changes in the contours of the land. Landscape architects also design gardens: Ask to see some installations they consider successful before engaging their services. If you are concerned only with design, you might enjoy working with a landscape designer, at least in the beginning. Garden designers may be very creative, but they are not always schooled in the engineering aspects of landscaping: drainage, runoff, and so on.

The plant bed that you will find easiest to work is a narrow bed or an island with access to all the plants from the edge: Stepping on freshly prepared earth

compacts it. A gently curved bed and plant groups whose silhouettes are mounded and softly rounded have the most charm. A very tall tree next to a very small house or shrub can seem angular and ungainly. When you are choosing long-lived plants, such as trees and shrubs, scale and proportion are important considerations. Try to make sure that the mature size of large plants will be in scale with the property and the dwelling. The gigantic blue spruce you often see dwarfing a small front yard probably started out as a charming little live Christmas tree. The property would be more attractive now if the owners had planted instead the slow-growing Colorado blue spruce (*Picea pungens*) 'Hunnewelliana', which takes thirty years to reach 15 feet. The heights of trees given in gardening literature are often those of full-grown specimens in the wild: The heights attained by trees in cultivation may vary considerably from those norms.

This isn't to say that I'm opposed to big plants in small spaces: Big, bold hostas and a tall rhododendron tucked into a corner of a small patio can give the space character without making it seem crowded—and a few big plants are less trouble to care for than a whole lot of small ones. Small dainty plants in a small space can be charming, or cloying: Small dainty plants with one or two big bold plants make a dynamic combo. Plant size also can be used to manipulate depth perception in a garden: Large plants up close coupled with smaller plants at a distance make the garden appear deeper than it really is. For example, you might plant a small-leaved Foster's holly up close and at a distance plant a small row of two or three *Ilex crenata* 'Sky Pencil', a Japanese holly that is naturally narrow and only 10 feet tall at maturity. (This technique is discussed at length in "Shade Gardens".)

BALANCE. When you're planning the overall composition of the garden, remember that plantings in balance create a sense of security and well-being. Pairs of same-sized shrubs or trees lining a walk or a driveway express balance and make a lovely approach to a formal dwelling, but

repeated duplications can seem static, rigid. You can add a dynamic to balanced plantings by duplicating a silhouette without duplicating the plants that create it: For example, you can balance a clump of shrubs on the left of a driveway with a similar-sized clump farther along on the right hand side, then repeat the groupings. You can balance a large evergreen, such as an Irish yew (*Taxus baccata* 'Fastigiata'), growing on one side of the yard, by planting on the other side three or four different evergreens that create a similar but texturally different mass: Choose among a hemlock, a spruce, an American arborvitae (*Thuja occidentalis*), or a Hinoki cypress (*Chamaecyparis obtusa*), for example, along with a dwarf Sawara cypress (*C. pisifera* 'Boulevard').

COLOR. The color wheel pictured here is used by designers in choosing flower colors. Moving clockwise around the wheel, the colors are violet, red, orange, and yellow, green, and blue. If you want to create a vibrant garden, one that makes you want to do cartwheels, combine the complementary colors opposite each other on the color wheel: red and green, blue and orange, yellow and violet or purple. For a sunny, cheerful garden, feature red, orange, and yellow; a combination of all the colors interspersed with lots of white has the same effervescent effect. For a cool, restful garden choose blue flowers with white and pale pink flowers nearby

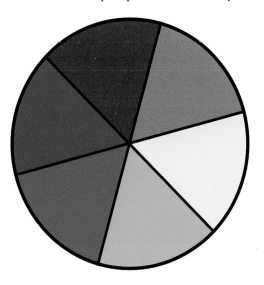

to make the blues stand out. For a harmonious garden, create a monochromatic scheme by using colors, and tints of those colors, that are side by side on the color wheel: red and orange, orange and yellow, blue and violet, and variations on these. For a romantic garden combine white with pink, blue, purple, and lavender. If you are home more at night than other times, then I think you would enjoy a Victorian moon garden featuring white flowers and white variegated foliage plants. Pale yellow, pale pink, and very pale blue or lavender also show up in the dark. For fragrance that is more intense after sundown, plant white nicotiana, gardenias, *Gladiolus tristis,* oleander, honeysuckle, the moonflower vine (*Ipomoea alba*), sweet woodruff, and white sweet alyssum. For perfume in the autumn, plant holly olives (*Osmanthus heterophyllus*): The small white flowers open late in the season when other fragrant flowers have gone by.

Tints are colors toned down by the addition of white: Pink is a tint of red and lavender, a tint of violet or purple. You can emphasize tints by combining white with a color, white petunias next to pink petunias, for example, with crimson on the far side. Shades are colors mixed with black—dark green, dark blue, dark red. You can use these deeper tones to give depth to your composition. I find the bold deep maroon foliage of 'Palace Purple' heuchera gives character to the front edges of a colorful flower border, and I like to use in the background tall 'Crater Lake Blue' veronica (*V. austriaca*) and *Veronica spicata,* blue salvia, and the darker shades of the magnificent Pacific Giant delphiniums.

Flowers are not the only source of color, of course. All the foliage plants—trees, shrubs, vines, ferns, and the ornamental grasses—can be used to layer in tints and shades. Evergreens may be the backbone of the garden, to be sure, but any good thing can be overdone. I think you'll enjoy your garden more if you include among the foundation plants some colorful deciduous shrubs. An ideal grouping includes an evergreen, a deciduous shrub that blooms over a long season, and one that has brilliant foliage in the fall. A grouping I find especially attractive in a mid-height hedge combines evergreen mugho pines (*Pinus mugo*) with potentillas (*Potentilla fruticosa*), which bear pretty yellow flowers all summer

long, and *Berberis thunbergii* 'Crimson Pygmy', a dwarf barberry that fairly glows in fall and has bright berries for the birds. All three will tolerate drought and saline soil. Only an occasional light pruning of the potentilla and the barberry will be required to keep this combination of plants in bounds, in a long hedge an especially important consideration.

MAINTENANCE CONSIDERATIONS. A beautiful garden is one that is well loved—and to love it, you need time to enjoy it. When your plant list is complete, make a rough estimate of the maintenance your plants will require; if it's more than you have time for, look for low-maintenance alternates. You may enjoy trimming a 10-foot long hedge of 'Nellie R. Stevens' hollies in spring and again toward the end of summer. But if the hedge is a hundred yards long, plant dwarf or slow-growing shrubs, such as Japanese boxwood, that will require less attention. You may enjoy caring for a few beautiful, high-maintenance rose bushes, but in combination with a kitchen garden, bed of perennials, and crape myrtles, the maintenance may become too much of a burden. A less-taxing garden would have one or at most two, high-maintenance beds and a low-maintenance summer-flowering tree. Crape myrtles need pruning before growth starts in spring, the removal of suckers in summer, and removal of seedheads in fall. Trouble-free American yellowwood (*Cladrastis lutea*) needs only a light pruning in summer. A small, slow-growing tree, its foot-long, pendulous clusters of fragrant white flowers resemble wisteria, and its foliage develops marvelous colors during the fall.

You can also save on maintenance by choosing top-quality, pest- and disease-resistant varieties of all plants. I consider resistant varieties of the ever-popular roses and crabapples, phlox and zinnias especially important. Monoculture invites problems. Cultivars of our lovely native plants introduce a healthy, and interesting, diversity. Be sure to choose varieties that thrive in your climate and soil.

I have found that young trees and shrubs, especially species that transplant with difficulty, adapt more easily and grow faster than mature transplants. If you need a big tree, you can hire a landscape service with mechanized equipment. I buy container-grown, or balled-and-burlapped plants, rather than bare-

root plants. They become established sooner and can be planted any time during the growing season. Bare-root plants can be planted successfully only when they are dormant, in very early spring or in the fall. Insist on having grafted or vegetatively propagated trees and shrubs; they are more consistent and usually better performers than trees and shrubs grown from seed.

When you choose ornamental trees and shrubs, consider their fruits as well as their form, foliage, and flowers. Bright, colorful berries decorate your garden in late summer and autumn, and they feed the birds. Some varieties provide double the pleasure—showy flowers *and* decorative fruits. Others make up for inconspicuous flowers with striking foliage, interesting all season (variegated holly, for example) or a blaze of color in the fall (e.g., *Euonymus alatus*), as well as a spectacular show of berries. Usually you need only one individual to grow a crop of colorful fruits, but a few species, notably the hollies, are dioecious, that is, the male and female flowers are on separate plants, and you will need to plant at least one male nearby for the female to produce its brilliant berries. You may choose to combine visual and gustatory pleasures: Some species of kiwi fruits are dioecious, and the pretty flowers of some plum trees will not set fruit unless cross-pollinated with a different variety. Your supplier will be able to advise you on special pollination requirements, if any.

There is a downside to fruiting trees and shrubs: They can be messy. If you wish to forego the chore of raking up rotten fruits, choose among the many showy cultivars of common fruiting ornamentals that produce small fruits the birds clean up or do not set fruit at all. The ancient, dioecious ginkgo tree is prized for its elegant form and unusual fan-shaped leaves that glow yellow in the fall; to avoid its messy, notoriously putrid fruits, be sure to plant only males.

I have always found the nearest well-established garden center to be a good source of reliable information and of plants that will perform well in my garden. Only experienced local horticulturalists and gardeners know for sure which varieties are most likely to perform best in your region. I have also found members of local garden clubs and plant societies helpful and well informed, and they usually share my interests.

CLIMATE ZONES

One of the first questions to ask yourself when choosing a perennial plant is whether it will thrive in your climate zone. Annuals, including many herbaceous flowers and most vegetables, live only one season; their hardiness (their tolerance of temperature extremes) affects only how early they can be planted in spring, and how long they will last in the fall. The zones ranges assigned to plants on my plant lists, and on most horticultural references, are keyed to the USDA Hardiness Zones and indicate the coldest and warmest regions in which the plants are known to do well. A city garden often is 5° to 10° F. warmer than a nearby country garden, enough to change the climate zone. Select only plants, shrubs, and trees that are clearly hardy in your garden's zone: Late frosts can really devastate flower buds.

The plants most at risk are those planted at the edge of their hardiness zones, but micro climates in your yard can increase your chance of success. (A microclimate is a small area whose climate differs from the average regional climate. It may be warmer or cooler than prevailing temperatures, the range in temperatures may be wider or narrower, and the humidity may be higher or lower.) Walls, corners, reflective surfaces (such as white walls, mirrors, and windows), windbreaks, and the shelter of large evergreen shrubs and trees raise the surrounding temperatures in winter and summer.

Temperatures are usually lower in the shade from a tree, under lathing or a vine-covered arbor, as well as at a site with a northern exposure. A winter or summer mulch over the roots buffers extremes of soil temperatures and sometimes air temperature near the ground. Climate near the ocean is usually more moderate than it is inland.

Snow cover can also be another great zone changer. Some tender perennials that usually don't survive icy winters may contradict the norms and survive where there's a deep winter blanket of snow. The tuberoses I grew years ago in my Zone 3 Vermont garden, for example, die of the cold here in mild Zone 7, where there's little snow.

This map shows the major North American hardiness zones as identified by the USDA. The temperature ranges in the key indicate the average minimum temperatures for each zone. If you do not live in North America and wish to know the suitability of plants listed in this book, use the minimum temperature in your locale to determine your zone.

	ZONE 1	-50 TO -40°F	-45 TO -40°C
	ZONE 2	-40 TO -30°F	-40 TO -34°C
	ZONE 3	-30 TO -20°F	-34 TO -29°C
	ZONE 4	-20 TO -10°F	-29 TO -23°C
	ZONE 5	-10 TO 0°F	-23 TO -18°C
	ZONE 6	0 TO 10°F	-18 TO -12°C
	ZONE 7	10 TO 20°F	-12 TO -7°C
	ZONE 8	20 TO 30°F	- 7 TO -1°C
	ZONE 9	30 TO 40°F	- 1 TO 4°C
	ZONE 10	ABOVE 40°F	ABOVE 4°C

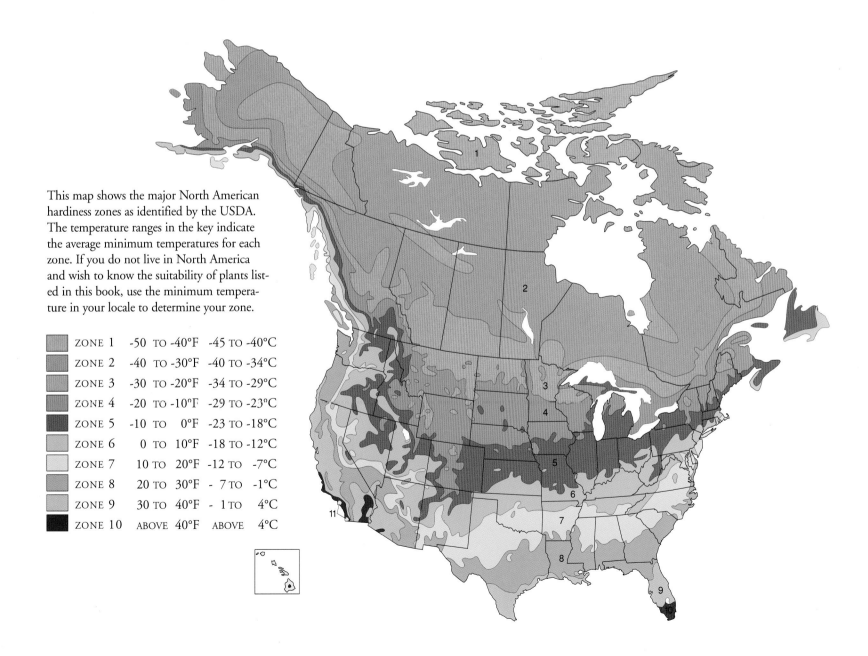

LIGHT

As you plan your garden and study the changing patterns of sunlight during the year, you will probably discover a variety of light climates, each offering its own challenges and opportunities. Some species thrive only in a minimum of 6 to 8 hours of full sunlight each day, while others tolerate only fleeting moments of direct sunlight, or none at all. Many plants fall between these extremes, requiring or tolerating varying degrees of sun under different conditions. Remember that more sunlight may also mean more heat: In the hottest parts of the country, some noon shelter—a trellis or the dappled shade of tall trees, for example—may be beneficial for many plants that normally thrive in full sun. Some species that require full sun cannot tolerate the heat that accompanies it in some climates: Rock garden plants that thrive in the intense sunlight of cool alpine meadows shrivel and die in the sizzling hot midsummer sun at low altitudes. Soil moisture is also important: Plants often tolerate more direct sun (and heat) when they grow in moist, humus-rich soil covered by a 3-inch mulch. Many lovely garden plants grow poorly in direct sun, regardless of the temperature, and only thrive in shade. The growth of plants in light and shade is discussed in greater detail in "Shade Gardens."

SOIL PREPARATION

You know your soil is fertile and in good condition by the way your plants look: Sturdy, vigorous plants that produce lots of flowers and healthy green foliage are growing in good garden soil. Soil structure or composition, soil pH, and fertility are the three key attributes of soil.

SOIL STRUCTURE. Loam is composed of roughly equal parts of sand, silt, and clay, perhaps a little more sand and silt and a little less clay. Sand particles provide spaces for movement of the air and water essential for root growth, the smaller silt particles hold water, and the fine clay particles absorb water and nutrients. A good garden soil is loam enriched with humus, that magic residue of decomposed organic matter that improves both the soil's structure and its fertility. Humus stores water and nutrients, and humus-rich soils are easy to till and support the vigorous growth of roots, as well as the earthworms, other soil animals, and microorganisms that keep the soil in good condition. In an active, healthy soil, humus is continually broken down; working compost into the soil every spring and maintaining an organic mulch help to replenish the soil.

When the proportions of the ingredients are just right, a ball of damp soil packs like a snowball and crumbles easily under light pressure; if it won't pack into a ball, it's too sandy (it may have too much humus, but that's rare), and if the ball won't crumble under light pressure, it probably has too much clay. To improve sandy soils, dig in a 2-inch layer of humus; dig in a 2-inch layer of builder's sand (never ocean beach sand!) to lighten a soil too high in humus.

To adjust clay soils, work in 2-inch layers of both humus and sand, along with gypsum and superphosphate applied at the rate of 25 pounds for every 500 square feet; if the soil is very heavy clay, double the application of gypsum. Amending clay soil in this way will often solve a drainage problem. A drainage problem that persists may be cured by a drainage well: Find the lowest point of the problem area, dig a hole that goes several feet below the clay subsoil, and fill the entire hole with crushed gravel. Another answer to poor drainage is a raised bed, as described on the following page.

SOIL PH. The pH of a soil is a measure of its acidity or alkalinity; it's important because it affects the availability of nutrients needed for plant growth. The pH scale ranges from 1 to 14: At pH 7, the soil is neutral; as pH decreases below pH 7, the soil becomes increasingly acidic; above pH 7, the soil becomes more alkaline. Nutrients are most readily available in slightly acid soils, and most garden plants grow well in soils of pH 5.5 to pH 6.8; some woodlands plants and evergreens prefer more acid conditions. Most will tolerate a range in pH. Barberries, euonymus, forsythias, hydrangeas, lilacs, and mahonias, for example, prefer near-neutral soils and will grow in limestone-derived soils up to pH 8. In general, soils in the eastern part of the United States tend to be acidic, and those in the prairies and farther west tend to be more alkaline, but soil pH also depends on the materials from which the

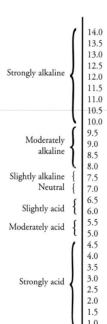

Strongly alkaline	14.0 13.5 13.0 12.5 12.0 11.5 11.0 10.5 10.0
Moderately alkaline	9.5 9.0 8.5
Slightly alkaline	8.0 7.5
Neutral	7.0
Slightly acid	6.5 6.0
Moderately acid	5.5 5.0
Strongly acid	4.5 4.0 3.5 3.0 2.5 2.0 1.5 1.0

soils were derived, age, drainage, and many other factors. With time and use, lawn and kitchen garden soils tend to become more acidic.

It's a good idea to check the pH of your soil before you begin major gardening projects, and every year as well. Farmers do, and they also check for soil deficiencies and fertilize only with the missing elements. Garden centers sell kits to test pH and also kits that test for nutrient deficiencies.

To raise the pH of soil that tests below pH 5.5, mix finely ground limestone into the soil in light doses once or twice a year and retest a few weeks after each application. To lower the pH of soil that tests above pH 6.8, ask your Agricultural Extension agent or your garden center about sulfur applications; the treatment is short-lived and must be repeated after eight months to a year. Using acidic mulches, such as peat moss, composted sawdust or bark, pine needles, or cottonseed meal, is a long-term approach to reducing alkalinity.

FERTILIZING BASICS. The granular materials called complete fertilizers add to the soil the three major elements needed by plants: nitrogen (N), phosphorus (P, as phosphate), and Potassium, or potash (K). Nitrogen is needed for stem and leaf production and maintenance of green foliage. Inadequate growth, yellowing lower leaves, and pale foliage are signs that nitrogen is lacking, a condition often remedied simply by application of a fertilizer with a higher proportion of nitrogen, 10-10-10, for example. Phosphate promotes good root growth, flowering, and fruiting. Dark red or green leaves and stunted growth suggest phosphorus deficiencies: try a fertilizer whose NPK ratio is 5-10-5. Potash also affects flower and fruit production and strengthens stems and resistance to diseases. Weak stems and a susceptibility to disease suggest a potassium deficiency: Change to a fertilizer that has a high proportion of potash, like 5-10-10.

Slow-release fertilizers deliver their nutrients over periods of several months, providing a steady supply of nutrients. Fast-acting inorganic fertilizers release their nutrients fairly quickly and need to be replenished often. I like to apply a slow-release fertilizer (5-10-10) for new beds and every year in late winter or early spring before I see the first signs of growth. Organic fertilizers, such as seaweed, fish emulsion, and manure tea (steeped dried manure) release their nutrients quickly, and you can use these to give your plants a boost at mid season. Another way to deliver a quick lift to ornamental plants is to apply a water-soluble fertilizer with a hose: It's called foliar feeding because the leaves, as well as the roots, absorb the nutrients.

As a rule of thumb, underuse fertilizer consistently. The National Park Service recommends fertilizing only when a soil test indicates a deficiency. Excess fertilizer running off from our lawns and gardens pollutes our ground water and inland and coastal waters. Naturally, I give different advice for fertilizing plants growing in containers in artificial soil mixes: Small plant containers need *light* applications at every watering.

DOUBLE DIGGING AND RAISED BEDS. Fall is the best time to prepare a new bed. If your soil or drainage is beyond remedy, I recommend that you create a raised bed by importing good topsoil. First outline the bed with markers or with a garden hose, then strip away the sod and double dig the area. To double dig, first excavate a foot-deep trench at one edge of the area you have marked off. Pile the soil into a wheelbarrow. Use a spading fork to loosen the sub-soil at the bottom of the trench. Then dig a second trench next to the first one, spading the soil into the first trench. Loosen the subsoil, and repeat the procedure until you've worked your way to the other side of the marked-off area. Use the soil from the first trench to fill the last one.

Now treat the soil with a weed killer, wait a week, water the area, and repeat the treatment. Or, in the heat of summer, cook the weeds to death under plastic. Let the garden rest another seven days, then cover the soil with enough new *weedless* garden soil from a reliable nursery to raise the soil level 12 to 15 inches above ground. The next steps are to test the soil, correct the pH, and add a fertilizer and soil amendment, such as gypsum and super phosphate. Cover the bed with 2 to 4 inches of humus (such as decomposed bark, compost, partially decomposed leaves, sphagnum peat moss, black peat humus, decomposed animal manures, or composted sewage sludge.) Then it's easier to use a rear-tine rototiller, which you can rent from a garden center, to thoroughly mix together the soil and the amenders. To keep the sides of a raised bed from eroding, mulch them, or frame them with low retaining walls of stone, painted cement blocks, red cedar or pressure treated wood, or railroad ties. Before planting, rake the bed smooth and discard clumps and stones; make the top surface a little concave in order to collect the rain and prevent runoff and erosion.

PLANTING AND TRANSPLANTING

Late winter and early spring are the preferred planting times at the U.S. National Arboretum in Washington, D.C., particularly for woody plants and for species that react poorly to transplanting, while they are still dormant and before their period of most vigorous growth. Early fall is also an excellent time for planting, providing the climate allows a couple of months for the roots to grow before the onset of winter.

TREES AND SHRUBS. Researchers now believe that trees and other woody plants take hold more successfully, adapt more quickly, and grow stronger and more resistant, if we subject them to natural stress. Apparently the quick growth that follows frequent fertilizing and watering often makes a tree more vulnerable to wind, drought, extremes of temperature, pests, and diseases. The very best help you can give to trees and large shrubs at planting time is to provide well-worked and generous planting holes, holes as large as a card table, to give the roots plenty of room to spread. If the plant is balled and burlapped, be sure to remove the burlap before planting. If the rootball breaks up, place the plant in the hole, then gently pull the wrapping away.

Often you will find roots of container-grown plants wound around the rootball: before planting, gently loosen the roots at the sides and the bottom. To plant bare-root plants, those without soil around their roots, soak the roots overnight in lukewarm water and spread them out over a prepared cone of soil in the planting hole. Do not fertilize trees or shrubs when you plant them. I find that staking is not really necessary unless the plant starts to grow at an angle. In cold regions a burlap windbreak is helpful the first winter, and, to protect the trunk from wildlife, circle it with a cylinder of 1-inch mesh chicken wire tall enough to project above the snow.

Several months before you move an established tree or a large shrub, cut a circle 2 or 3 feet deep in the soil all around the trunk to sever the side roots. When moving time comes, dig a trench around the outside of the root-pruned circle, wrap the rootball in burlap or chicken wire, and then pry it up.

Contrary to traditional practice, current research suggests that pruning newly planted trees and shrubs may actually slow root growth; just prune to remove broken branches or to shape the plant.

For established plants, I prune flowering shrubs that bloom on new wood in late winter or early spring *before* growth begins; prune those that bloom on mature wood *immediately after* they flower, just before bud initiation begins for the next season's bloom. Prune young foliage shrubs during active growth: Cut just above a lateral bud, those succulent stems will grow lateral shoots. When the plants have reached the desired height, prune only after the season's new growth is fully developed and cut back a little into the old wood. Pines will branch if you cut the candles back by half in early summer, and other conifers can be made to branch by pruning new wood. You can shape young conifers by lightly pruning new growth. In areas with cold winters, do not prune woody plants in the fall, as late-season new growth may be damaged by frost. The exceptions are dead or diseased branches, which you should remove as soon as you see them.

GROUND COVERS. Choose ground covers appropriate for your site and soil, especially when the area is large. In fall or in early spring remove the sod if necessary, and cultivate the soil 8 inches deep three times over a two-week period. Before the final rototilling, cover the area with 2 or 3 inches of compost or decomposed leaves; if the soil is very acid, add limestone according to the package directions; in the eastern United States, add 5 pounds of super phosphate for every 100 square feet; and add a slow-release fertilizer. Cover the area with 2 inches of mulch and plant through the mulch. Allow the plants at least two years to spread enough to cover completely. In the first three years, apply a complete fertilizer at half the recommended rate in late winter, and again in late spring, and keep ahead of the weeds.

PERENNIALS/DIVIDING. The come-back plants, the perennials and some of the flowering bulbs, are the mainstay of flower gardens. But, contrary to popular myth, they don't come back forever, (except possibly peonies, which live for a century and more). Perennials are more likely to come back year after year if you treat them well. The first flowers to bloom will be the bulbs you planted the preceding fall and those that have become established, such as daffodils and some of the charming little late winter and early spring flowers that do well in grass and among low ground covers. All the hardy bulbs are planted in fall and most need winter's cold to come into bloom.

Another group of spectacular flowering bulbs blooms in the summer and early fall: the stately perfumed lilies, dahlias, bright begonias, and elegant fall-flowering crocuses. Some remarkable summer flowering bulbs, such as lily-of-the-Nile and nerine, are natives of tropical climates; where winters are cold, they are planted in spring for summer bloom and taken indoors for the winter, or discarded. In a flowering border, I plant the bulbs in groups spaced to come up between or through clumps of perennials, and those that bloom and fade in spring I screen or replace sometime later by annual flowers.

Most perennials bloom only the second year, so I recommend that you start your garden with one-year-old seedlings, root divisions or container-grown plants, so that you'll have blooms the first season. Plants labeled "tender perennials" (geraniums, for example) don't survive frost, so in cool regions they're grown as annuals. Biennials have a two-year growth cycle: A biennial grows foliage the first year, it will flower the next year, then it

dies. Examples are parsley, some foxgloves, black-eyed Susans, and the beautifully scented, spring-blooming English wallflower. To keep biennials in the garden year after year, I sow seed around the plants as they begin to mature the second season: The seedlings from that sowing will bloom the following year. They may also seed themselves.

To keep your perennials in top form, you will have to divide and replant most species every four or five years, or when they show loss of vitality and bloom: Garden mums should be divided early every spring. Plants that recover slowly from transplanting, such as peonies, I divide only when they show signs of deterioration. You must divide some types, such as poppies after they have flowered and the foliage has died down, as they become dormant. Garden literature and good catalogs tell you which flowers require this treatment. In cool regions, spring, before growth begins, is the best time to divide and transplant. Where winters are mild, mid fall is as good as spring for all flowers excepting plants that recover slowly from transplanting: Plant those in early spring. In the South, divide and transplant in winter, when the plants are dormant.

To divide a perennial, outline and dig up the clump, or crown, and locate its natural lines of division. If you find several divisions, break them apart with a spade or a knife, discard the central portion, and replant the portions that have young shoots. Clumps that have a single crown, and also rhizomes, must be cut or broken into sections, each containing an eye, or bud, and a healthy set of roots. To divide a plant that roots by runners, or stolons, cut the connection between the new plants and the parent, then dig and replant the plantlets. After you have transplanted or divided a growing plant, prune it back by a third, and the plant will repay you by recovering very quickly from the move.

Most healthy plants don't need staking, except tomatoes and very tall plants like lilies and delphiniums, and those with many small stems, such as baby's breath and coreopsis. In windy locations other plants need help, and sun-loving plants grown in semi-shade may also require support. Plant a single unobtrusive stake to one side of the clump, and screen it as much as possible with branches and leaves, then use green garden tape to gently tie the central stem to the stake.

Plants with many small stems may be supported by a nest of twigs. Local garden centers generally offer a variety of perennial supports.

SEEDS. Sow seeds in the open garden in early or mid spring in soil that is slightly damp but not wet. Sow large seeds in zigzag rows at a depth equal to about three times their width; broadcast (scatter) small seeds evenly over the soil surface, and tamp them firmly into place. Some annuals and biennials reseed themselves, and you can help them by spreading a 1- to 2-inch layer of fresh soil around the plants and by gathering the seeds as they ripen and scattering them over the soil. After planting, water the seedbed with a fine spray and keep it damp until you see that the seedlings are growing lustily.

SEEDLINGS. Annuals, and many perennials, are set out in the garden as seedlings. The rules for planting trees and shrubs applies to flowers as well: Provide the right light, good soil, and a generous, well-worked planting hole. Loosen roots that are binding the rootball, and after planting, water with a light application of a soluble fertilizer. To encourage branching and flowering, I pinch out the central stem and the branch tips of seedlings of branching annuals and perennials, such as snapdragons and stock. I pinch off, or deadhead, spent blossoms whenever the weather is pleasant. It's a delightful chore that encourages more blossoms; deadheading is especially helpful to roses, petunias, and pansies.

CONTAINERS. I provide fresh soil for hanging baskets, tubs, and planters before I plant in them in spring. The tubs and planters of perennials I give a top dressing of 2 to 3 inches of compost or fertile soil in late winter before new growth begins. When preparing soil for containers, I mix in half as much soil-less potting mix. I mix a water-holding gel into the soil for all the small container plants; these starch-based super-absorbents really do help to keep the soil moist. They come either as granules or as sticks of stuck-together grains, and they can hold water amounting to hundreds of times their own weight. Try to mix gel grains thoroughly with the soil, otherwise they will clump into jellylike globs. For a more detailed discussion of container soils, turn to "Small Gardens."

MAINTENANCE

Once you've installed your new garden, treat the plants well and they will give you many years of pleasure.

WATERING. Plants thrive in uniformly moist, well-aerated soil. It's possible to replace the water lost to maintain this ideal condition, but to do so daily would be time-consuming, wasteful, and expensive. Most gardeners opt for the cheaper and easier alternative of watering deeply, then watering deeply again only when signs of mild stress appear. Rather than following an arbitrary watering regime, water when the garden needs water. Spend time in the garden and study the soil and the plants, and you'll learn the signs that it's time to water again.

When you're starting a new garden, turn to "Xeriscape Gardens" for information on water-conserving plants and techniques. Consider installing a drip irrigation system. Coupled with mulch, a drip system will save time and money. Electric timers are available, but, if they are set to an arbitrary schedule, you may find yourself watering in the middle of a downpour.

The most elaborate systems consist of networks of tubes that deliver water under low pressure to specific locations and plants. A simple and less costly system is a series of soakers, or leaky hoses, and that's what I use in my small D.C. garden. In the heat of summer I turn the water on manually with the pressure set to ooze water slowly, and leave it on about an hour.

I also use a hose and a sprinkler now and then. Overhead watering is the best way to provide a humid environment for just-sown seeds to keep the seedbed moist until they germinate and the seedlings emerge. I also use overhead watering to refresh the garden at the end of very dry, windy, hot days, and when the New Guinea impatiens or some other tender plants wilt in the noonday sun. Watering during the day lowers leaf temperatures and reduces stress. Evening watering conserves water and is not harmful: The foliage is wet by the dew anyway. But watering in the morning is generally best.

MULCHING. Mulch is a protective blanket for the soil that discourages weeds, tempers extremes in soil temperatures, helps to conserve moisture, and gives the garden a trim, tidy, professional look. Organic mulch is beneficial in yet another way: It slowly decomposes (composts),

adding humus to the soil. Among the most attractive mulches are fine-grade hammermill bark, pine bark, hardwood bark, or the barks of West Coast fir, cedar, and cypress. The finer the bark, the more quickly it will decompose and allow weeds to grow. You can also mulch with compost or leafmold, but they're less effective at suppressing weeds. If you see weeds, pull them up immediately before they grow into monsters or you will have to hack them out with a hoe. The best time to lay down mulch is after newly set plants have been watered. Replenish the mulch during the season, if necessary, and again every spring after the ground has warmed and before summer heat arrives. Make your mulch 3 inches deep, and keep it 3 inches away from the stems of shrubs and trees.

Winter mulches are recommended for some plants growing in southern gardens and for those on the edge of their cold hardiness. Apply it only after the ground has frozen, and remove it when you first spot signs of active growth in the plants.

COMPOSTING. Most plants grow especially well in soils rich in humus, and one of the best sources of humus is compost: Any gardener can make it. Composting is essentially just layering piles of organic matter—leaves, clippings, kitchen waste, sod, manure, and sawdust are just a few of the materials that make good compost—so that they will decompose. There are two basic approaches: hot and cold. In hot composting, the pile is constructed and tended so that decomposition occurs rapidly, at a high temperature; it is a fairly complex process and requires a lot of work and attention. Cold composting is the slower, more laissez-faire approach, and that's what I do. I simply layer the materials and keep them damp (but not wet) and aerated, and they composta in a few months.

Decomposition of organic matter requires nitrogen and will occur more quickly if manure, grass clippings, and fertilizer are added to the compost pile. To each 32-gallon bag of dried leaves, we add two cups each of a high-nitrogen fertilizer and of gypsum to improve our clay soil. I use an acidic fertilizer for compost that will be placed around acid-loving azaleas and rhododendrons. We spread the mixture out in the compost bin and top each batch with a thin layer of green waste such as fresh weeds, spent annuals,

and prunings from the ivies and other ground covers. Vegetable peelings from the kitchen can go in, too.

HEAD START PROGAMS. You can lengthen the growing season in spring and in fall by starting seeds and growing seedlings in a cold frame, a hotbed, or in the open garden under hot caps, cloches, and various types of plastic tenting.

COLD FRAME. In cold regions where the soil is slow to warm in spring, a cold frame is a great place to start seedlings for the vegetable garden and the flower beds (lettuces and marigolds, for example). Where winters are mild, salad greens and other cold weather crops, for example, arugula, the early leaf lettuces, radishes, mâche, and chives, can be grown in a cold frame all through the cool months. In late summer, when it is too hot to grow seedlings in the open garden, you can start seeds for perennials and fall crops there. In warmer climates, a cold frame is also a great place to store dormant plants over winter, for example tender perennials that can stand some chill, like geraniums and begonias, and rhizomes and tubers, not bulbs and corms.

A cold frame is a bottomless box sunk into the earth and roofed over with glass or plastic. It is slanted to the south at a 45° angle, to catch the sun and so that water and snow slide off. The heat absorbed during the day warms the box at night. Garden centers offer pre-cut ready-to-assemble cold frames and lightweight, portable frames that can be moved around in the garden to protect late and winter crops. You can make a cold frame from pressure-treated boards. Provide the box with good soil, and check the water needs of the plants frequently. Place a shaded thermometer inside so that you can monitor the air temperature, and vent the frame when the heat exceeds 90°F. (or your determined upper limit). Sophisticated cold frames are available equipped with solar-powered frame openers triggered by high temperatures.

HOTBED. A hotbed is just an insulated cold frame equipped with an underground heating cable regulated by a thermostat. It allows you to start seeds and to grow seedlings earlier in spring than a cold frame does, to grow cool weather crops in colder regions in winter, and as a cold frame at other seasons.

MAIL ORDER SOURCES

The mail order providers here are only a few of hundreds in the United States and Canada.
Many other sources are listed according to their specialty in Barbara Barton's *Gardening by Mail* (Houghton Mifflin, 222 Berkeley St., Boston, MA 02116-3764)
and Gardener's Source Guide (P.O. Box 206, Gowanda, NY 14070).

Abundant Life Seed Foundation
P.O. Box 772,
Port Townsend, WA 98368
(Heirloom grains, vegetables,
flowers, natives)

Arrowhead Alpines
P.O. Box 857,
Fowlerville, MI 48836
(Alpine seeds and plants)

Kurt Bluemel, Inc.
2740 Greene Lane,
Baldwin, MD 21013-9523
(Ornamental grasses)

Bobtown Nursery
16212 Country Club Rd.,
Melfa, VA 23410
(Native, wetland, and salt-tolerant
plants)

Bountiful Gardens
18001 Shafer Ranch Rd.,
Willits, CA 95490
(Heirloom vegetable, flower, herb
seeds)

W. Atlee Burpee & Co.
300 Park Ave.,
Warminster, PA 18974
(Vegetable and flower seeds)

Canyon Creek Nursery
3527 Dry Creek Rd.,
Oroville, CA 95965
(Perennials)

Carroll Gardens
P.O. Box 310,
Westminster, MD 21158
(Trees, shrubs, vines, perennials)

Catnip Acres Herb Nursery
67 Christian St.,
Oxford, CT 06483-1224
(Herbs and everlastings)

Colorado Alpines, Inc.
P.O. Box 2708,
Avon, CO 81620
(Alpines and unusual plants)

The Cook's Garden
P.O. Box 535,
Londonderry, VT 05148
(Flower and gourmet vegetable
seeds)

Crownsville Nursery
P.O. Box 797,
Crownsville, MD 21032
(Perennials, herbs, grasses, ferns,
hostas)

Clyde Robin Seed Company, Inc.
3670 Enterprise Ave.,
Hayward, CA 94545
(Wildflower seeds and seed mixes)

The Daffodil Mart
7463 Heath Trail,
Gloucester, VA 23061
(Flowering bulbs)

Deep Diversity
P.O. Box 15189,
Santa Fe, NM 87506-5189
(Seeds of many heirloom and rare
varieties)

Evergreeen Y. H. Enterprises
P.O. Box 17538,
Anaheim, CA 92817
(Asian vegetable seeds)

Filaree Farm
Conconully Hwy.,
Okanogan, WA 98840
(Garlic, Asian vegetable seeds)

Fox Hollow Herb & Heirloom Seed
Company
P.O. Box 148,
McGrann, PA 16236
(Flower, herb, heirloom vegetable
seeds)

The Fragrant Path
P.O. Box 328,
Fort Calhoun, NE 68023
(Fragrant, rare, heirloom plants and
seeds)

Garden City Seeds
1324 Red Crow Rd.,
Victor, MT 59875-9713
(Vegetable and flower seeds for cool
climates)

Goodness Grows, Inc.
P.O. Box 311,
Lexington, GA 30648
(Herbs, native plants, ferns)

The Good Earth Seed Company
P.O. Box 5644,
Redwood City, CA 94063
(Asian vegetable seeds)

The Gourmet Gardener
8650 College Blvd.,
Overland Park, KS 66210
(Gourmet and European vegetable
seed)

Gleckler's Seedsmen
Metamora, OH 43540
(Unusual vegetable varieties)

High Altitude Gardens
P.O. Box 1048,
Hailey, ID 83333
(Cold-tolerant vegetable, wildflower,
herb seeds)

Jackson & Perkins Co.
PO Box 1028
Medford, OR 97501
(Roses; bulbs; trees)

Klehm Nursery
4210 N. Duncan Rd.,
Champaign, IL 61821
(Perennials, grasses, hostas, peonies)

Le Jardin du Gourmet
P.O. Box 75, St. Johnsbury Center,
VT 05863-0075
(French vegetable varieties)

Lilypons Water Gardens
P.O. Box 10,
Buckeystown, MD 21717-0010
(Waterlilies, water garden plants and
equipment)

Lockhart Seeds
P.O. Box 1361,
Stockton, CA 95201
(Vegetable, oriental vegetable seeds)

Logee's Greenhouses
141 North St.,
Danielson, CT 06239
(Exotic greenhouse, warm-climate
plants)

Moon Mountain
P.O. Box 725,
Carpinteria, CA 93014
(Annuals, perennials, wildflowers)

Native Seeds/SEARCH
2509 N. Campbell Ave.,
Tucson, AZ 85719
(Southwest native American vegetable seeds)

Nichols Garden Nursery
1190 S. Pacific
Albany, OR 97321
(Herbs, flowers, vegetable seeds;
herb plants)

George W. Park Seed Co., Inc.
Cokesbury Rd.,
Greenwood, SC 29647-0001
(Vegetable and flower seeds)

The Pepper Gal
P.O. Box 23006,
Fort Lauderdale, FL 33307-3006
(Seeds of many varieties of peppers)

Peaceful Valley Farm Supply
P.O. Box 2209,
Grass Valley, CA 95945
(Organically grown seeds, pest
controls)

Rice Creek Nurseries
11506 Hwy. 65,
Blaine, MN 55434
(Alpines, rock garden plants, dwarf
conifers)

Ronniger's Seed Potatoes
Star Route 59,
Moyie Springs, ID 83845
(Many varieties of seed potatoes)

Roses of Yesterday and Today
802 Brown's Valley Rd.,
Watsonville, CA 95076
(Old-fashioned, modern, species roses)

Seeds of Change
Box 15700,
Santa Fe, NM 87506-5700
(Heirloom, native American seeds)

Seeds West Garden Seeds
P.O. Box 27057,
Albuquerque, NM 87125-7057
(Varieties for the Southwest)

Shady Hill Gardens
821 Walnut St.,
Batavia, IL 60510
(Geranium plants and seeds)

Shepherd's Garden Seeds
30 Irene St.,
Torrington, CT 06790
(Vegetables, herbs, flowers for
butterflies)

R. H. Shumway, Seedsman
P.O. Box 1,
Graniteville, S.C. 29829
(Heirloom vegetable seeds)

Siskyou Rare Plant Nursery
2825 Cummings Rd.,
Medford, OR 97501
(Alpine and rock garden
plants)

Southern Exposure Seed Exchange
P.O. Box 170,
Earlysville, VA 22936
(Heirloom vegetable and herb
seeds)

Southern Seeds
P.O. Box 2091,
Melbourne, FL 32902
(Vegetables and herbs for hot
climates)

Sunlight Gardens
174 Golden Lane,
Andersonville, TN 37705
(Wildflower plants)

Stokes Seed Company
P.O. Box 548, Buffalo,
NY 14240-0548
(Vegetable and flower seeds)

Territorial Seed Co.
P.O. Box 157,
Cottage Grove, OR 97424
(Varieties for the Pacific North-
west)

Thompson & Morgan, Inc.
P.O. Box 1308,
Jackson, N.J. 08527
(Vegetable and flower seeds)

André Viette Farm & Nursery
Rt. 1, Box 16,
Fishersville, VA 22939
(Wide variety of perennials)

Wayside Gardens
P.O. Box 1,
Hodges, SC 29695-0001
(Trees, shrubs, perennials,
roses)

We-Du Nurseries
Rt. 5, Box 724,
Marion, NC 28752
(Rock garden and woodland
plants)

Wetsel Seed Co., Inc.
P.O. Box 791,
Harrisonburg, VA 22801
(Shrubs, bulbs; farm, lawn, and
garden seeds)

White Flower Farm
Litchfield, CT 06759-0050
(Shrubs, perennials, bulbs)

Wildlife Nurseries
P.O. Box 2724,
Oshkosh, WI 54903
(Aquatic wildflowers)

Wildseed Farms
P.O. Box 308,
Eagle Lake, TX 77434
(Grasses, wildflower seeds)

Woodlanders, Inc.
1128 Colleton Ave.,
Aiken, SC 29801
(Native S.E. trees, shrubs, vines)

INDEX

Numbers in **boldface** type inidicate illustrations